Speechless
Dialect

Speechless Dialect

Shakespeare's Open Silences

Philip C. McGuire

University of California Press

Berkeley / Los Angeles / London

University of California Press
Berkeley and Los Angeles, California

University of California Press, Ltd.
London, England

Library of Congress Cataloging in Publication Data

McGuire, Philip C., 1940
   Speechless dialect.

   Bibliography: p.
   Includes index.
   1. Shakespeare, William, 1564–1616—Dramatic production.
2. Silence in literature.   I. Title.   II. Title:
Shakespeare's open silences.
PR3091.M27   1985   822.3'3   84–24115
ISBN 0–520–05373–7

Printed in the United States of America

1 2 3 4 5 6 7 8 9

For Mimi Pete

Contents

There is a prone and speechless dialect,
Such as move men. . . .
    Measure for Measure I.ii.178–79

Acknowledgments

No one writes about Shakespeare's plays in a vacuum, and this book would not have been possible without the exemplary work of many people, especially Bernard Beckerman, John Russell Brown, J. L. Styan, and Marvin Rosenberg. After reading the typescript, Michael Warren, Jay Halio, and Frederick Crews generously offered suggestions that by challenging my thinking improved the book, which also benefitted from the expert aid of editors Dan Dixon, Mary Lamprech, and Lydia Duncan. I also wish to thank Daniel W. Ladell, the archivist for the Stratford Shakespearean Festival of Canada, as well as Levi Fox, director of the Shakespeare Centre in Stratford-upon-Avon, and the members of the staff of the centre's library.

I am also grateful for the financial support provided by Michigan State University's Department of English, College of Arts and Letters, and Office of International Studies and Programs, as well as for grants from the All-University Research Fund. This assistance allowed me to present conference papers in which I began to articulate the ideas from which this book developed. One such paper, presented at the 1984 Shakespeare Symposium at Iowa State University, was published under the title "Silence and Genre: The Example of *Measure for Measure*" in the *Iowa State Journal of Research* 59, no. 3 (1984): 241–51—a special issue entitled "Aspects in Renaissance Scholarship IV: Papers Presented at 'Shakespeare and his Contemporaries,' Symposium 1984," edited by Linda R. Gaylon and Kenneth G. Madison.

To Carmela Pinto, Carol Duane, and Jo Grandstaff, and to my colleagues at Michigan State, especially Douglas L. Peterson, I wish to express thanks for encouragement and help. One of those colleagues is also my wife, Sheila Roberts McGuire, and to her my gratitude and debt are deepest. Any words I could put down here would fall short of what I feel and what is her due. In her case, loving silence must suffice.

Introduction

Somewhat perversely, I wish to begin this study of a certain kind of silence that occurs within several of Shakespeare's plays by stressing what he and his contemporaries regarded as the distinctively human capacity to speak. In *A Defense of Poesy*, Sir Philip Sidney declares that "*oratio* next to *ratio*, speech next to reason, be the greatest gift bestowed upon mortality."[1] Ben Jonson, arguably the greatest playwright among Shakespeare's contemporaries, echoes Sidney when he notes in *Timber: or Discoveries* that "*speech* is the only benefit man hath to expresse his excellencie of mind above other creatures."[2] In the same work, Jonson also observes that

> *language* most shewes a man: speake that I may see thee. It springs out of the most retired, and inmost parts of us, and is the Image of the Parent of it, the mind. No glasse renders a mans forme, or likenesse, so true as his speech.[3]

For Shakespeare speech is not only the most direct manifestation of that rational faculty "without the which we are pictures or mere beasts" (*Hamlet* IV.v.86), it is also a sign of being alive and participating fully in human life. When, toward the end of *Henry IV, Part I*, Hal finds Falstaff, whom he had left for dead, carrying Hotspur's corpse, he calls for him to demonstrate that he is truly alive by speaking:

> . . . Art thou alive,
> Or is it fantasy that plays upon our eyesight?
> I prithee speak. We will not trust our eyes
> Without our ears. . . .   (V.iv.132–35)

During a parallel scene in *Henry IV, Part II*, Hal discovers that his father, whom he had thought dead, is still alive, and his first response to that discovery indicates again the close association of speaking with living: "I never thought to hear you speak again" (IV.v.91). Another example of the same association occurs near the conclusion of *The Winter's Tale*. The sight of Hermione's "statue" coming to life and embracing Leontes prompts Camillo to call for proof that this woman long thought dead now truly participates in life in a way that is distinctively human: "If she pertain to life, let her speak too" (V.iii.113).

The obverse of that close connection between living and speaking evident in Shakespeare's dramas is the linking of silence with death. Hamlet's last words are "The rest is silence" (V.ii.347), and during *Richard II* Northumberland reports the death of Gaunt in words that stress the dead man's inability to speak: "His tongue is now a stringless instrument; / Words, life, and all, old Lancaster hath spent" (II.i.149–50). During the same play, Mowbray equates the endless banishment to which Richard has sentenced him with death precisely because exile will deny him the use of his powers of speech:

> The language I have learnt these forty years,
> My native English, now I must forgo,
> And now my tongue's use is to me no more
> Than an unstrung viol or a harp,
> Or like a cunning instrument cased up
> Or, being open, put into his hands
> That knows no touch to tune the harmony.
> Within my mouth you have enjailed my tongue,
> . . . .
> What is thy sentence then but speechless death,
> Which robs my tongue from breathing native breath?
>   (I.iii.159–66, 172–73)

My concern in this book is not with the lasting silences into which Shakespeare's characters lapse when they die but with certain silences that Shakespeare's words impose upon characters who remain alive. I call them open silences. For my purposes, it is crucial to distinguish between silences that are mandated by a Shakespearean playtext and those that a playtext allows but does not require. Isabella's silence each time the Duke proposes marriage to her during the final scene of *Measure for Measure* is required, since Shakespeare provides no words for her to speak. In contrast, during the same scene Shakespeare allows the actress playing Isabella and the director to decide how long—if at all—Isabella will remain silent

before responding to Mariana's plea to join her in asking the Duke
to spare Angelo's life. Isabella may hesitate a short while or a long
while before speaking, or she may not hesitate at all, but sooner or
later she must respond to Mariana's plea by speaking, on Angelo's
behalf, the words that Shakespeare has assigned to her:

> Most bounteous sir,
> Look, if it please you, on this man condemned
> As if my brother lived. I partly think
> A due sincerity governed his deeds
> Till he did look on me. Since it is so,
> Let him not die; . . .   (V.i.440–45)

The freedom Shakespeare allows at this point can be an extremely significant feature of any performance of *Measure for Measure*. An Isabella who is silent only briefly or even not at all before
beginning to speak for Angelo conveys a capacity for showing
mercy and forgiveness that is, or is becoming, virtually spontaneous, almost instinctive. The longer Isabella pauses before speaking the lines the playtext gives her—that is, the more sustained her
silence—the greater will be the audience's sense of the anguish and
bereavement she must struggle to overcome before bringing herself
to ask that mercy be shown to the man who, she thinks, is responsi-
ble for her brother's death. The effect of sustaining Isabella's silence
can reach beyond her to affect the audience's responses to other
characters, especially the Duke. The greater the audience's sense of
her anguish and grief while silent, the more possible it is that the
audience will be less sympathetic toward the man who imposes such
suffering upon her even while he knows that the brother for whom
she mourns is in fact alive.

What is an "open" silence? The full answer to that question will
emerge from the chapters that follow. Here I shall simply provide an
abstract definition and one detailed example. An open silence is one
whose precise meanings and effects, because they cannot be determined by analysis of the words of the playtext, must be established
by nonverbal, extratextual features of the play that emerge only in
performance. Such silences are usually required by Shakespeare's
words, and they occur most often during the final scene of a play.

Barnardine's silence all the while he is on stage during the final
scene of *Measure for Measure* offers a relatively simple example of
an open silence. The words of Shakespeare's playtext establish that
Barnardine is a duly convicted murderer whose guilt is "most mani-

fest and not denied by himself" (IV.ii.135). During act IV, scene iii, Barnardine defiantly refuses to submit to his own execution, thus thwarting the Duke's plan to use his head to convince Angelo that Claudio has been executed:

> Barnardine: I will not consent to die this day, that's certain.
>   Duke: O, sir, you must; and therefore I beseech you look forward on the journey you shall go.
> Barnardine: I swear I will not die to-day for any man's persuasion.
>   Duke: But hear you—
> Barnardine: Not a word; if you have anything to say to me, come to my ward, for thence will not I to-day.
>   [*Exit*]   (IV.iii.52–60)

Nowhere in the playtext of *Measure for Measure* does Shakespeare give to Barnardine or to any other character words that convey any sense of sorrow or repentance on Barnardine's part, and the timing of Barnardine's entrance during the final scene makes the absence of such words particularly striking. Barnardine, the murderer who has defiantly refused to be executed, is brought on immediately after Angelo has voiced his sorrow and asked to be executed for (as he thinks) killing Claudio:

> I am sorry that such sorrow I procure,
> And so deep sticks it in my penitent heart
> That I crave death more willingly than mercy;
> 'Tis my deserving, and I do entreat it.   (V.i.470–73)

Barnardine remains silent even after the Duke grants him life:

>   . . . Thou'rt condemned;
> But for these earthly faults, I quit them all,
> And pray thee take this mercy to provide
> For better time to come.   (V.i.478–81)

Does the unbroken silence that the Shakespearean playtext requires of Barnardine during the final scene signify his tongue-tied shock at having been given life? Is that silence a way of expressing Barnardine's gratitude, a gratitude beyond words, for the mercy the Duke has granted with words? Or is Barnardine's unremitting silence a sign of indifference to the Duke's mercy or even of an incorrigibility that such mercy can never touch? If so, is the audience watching a performance of *Measure for Measure* moved to question the Duke's wisdom in granting life to Barnardine? Does the audience reassess the relationship between justice and mercy that the Duke has established, perhaps doubting its appropriateness in this case? Or does the Duke's act of sparing a murderer who never voices any sense of guilt or repentance strike an audience as confirmation of the Duke's unconditional acceptance of the principle that human life is of such value that it must be preserved and cherished, no matter how viciously lived? Even if the Duke himself accepts that principle, and acts upon it, is the audience also convinced of its validity or its practicality?

A comparison of Barnardine's silence with the silence in which Iago wraps himself at the end of *Othello* can further clarify what I mean by an open silence. After Othello asks, "Will you, I pray, demand that demi-devil / Why he hath thus ensnared my soul and body," Iago speaks his final words: "Demand me nothing. What you know, you know. / From this time forth I never will speak word" (V.ii.300–305). Considered in the abstract, Iago's silence could be construed as a sign of remorse, particularly when one considers that in falling silent, Iago is in effect renouncing the power of speech that enabled him to destroy Othello by pouring "this pestilence into his ear" (II.iii.339). However, the responses Shakespeare gives to two of those who hear Iago vow not to speak establish that his silence is not only an act of defiance directed against Othello and those who now speak on Cyprus for the state of Venice but also a denial of the very possibility of prayer and remorse:

Lodovico: What, not to pray?
Gratiano: Torments will ope your lips.   (V.ii.306)

The final speech of the play, assigned to Lodovico, includes words that make it clear that, even after Othello's suicide, Iago's silent defiance remains untempered by any hint of remorse:

> O Spartan dog,
> More fell than anguish, hunger, or the sea!
> Look on the tragic loading of this bed.
> This is thy work. . . .   (lines 361–64)

Lodovico then assigns to Cassio, Othello's successor as "lord governor" of Cyprus, "the censure of this hellish villain, / The time, the place, the torture. O, enforce it" (lines 367–69). By giving words to other characters, Shakespeare makes clear that Iago's silence signifies defiance. It remains possible, of course, to vary Iago's defiance. He could, for example, refuse to obey Lodovico's command to "look on the tragic loading of this bed," or he might express his resolute defiance by smiling in silent triumph if he is forced to "look on it." That such variety is possible does not, however, undercut the fact that Iago's silence is an act of defiance.

Shakespeare does not use the words at his command to define a comparable focus for Barnardine's silence. Barnardine says nothing, and no character says anything in response to his silence. Barnardine's silence and others like it in Shakespeare's plays help us to realize the limits inherent in the approach that has dominated the study of Shakespeare's plays since at least the time of Dr. Johnson. Those who utilize that approach, which has reached its zenith in this century, seek to understand Shakespeare's plays by treating the words that Shakespeare wrote as if they were elements of a literary text rather than parts of a dramatic script. They take assumptions, concepts, and processes of analysis developed for and appropriate to works written to be read by individuals in silent solitude and apply them to works designed to be heard and seen by people who have come together as a group and in public in order to see and hear a play. The fundamental premise of what might be called the "literary" or "textual" method is that studying the words of a Shakespearean play will give adequate, even full, knowledge of the play itself. Applied to what Shakespeare wrote, the literary method has yielded and will continue to yield insights of power and beauty, and it should not be abandoned. However, we need to employ it now with a much sharper sense of how much it reveals and how much it obscures as it is used to convert the words of a play into a literary text, a work of literature in its own right.

What literary analysis tends by its nature to dismiss or to disregard is precisely the kind of problem posed by a silence such as Barnardine's. That silence cannot be dismissed as trivial or peripheral. It is, after all, a silence mandated by the fact that Shakespeare provides no words for Barnardine to speak during the final moments of *Measure for Measure*. In addition, Barnardine's silence bears directly on such major concerns of the play as the morality of capital punishment and the relationship between justice and mercy in society. The meanings and effects that his silence yields can significantly shape an audience's perceptions of how the play presents those issues—issues that continue to trouble and divide societies to this day.

A mode of analysis that takes as its exclusive point of reference the words of *Measure for Measure* cannot enable us to understand the precise meaning(s) and effect(s) of Barnardine's failure or refusal or inability to speak when he is granted life. Barnardine's silence is textually indeterminate; it is open. A silence like his takes on distinct coherence—a set of specific meanings and effects—only within the particular contexts established during actual performances of the play. Those contexts are primarily nonverbal and extratextual, and they can vary in remarkable, even contradictory, ways, endowing Barnardine's silence with a broad span of potential meanings and effects. Without contradicting Shakespeare's playtext, Barnardine's silence can be played as a sign of gratitude or of repentance that justifies the Duke's mercy. However, that same silence can, on another occasion and, again, without contradicting what Shakespeare wrote, be played as an act of indifference or even incorrigibility that elicits from the audience a far more qualified, ambivalent response to the Duke's mercifulness. Thus, granting life to Barnardine may be fully appropriate within the context established during one performance of *Measure for Measure* and entirely inappropriate within the context of a different performance of the play. The presence of open silences such as Barnardine's—silences whose meaning and effects are central yet can vary legitimately from production to production—requires a process of inquiry that unites close analysis of the words of Shakespeare's playtexts with equally rigorous analysis of performances.

□   □   □

Analysis of Shakespeare's open silences requires that we rethink our conception of the relationship between Shakespeare and those who perform and produce his plays. We also need to set aside the common and deeply engrained conviction that the process of creating a play by Shakespeare was completed in all essential detail when Shakespeare put down his quill. The prevailing expectation is that directors, actors, and designers should conform to Shakespeare's intentions as expressed in the words he wrote. Helene Keyssar has provided an account of what putting that expectation into practice entails:

> In speaking specifically of the strategy of drama, there are two sepa-
> rate but interrelated strategic processes: the strategy of the text as de-
> signed by the playwright and the strategy of the performance as com-
> manded by the director, actors, and designers. While it is not always the
> case, the latter should be dependent upon the former; that is, part of the
> importance of the notion of strategy to drama is that the director's
> knowledge of the strategy of the text should be the basic resource for
> production decisions of every kind.[4]

Open silences offer evidence that the relationship between the two "strategic processes" is more complex. Open silences are estab-lished by "the text as designed by the playwright," but because they do not allow us to deduce what Shakespeare intended should hap-pen during them, they make it impossible to use the text as "the basic resource for production decisions of every kind."

Open silences testify to the presence within Shakespeare's designs or strategies of moments that give full scope to the creative energies and talents of those who make performances of his plays possible. Perhaps the most remarkable feature of what Shakespeare wrote is the way in which he used his creativity to summon those who per-form and produce the play to exercise theirs. I prefer to think of the moment when Shakespeare finished setting down on paper the words of a particular play as the end of the first stages of a process of creation that is completed with each performance of the play. Open silences mark a relaxation, a suspension, of the total control that it is Shakespeare's prerogative as a playwright to exercise. On the actors, directors, and designers who perform and produce his plays, open silences confer the power to be virtual cocreators with him, to employ their power to fulfill the process that he began and framed but did not complete.

The advice that Shakespeare has Hamlet give to the players testi-fies to the importance of their creativity. "The purpose of playing," Hamlet tells them, is "to hold, as 'twere, the mirror up to nature" (III.ii.19–21). Hamlet's emphasis is on *playing*, on performing a play rather than writing one, and it is, he says, the process of playing that makes it possible for a play to illuminate the world within which it is performed—"to show virtue her own feature, scorn her own image, and the very age and body of the time his form and pressure" (lines 21–23). As Hamlet himself notes when he warns against the excesses of "those that play your clowns" (lines 36–37), it is possible that those who perform Shakespeare's plays will not measure up to the responsibilities placed upon them. Through ignorance, through lack of talent, or, most reprehensibly, through self-indulgence, they may fail to ally their creative powers with his. However, the proper response to the possibility or even the fact of such failures is not to ignore or deny the contributions that performers make to the creation of a Shakespearean play. We need instead to find better ways of understanding and evaluating the creative alliance of playwright with performers that Shakespeare's plays require.

Shakespeare's open silences also exemplify the freedom that is fundamental to all drama and that is particularly important to his plays. Such silences grant to those who perform and produce the plays the power to give them shape and coherence, thus ensuring that the plays will vary from production to production, even from performance to performance. Open silences are only one source of the freedom that Shakespeare's plays generate, but these silences serve especially well to illustrate that such freedom is not merely accidental and peripheral but extends to how major issues posed during a given play are resolved. The playtext of *Measure for Measure*, for example, clearly establishes that the relationship between justice and mercy is a primary concern of the play, but that same playtext, through silences such as Barnardine's, leaves for resolution during performance the question of just what the precise balance between those virtues is, should be, or can be. The freedom incorporated into Shakespeare's plays by such means as open silences gives his dramas an unparalleled capacity to adapt to and be enriched by external changes—changes in the composition and responses of audiences, in conventions of acting and staging, in the technical resources of the stage and in theater architecture, in conceptions of what drama is and does, and in the values of a given society moving through history.

The prevailing response to the fundamental freedom of Shakespeare's plays has been to ignore or deny it. In general, we have long preferred to equate his plays with the words that are present in them. Rendered in print, those words seem fixed, stable, available for sustained and repeated scrutiny. Words in print, words that have been textualized, conform to criteria for what is a proper object of study that, as I discuss in Chapter 6, have roots in cognitive and cultural patterns fostered by the introduction of typography and the related development of modern physical sciences. The play itself—fluid, changing, contingent—cannot meet those criteria. My fifth chapter includes a discussion of how stage traditions and the desire to settle upon a fixed, standard text for *King Lear*—to agree upon words that all can scrutinize—have had the effect of minimizing the freedom of the play's final moments.

Certainly the words of a Shakespearean play constitute a text rich enough and complex enough to merit study in its own right. My quarrel is not with the study of such texts but with the practice of substituting that study for study of the plays themselves. My controlling premise is that a play is not identical with its words and that the proper object for us to study is Shakespeare's plays, which include considerably more than the words preserved in the printed texts that have survived from his era or have been devised by subsequent editors. In the final chapter of this book I argue that the open silences within Shakespeare's plays and the freedom they generate pose epistemological and ontological problems that defy the methods and assumptions of textual or literary analysis. To solve those problems I apply to the study of Shakespeare's plays the principles of superposition and complementarity that physicists formulated during the early decades of this century in order to understand the atomic and subatomic levels of the material world.

Many will insist that to accept an inherent freedom in Shakespeare's plays is to distort or devalue what Shakespeare wrote. To me the contrary seems true. To acknowledge that a play can vary in crucial respects from performance to performance is to express the deepest respect for what Shakespeare wrote because it permits us to accept and preserve moments of freedom generated by the open silences that his words bring into being.

Did Shakespeare consciously craft the open silences in his plays? Since we lack such documents as Shakespeare's various drafts of each play and his notebooks, there is no way to answer that question definitively. Perhaps, perhaps not. If Shakespeare were conscious of open silences, what of the possibility that he had specific ideas about what he wanted to happen during them and that the acting company of which he was both a member and a shareholder then enacted his ideas in performance? Could it be, in other words, that what I have called open silences were not in fact "open" for Shakespeare himself? The possibility is one that we can neither dismiss nor confirm, for we have no conclusive evidence that Shakespeare functioned within his acting company, the Lord Chamberlain's Men (later the King's Men), as a "director" in any modern sense of the term.

Our uncertainty becomes greater if we keep in mind G. E. Bentley's demonstration, in *The Profession of Dramatist in Shakespeare's Time, 1590–1642*,[5] that what a playwright of that era wrote was generally the property of the acting company for whom he wrote it. Thus, as far as we can tell, what we today call Shakespeare's plays were not then thought of as "his" in the modern sense of the term. The fact that he was the author of "his" plays may very well not have given him stature within the King's Men equivalent to or even approaching the authority that subsequent generations, down to our own, have granted him. Indeed, it is conceivable (but, again, not demonstrable) that it was not Shakespeare's ideas that were enacted during an open silence but the ideas of another member of the company—Richard Burbage, perhaps, or Will Kempt—or even ideas that were, as John Russell Brown argues in *Free Shakespeare*,[6] formulated collectively and that remained subject to change.

Whether or not the open silences within Shakespeare's plays were "open" for him and for the King's Men, the fact remains that we do not know what the actors of his company did during those silences. A point of even greater importance is that we cannot deduce what their actions were by studying those words of Shakespeare that have come down to us. Whatever Shakespeare's intentions (if any), history has ensured that the silences that are my subject are "open" for us. Using Shakespeare's words as we have them, we can demonstrate that such silences do exist within specific plays. We can also demonstrate that they have major impact on the meanings and the effects those plays convey as well as serious implications for how we study plays by Shakespeare.

☐   ☐   ☐

This book is not a survey of all the open silences within Shakespeare's plays. My focus is upon open silences that occur during five plays written across the full span of Shakespeare's career: *A Midsummer Night's Dream, Twelfth Night, Measure for Measure, King*

Lear, and *The Tempest*. I have selected them because they illustrate both the diverse uses made of open silences and the kinds of problems those silences pose for those who study his plays—problems touching on issues of structure, theme, tone, and genre.[7]

My discussion of each of the plays upon which I focus includes analysis of particular productions—including productions for cinema and television—performed since the 1950s. I do not provide a comprehensive history of productions of those plays, and I do not discuss any one production in all its aspects. I chose for discussion productions that provide a sense of the range of possibilities that flow from particular moments of open silence. Unless otherwise noted, I have seen each of the stage productions discussed in detail at least once and studied the promptbook or the stage manager's book.

I should also like to direct attention to some of my terminology. In conformance with American usage, I treat "audience" as a noun that takes a singular verb. I realize, however, that phrases such as "the audience is" or "the audience feels" foster an impression of uniformity that is misleading because it obscures the possibility, perhaps even the likelihood, that individual members of the same audience have different responses. To emphasize that a play is a process unfolding in time, I use "during" rather than "in" as much as possible. I prefer, for example, to speak of what occurs "during" a scene or an act rather than "in" it. I use the word "script" to refer to a written (or printed) document intended to serve as the basis for a performance. Shakespeare wrote scripts, but each of them has become a "text," a document that in itself provides, as Hans-Georg Gadamer has explained, "the authoritative datum to which understanding and interpretation have to measure up."[8] When referring to the words that are components of Shakespeare's plays, I generally use the term "playtext," in order to convey a sense of both the status those words have acquired apart from the plays and the danger such status carries. Use of "playtext" will serve, I hope, as a recurring reminder that, even when printed and edited, the words of a play by Shakespeare are not a "text" in the same sense that a novel or *Paradise Lost* is a "text."

The words that make up what many would call the "text" of a play by Shakespeare have an authority that cannot be denied. Indeed, without those words, the open silences would not exist. The existence of open silences, however, compels us to acknowledge the limits of textual authority. The words of the text do not provide us with the means—"the authoritative datum"—for understanding the open silences that the words themselves generate. For such understanding we must turn to performances. What we can learn from performances is something other than, something different from, something outside of the knowledge that the text can provide. It is something without which our knowledge of the play is less than complete. For me a play is not identical with the words that make up its text (or texts), even if those words are Shakespeare's. A play by Shakespeare consists of—is—both its words and its performances.

Note on Sources

Aside from a few instances that are clearly identified, all quotations from Shakespeare's plays are from *William Shakespeare: The Complete Works*, Pelican text revised, general editor Alfred Harbage, first published in 1969 by Penguin Books and reprinted in 1969, 1970, 1971 (twice), 1972, 1974, and 1975; the specific reprint from which I quote was published in 1977 by Viking Press (New York). In quoting from the 1608 Quarto of *King Lear* and from the 1623 Folio, I have changed the Renaissance long "s" to modern "s" and normalized u/v and i/j in accordance with modern practices.

1. Hippolyta's Silence and the Poet's Pen

The opening moments of *A Midsummer Night's Dream* include a silence—Hippolyta's—that has reverberations that, reaching beyond the scene of which it is a wordless yet crucial element, touch upon the issue of how much (and how little) the words Shakespeare penned reveal about the play. The first words of the play are those of Theseus telling Hippolyta of the approach of their wedding day:

> Now, fair Hippolyta, our nuptial hour
> Draws on apace. Four happy days bring in
> Another moon; but, O, methinks, how slow
> This old moon wanes! She lingers my desires,
> Like to a stepdame or a dowager
> Long withering out a young man's revenue.   (I.i.1–6)

Hippolyta replies with the only words she speaks during the opening scene:

> Four days will quickly steep themselves in night,
> Four nights will quickly dream away the time;
> And then the moon, like to a silver bow
> New bent in heaven, shall behold the night
> Of our solemnities.   (lines 7–11)

When Theseus says that, having conquered her in battle, he will now make her his wife "in another key, / With pomp, with triumph, and with revelling" (lines 18–19), Hippolyta says nothing, and she maintains that silence the rest of the time she is onstage. The defeated Queen of the Amazons becomes a mute observer as the man who "won" her love by doing her "injuries" (line 17) rules that a young woman who is one of his subjects must die or live a life cloistered among women if she does not obey her father and enter into a marriage that she does not want.

The words Hippolyta does speak are of very limited use when we attempt to clarify the meanings and effects of her silence. What she says is part of a dialogue with Theseus that clearly reveals that each of them responds differently to the passage of time. For Theseus, time moves slowly toward their "nuptial hour," but for Hippolyta time moves swiftly. He laments "how slow / This old moon wanes," whereas she twice uses the word "quickly" to describe the passing of time: "Four days will quickly steep themselves in night, / Four nights will quickly dream away the time."

The words that Shakespeare assigns to Theseus and Hippolyta allow us—if we wish—to see the differences in their temporal responses as facets of an underlying harmony. In emphasizing how "quickly" time will move, Hippolyta can be reassuring Theseus that the hour for which he longs will soon arrive, and her words of reassurance can also convey her own sense of excited anticipation. Theseus and Hippolyta have differing senses of time's pace, but each can be accurate. Time can move both quickly and slowly, traveling, as Rosalind notes in *As You Like It*, "in divers paces with divers persons" (III.ii.293–94). The differences underscored by Hippolyta's use of "quickly" can suggest that, when they are together, the Duke of Athens and the Queen of the Amazons have a fuller sense of the complexity of time than either does in isolation.[1] The "nuptial hour" toward which each moves at a different pace becomes, then, a moment when they will complete a union that does not obliterate their differences but allows them to complement one another. Their differences become, in effect, the basis for a harmony that is more inclusive, more resilient, than would otherwise be possible.

The words Theseus and Hippolyta exchange at the start of the play permit us to see their differences as facets of an underlying harmony, but the words do not compel such a conclusion. The differences brought into focus by Hippolyta's use of "quickly" can, without distorting the words of Shakespeare's playtext, just as plausibly be taken as reflecting a conflict between Theseus and her. If the nuptial hour approaches so slowly for Theseus because he desires it so much, then perhaps it approaches so quickly for Hippolyta, the newly conquered queen of a society of women who had long resisted male domination, precisely because she desires it so little. In explaining that "time travels in divers paces with divers persons," Rosalind notes that it moves most swiftly for "a thief [going] to the gallows; for though he go as softly as foot can fall, he thinks himself too soon there" (III.ii.293–94, 311–12). In contrast, time, which gallops by for the thief, moves at a trot, Rosalind says, for

> . . . a young maid between the contract of her marriage and the day it is solemnized. If the interim be but a se'nnight, Time's pace is so hard that it seems the length of seven year.   (lines 299–302)

The opening lines of *A Midsummer Night's Dream* reverse those relationships. Theseus feels time moving slowly as if he were a maid awaiting her wedding day, whereas the response of the woman whom he has taken to be his bride is like that of a thief approaching the gallows. For her, as for the thief, time moves "quickly." Before the scene concludes, Theseus decrees, in the presence of a silent Hippolyta, that the wedding day she said will "quickly" arrive will also be the day on which Hermia must

> > . . . either prepare to die
> For disobedience to your father's will,
> Or else to wed Demetrius, as he would,
> Or on Diana's altar to protest
> For aye austerity and single life.   (lines 86–90)

Theseus' decree means that Hippolyta's movement through time, toward what will be the day of her marriage, becomes congruent with Hermia's movement through time, toward the same day, which will find her facing an involuntary marriage, the single life, or death. Each woman might think herself, like the thief on his way to the gallows, "too soon there."

The more closely we analyze the opening exchange between Theseus and Hippolyta, the more likely we are to see it with what Hermia calls a "parted eye, / When everything seems double" (IV.i.188–89). As they exist on the printed page, the words that make up that exchange are "double" in the sense of being radically ambiguous, of being equally capable of expressing harmony or conflict or even a combination of both. Because they are ambiguous, those words cannot provide the basis for specifying the precise meanings and effects of Hippolyta's silence. In fact, even if the meaning of the words were absolutely clear, they would not suffice as the basis for interpreting Hippolyta's silence. If, for example, we could determine beyond doubt that the dialogue between Theseus and Hippolyta established a fundamental harmony between them,

Hippolyta's subsequent silence could indicate either a continuation of that harmony (since she utters no objection to what Theseus does) or a breakdown of that harmony (since she does not verbally agree with what he does). The converse is also true. If the opening dialogue were taken as establishing conflict between them, Hippolyta's ensuing silence could then reflect either the continuation of that conflict or, since she is no longer voicing any disagreement with Theseus, the cessation of that conflict.

Because no character comments upon Hippolyta's silence, there is no way to discriminate among the possibilities her silence allows by using a mode of analysis that focuses exclusively upon the words of *A Midsummer Night's Dream* and thus treats what is a play as if it were a work of literature. Hippolyta's silence is textually indeterminate. It is open in the sense that it is established by the words that constitute the playtext, but once established, it is capable of having meanings and effects that are not fixed by those words and that take on distinct form and shape only during performances of the play. We cannot probe her silence with any precision unless we attend to what has happened during performances.

□   □   □

Four specific productions of *A Midsummer Night's Dream* since 1959 demonstrate the range of meanings and effects that Hippolyta's silence can generate without contradicting the words of Shakespeare's playtext. During Peter Hall's 1959 production at the Shakespeare Memorial Theatre in Stratford-upon-Avon, Hippolyta's silence confirmed the harmony between her and Theseus that was expressed during the opening dialogue.[2] She and Theseus sat side by side as he listened to Egeus' accusation and Hermia's reply. After warning Hermia to "take time to pause," Theseus stood and raised an unresisting Hippolyta to her feet. As they walked toward the staircase that dominated the set, Theseus stated that Hermia's decision must be made "by the next new moon— / The sealing day betwixt my love and me / For everlasting bond of fellowship" (lines 83–85). They reached the staircase and stood there together while Theseus set forth the third of Hermia's alternatives: "on Diana's altar to protest / For aye austerity and single life" (lines 89–90). The consistent pairing of Theseus and Hippolyta underscored the contrast between what that "sealing day" would bring for Hippolyta and what it would bring for Hermia. Their movements together also established that both Theseus and Hippolyta were oblivious to the contrast.

That pairing was interrupted briefly later in the scene, when Theseus walked away from Hippolyta and toward Hermia while advising her to "arm yourself / To fit your fancies to your father's will" (lines 117–18), but the interruption did not signify any breach in the relationship between Theseus and Hippolyta. Having warned Hermia that the Athenian law sentenced her "to death or to a vow of single life" if she failed to obey her father, Theseus turned immediately to the woman who was soon to become his bride and said, "Come, my Hippolyta" (line 122). Hippolyta's silent response was a model of the very type of obedience that Hermia had outspokenly refused to accept. Without hesitation, Hippolyta crossed toward Theseus and he toward her and, hands joined, they walked together toward the exit as he asked solicitously, "What cheer, my love?" (line 122).

Hall's production, in which Hippolyta's silence conveyed her untroubled, obedient acquiescence in the sentence imposed on Hermia, stands in pointed contrast to the production of *A Midsummer Night's Dream* that John Hirsch directed at the Stratford (Ontario) Shakespearean Festival in 1968. In Hirsch's production, the opening exchange between Theseus and Hippolyta established that theirs was a relationship marked by conflict rather than by harmony. Theseus was a nearly doddering old man in military dress uniform of the late nineteenth century; Hippolyta was a desirable woman of middle years who entered carrying a red rose and wearing a black dress that, in contrast to what Hermia and Helena wore, showed her shoulders. As Hippolyta spoke of how quickly "the night of our solemnities" would arrive, she stepped away from Theseus and stood, downstage right, on the lower of the two steps around most of the perimeter of the Festival Theatre's thrust stage. Theseus followed her, and when he ordered Philostrate to "stir up the Athenian youth to merriments" (line 12)—an order that took on sexual overtones and stressed his own age—Hippolyta again distanced herself from him. Using the bottom step, she crossed to the downstage left corner, where she sat on the first step. Theseus followed her again and, dropping to his hands and knees, tried to kiss her at the conclusion of his pledge to wed her "with pomp, with triumph, and with revelling." Hippolyta avoided the kiss by drawing back without ris-

ing—a gesture that conveyed both her distaste and Theseus' awkward, futile amorousness as he sought to convert his military victory
over the queen of the Amazons into a sexual conquest. The entrance
of Egeus, Hermia, Demetrius, and Lysander caught Theseus unpre-
pared. His failure as a wooer was obvious to them, and his subsequent exercise of ducal power became in part a compensation for
that failure.

Hirsch's production intensified the conflict between Theseus and
Hippolyta by using her silence to emphasize Hippolyta's recognition of the affinities between herself and Hermia. In this production,
in contrast to Hall's, Hippolyta was not at Theseus' side as he listened to and acted upon Egeus' complaint against Hermia. Theseus,
standing center stage, addressed himself to Hermia, who stood at
the downstage right corner while Hippolyta remained seated on the
top step at the downstage left corner. That triangular configuration
aligned the two women in their resistance to male authority, and
that alignment eventually became a pairing. Hippolyta stood up
when Demetrius called for Hermia to "relent" (line 91), and when
Lysander defiantly asked, "Why should not I then prosecute my
right?" (line 105), Hippolyta moved toward Hermia along the same
step that she had earlier used to dodge Theseus. The pairing of the
two women was completed following Hippolyta's response to Theseus' words, "Come, my Hippolyta." She crossed not to Theseus but
to Hermia. Although he stood holding his hand out toward her,
Hippolyta turned her back to him and handed to Hermia the red
rose she had carried since her entrance. She then exited, leaving
Theseus to ask, "What cheer, my love?" to her departing back. Hippolyta's demonstration that she felt neither duty toward nor desire
for Theseus gave a special flavor to the words Egeus used when he
and Demetrius obeyed Theseus' order to accompany him as he exited after Hippolyta: "With duty and desire we follow you" (line
127).

The rose that Hippolyta passed to Hermia extended the correspondences between the two women beyond the fact that both faced
marriages that were being imposed on them by men whose control
rested on law or military conquest. That rose made it easier for the
audience to realize that Hippolyta's life among the Amazon women
is analogous to that "single life" available to Hermia if, resisting her
father's will, she elects "to abjure / For ever the society of men"
(lines 65–66) and to live instead among women "in shady cloister

mewed" (line 71). The use of the rose to draw attention to the analogy was particularly appropriate because Theseus uses the rose metaphorically when he dismisses a life lived among women and without men:

> Thrice blessed they that master so their blood
> To undergo such maiden pilgrimage;
> But earthlier happy is the rose distilled
> Than that which, withering on the virgin thorn,
> Grows, lives, and dies in single blessedness.   (lines 74–78)

Passed from Hippolyta to Hermia and then to Helena, the only woman in the opening scene whom no man seeks to marry, that rose came to signify the "single blessedness" that Theseus dismisses. Hermia's response to his words is a defiant vow to undertake "such maiden pilgrimage":

> So will I grow, so live, so die, my lord,
> Ere I will yield my virgin patent up
> Unto his lordship whose unwished yoke
> My soul consents not to give sovereignty   (lines 79–82)

The sovereignty that Hermia explicitly refuses to accept is the sovereignty that, in Hirsch's production, the conquered Queen of the Amazons resisted in silence, and the life of "a barren sister" (line 72) that Hermia prefers to wedded life with Demetrius points toward the life in sisterhood that Hippolyta lost when Theseus triumphed in battle.

Celia Brannerman's 1980 production of *A Midsummer Night's Dream* for the New Shakespeare Company at the Open Air Theatre in Regent's Park, London, endowed Hippolyta's silence with quite different meanings and effects.[3] Theseus once again wore a military dress uniform of the late nineteenth century, but he was middle-aged and vigorous; Hippolyta wore vaguely near-Eastern garb, including what one reviewer called "Turkish harem pants."[4] Hippolyta did not move away when, kneeling on one knee, Theseus declared, "But I will wed thee in another key, / With pomp, with triumph, and with revelling." That posture suggested that the conqueror was submitting to the conquered, and thus Theseus' words became a conciliatory pledge rather than a self-aggrandizing announcement of his capacity to shift styles as martial affairs gave way to marital concerns.

Standing side by side, Theseus and Hippolyta both found Egeus' complaint against Hermia and Lysander amusing at first. Egeus concluded his initial speech by opening a book he carried and citing the law that entitled him, as Hermia's father, to "beg the ancient privilege of Athens":

> As she is mine, I may dispose of her,
> Which shall be either to this gentleman
> Or to her death, according to our law
> Immediately provided in that case.   (lines 41–45)

Theseus himself checked Egeus' citation and handed the book, still open, to Hippolyta, before he turned to Hermia and said, "Be advised, fair maid, / To you your father should be as a god" (lines 46–47). As Theseus listened to Hermia's reply, Hippolyta stood slightly away from him studying the book of laws. When Hermia asked to "know / The worst that may befall me in this case / If I refuse to wed Demetrius," Theseus replied, "Either to die the death, or to abjure / For ever the society of men" (lines 62–66). Having different characters consult the book of laws brought into focus the fact that Theseus here allows Hermia an alternative that her father had not mentioned when he called for either her obedience or her death, "according to our law / Immediately provided in that case." In offering Hermia the opportunity to live a life outside "the society of men," Theseus made the first of several efforts to mollify the silent woman who would soon be his wife and who had been until very recently the head of a society that consisted entirely of women.

On hearing Theseus fix as Hermia's deadline "the sealing day betwixt my love and me / For everlasting bond of fellowship," Hippolyta angrily and loudly snapped shut the book of laws—a gesture sharply different from the actions of Hippolyta and Theseus at the comparable point in Hall's production, when their gestures demonstrated their unbroken fellowship. Theseus rose and raised Hippolyta to her feet, after which they walked hand in hand toward the staircase as he set the deadline. The Theseus of Brannerman's production tried again to mollify a Hippolyta whose displeasure was unspoken but also unconcealed as he spoke his final words of counsel to Hermia:

> For you, fair Hermia, look you arm yourself
> To fit your fancies to your father's will;
> Or else the law of Athens yields you up

(Which by no means we may extenuate)
To death, or to a vow of single life.   (lines 117–21)

In most productions of *A Midsummer Night's Dream*, the words "which by no means we may extenuate" are spoken to Hermia and emphasize the certainty of "death" or "single life" if she persists in defying her father's will. Brannerman's Theseus, however, addressed the words to Hippolyta rather than to Hermia, and they become, because of that interpretation, an effort by Theseus to ease Hippolyta's displeasure by explaining his own inability to mitigate the workings of Athenian legal processes. The effort failed. Hippolyta responded to the next words Theseus spoke ("Come, my Hippolyta") by stepping toward him, slapping the book of laws into his hands, and proceeding to exit without him. He was left to ask after her, in a last, futile effort at reconciliation, "What cheer, my love?" In Brannerman's production, Hippolyta's silence was part of a process whereby, as she witnessed Theseus' handling of Hermia's predicament, Hippolyta suspended her initial receptiveness to marriage with Theseus.

In his much acclaimed 1970 production of *A Midsummer Night's Dream* for the Royal Shakespeare Company (RSC), Peter Brook used Hippolyta's silence to deepen a split between her and Theseus that was present but muted during the play's opening dialogue.[5] Theseus and Hippolyta stood together during that exchange, and Hippolyta did not give the word "quickly" an overtly hostile emphasis, but she walked away, crossing from stage right to stage left after Theseus voiced his pledge to wed her "with pomp, with triumph, and with revelling."

When Egeus presented his case against Hermia and Lysander, Theseus and Hippolyta remained apart, seated downstage right and downstage left, respectively. That configuration fixed and emphasized their separation.[6] Hippolyta stayed seated until after Hermia's declaration that she would not marry Demetrius, to "whose unwishèd yoke / My soul consents not to give sovereignty." A sustained pause followed the word "sovereignty," during which no one moved or spoke. Then Hippolyta rose to her feet. The timing of her movement brought into focus her unspoken resistance to the sovereignty over her that Theseus had won in battle and would now exercise in marriage. That resistance, in turn, sharpened the words with which Theseus broke the stillness that followed the word "sovereignty." "Take time to pause," he cautioned Hermia. He then set the deadline for Hermia's decision, and in the specific context of Brook's production, this announcement of that deadline was also a declaration of his resolve to demonstrate his sovereignty over Hippolyta. Hermia must decide "by the next new moon," which would also be, Theseus stressed, "the sealing day betwixt my love and me / For everlasting bond of fellowship."

Another distinct pause followed Theseus' final warning to Hermia that if she chose to resist her father's authority and did not marry Demetrius, the law of Athens would yield her up "to death, or to a vow of single life." That pause ended when Theseus said, "Come, my Hippolyta." Hippolyta, however, stood motionless as Theseus crossed toward her, and before reaching her, he stopped to ask, "What cheer, my love?" When she still did not step toward him or speak, he turned in embarrassed anger to address Demetrius and Egeus. The Queen of the Amazons continued to stand motionless and silent as he spoke to the two men, and she did not join Theseus when he exited through the door upstage right. Instead, Hippolyta walked alone toward the door upstage left, silently challenging Theseus' claim that she is "*my* Hippolyta," "*my* love" (emphasis added). On reaching the doors, Theseus and Hippolyta stopped and looked briefly at one another before each exited separately. With "duty and desire," Egeus and Demetrius then followed Theseus through the door upstage right. Their eager compliance with his order to "go along" gave a final definition to Hippolyta's silent and Hermia's explicit refusal to submit to the sovereignty that men claimed over them.

Another way of demonstrating the impact that Hippolyta's silence can have is to consider a production—Elijah Moshinsky's in 1981 for BBC-TV[7]—that obliterated it. Moshinsky split Shakespeare's single opening scene into several "scenes" set in different locations. The first of Moshinsky's scenes opened by having the camera show Hippolyta, dressed in black, pacing restlessly, even angrily, in front of a line of attendants who stood along one wall of a room. The voice of Theseus speaking the play's first lines intruded as the audience watched Hippolyta. Then the camera showed him, still wearing armor, standing in front of his attendants, ranged along the opposite wall. Facing him across that intervening space, Hippolyta replied without in any way narrowing the distance, both physical and emotional, between them. After Hippolyta finished speaking, Theseus first ordered Philostrate to "stir up the Athenian youth to merriments," then crossed until he stood face to face with an unsmiling, defiant Hippolyta. In an assertion of his will and dominance, he declared to her his resolve to wed her "with pomp, with triumph, and with revelling."

Moshinsky's production then shifted directly to the arraignment of Hermia, which, set in a different room, became a scene distinct from the exchange between Theseus and Hippolyta that began the play. Hippolyta was not present during this second scene to watch in silence as Theseus heard the "complaint" against Hermia and passed judgment. Her absence negated all possibility of establishing visual correspondences between Hippolyta's situation and Hermia's, and Moshinsky squandered the potential established by his interpretation of the opening dialogue between Theseus and Hippolyta. Moshinsky thus wasted the opportunity presented by the silence that Shakespeare's words impose on Hippolyta—the same opportunity that Hall, Hirsch, Bannerman, and Brook exploited in sharply divergent ways.

□ □ □

The diverse meanings and effects that Hippolyta's silence yields have an impact that reaches beyond the opening scene. Her silence can be the primary factor in defining the nature of her relationship with Theseus, and that relationship in turn can shape the alignments among the various characters and even alter the structure of the play. Consider the possible consequences of endowing Hippolyta's silence with meanings and effects that establish—as Hall's production did—that the relationship between Theseus and Hippolyta is harmonious from the start of the play. Their harmony then contrasts with the discord that characterizes the relationship between Oberon and Titania and the interactions of Hermia, Lysander, Demetrius, and Helena.

Shakespeare's positioning of Theseus' and Hippolyta's first appearance after the opening scene illustrates how the Duke of Athens and the Queen of the Amazons, who are soon to be married, can function as a mean between the King and Queen of the Fairies, who are already married, and the four young Athenians who are seeking spouses. Shakespeare has Theseus and Hippolyta, whose amity has never been in doubt, enter immediately after Oberon and Titania

find that they are "new in amity" (IV.i.86). Consequently, Theseus
and Hippolyta are present when the four young Athenians awake to
find that, after the confusions of the night, they are paired in combinations that Theseus then validates when he declares that "in the
temple, by and by, with us, / These couples shall eternally be knit"
(lines 179–80). In productions such as Hall's, the harmony that
Oberon and Titania attain is the harmony that Theseus and Hippolyta have enjoyed since the opening moments of the play, and it is
through Oberon's manipulations that the four young lovers find
their affections realigned in ways that allow them to participate in
that harmony. If Hippolyta's silence signifies concord between Theseus and Hippolyta, *A Midsummer Night's Dream* becomes a play
whose structure is based on the principle of repetition. The opening
exchange between Theseus and Hippolyta establishes the harmony
that emerges from conflict, the amity in union that follows enmity
in battle. The audience then watches a variety of characters go
through variations of the same change from discord to concord.

If, however, Hippolyta's silence signifies a conflict with Theseus,
alignments among the various characters shift. The relationship between Theseus and Hippolyta at the start of the play does not establish a concordant order in which other characters eventually participate. Instead, the conflict between the Duke of Athens and the
Queen of the Amazons is the initial manifestation of a more fundamental disorder that surfaces again in the quarrel between father
and daughter and in the squabbling over which young man will be
paired with Hermia and which with Helena. The source of that
disorder lies, one learns at the start of act II, outside the human
realm, in the battle under way between the King and Queen of the
Fairies that disrupts everything from the cycle of the seasons to the
patterns of the Morris dancers. "And this same progeny of evils
comes," Titania advises Oberon,

> From our debate, from our dissension;
> We are their parents and original.   (II.i.115–17)

The occasion of their quarrel is Titania's refusal to give to Oberon
the changeling boy whom she prizes because of her affection for his
mother, who died giving birth to him: "And for her sake," Titania
tells Oberon, "do I rear up her boy; / And for her sake I will not
part with him" (II.i.136–37). In her insistence on keeping the boy,
Titania, like Hermia, explicitly refuses to submit to a male who

claims authority over her. She defies her husband just as Hermia defies both her father and her duke. In performance, Hippolyta's silent defiance of the man who has conquered her and will be her husband can be just as pointed, even if unspoken. In her silence the defeated Queen of the Amazons can even convey a commitment, like Titania's, to the primacy of the bonds that link one woman to another—a commitment that marriage does not extinguish. The pattern of resistance to an authority figure can be extended to include the scenes involving the "rude mechanicals" (III.ii.9), during which Bottom and to a lesser extent the other would-be actors repeatedly challenge Quince's decisions as director.

Peter Brook's production of *A Midsummer Night's Dream* illustrates the force such parallels can exert. He had the same actor play both Egeus and Quince, thus linking the father who tries to force his daughter to fit her fancies to his will and the novice director who struggles to force his performers to make their various and erratic fancies conform with his befuddled conception of dramatic order. Brook also doubled the roles of Oberon and Theseus, of Hippolyta and Titania, and of the courtiers and fairies. Probably the most striking instance of doubling involved Philostrate, the official charged with providing entertainment to the Athenian court, and Puck, the agent through whom Oberon seeks to execute his designs and the figure through whom, in the Epilogue, Shakespeare articulates the correspondence between what happens to the characters and what happens to the audience during the play:

> If we shadows have offended,
> Think but this, and all is mended—
> That you have but slumb'red here
> While these visions did appear.
> And this weak and idle theme,
> No more yielding but a dream,
> Gentles, do not reprehend.   (V.i.412–18)

The extensive doubling enabled Brook to use the process of seeing to give nonverbal but compelling confirmation to Puck's summary of the dreamlike visions experienced by the theater audience during *A Midsummer Night's Dream*. How audiences saw during performances of Brook's production was similar to how Hermia says she sees on awakening after her night in the forest: "Methinks I see these things with parted eye, / When everything seems double."[8]

When Hippolyta's silence is used to establish or to deepen her conflict with Theseus, the structure of *A Midsummer Night's Dream* changes accordingly. The principle of repetition is replaced by the principle of gradual intensification, followed by sudden, almost explosive transformation.[9] In the first four acts, the prevailing movement is toward disorder, which becomes ever more baffling to those caught up in it. At the moment during act IV, scene i when that disorder seems greatest, it is—to use Quince's not inappropriate malapropism—"translated" into order.[10] Titania awakes to find herself loathing the man with the head of the ass, whom she has taken to her bed, and willing to join hands and dance with Oberon without any thought of the changeling boy or his mother. The four young Athenians, each of whose last conscious memories were of hunting a member of the same sex in order to do battle,[11] awake to find themselves peacefully paired, male and female. With Theseus, Hippolyta, and Egeus standing before them, they learn, to their own amazement, that the answer to Theseus' question ("Begin these woodbirds but to couple now," line 139) is yes. His affections changed "I wot not by what power" (line 163), Demetrius, dazed but certain, declares that he now loves Helena, leaving Egeus with no one whom he can compel Hermia to marry. The process of "translation" even touches Theseus. Overruling Egeus, he sets aside without explanation the law whose validity he had upheld during the opening scene while Hippolyta looked on in silence, and he sanctions the union of Hermia with Lysander and of Helena with Demetrius.

The decision to have Hippolyta's silence convey that she and Theseus are (or come to be) in conflict during the opening scene requires that another decision be made about when that conflict ends, allowing Theseus and Hippolyta to participate in the "amity" engendered by the reconciliation of Oberon and Titania. One possibility is that the conflict has already ended when Theseus and Hippolyta enter in act IV, scene i, immediately after Oberon and Titania have exited together "new in amity." Theseus says,

> We will, fair Queen, up to the mountain's top
> And mark the musical confusion
> Of hounds and echo in conjunction.   (lines 108–10)

Then Hippolyta speaks for the first time since falling silent during the opening scene. The very fact that she breaks her silence can testify to a reconciliation with Theseus, and that possibility is strengthened when one considers that what she says can be an endorsement of Theseus' sense of the thrill of the hunt:

> I was with Hercules and Cadmus once
> When in a wood of Crete they bayed the bear
> With hounds of Sparta. Never did I hear
> Such gallant chiding; for, besides the groves,
> The skies, the fountains, every region near
> Seemed all one mutual cry. I never heard
> So musical a discord, such sweet thunder.   (lines 111–17)

However, the words Hippolyta speaks when she breaks her silence—like those she uttered at the start of the play before falling silent—need not necessarily signify harmony with Theseus. Twice she uses the word "never" ("Never did I hear" and "I never heard"), each time in a phrase that can convey her belief that the hunting that Theseus now proposes cannot measure up to what she has known in the past. Delivered with a skeptical or belittling edge, her words can convey continuing discord with Theseus, and if they do, the moment when she and Theseus are joined in amity must come later in the scene, perhaps after Theseus says, "Egeus, I will overbear your will" (line 178) and gives his approval to the marriages of Hermia with Lysander and Demetrius with Helena. With that decision Theseus disregards the Athenian law defining Egeus' paternal rights over Hermia, a law that, he had earlier said, "by no means we may extenuate." In Brannerman's production especially, those words emphasized Theseus' respect for Athenian law. By exploiting the parallels between the exit Theseus and Hippolyta make in this scene and the exit they make during the opening scene, Brannerman had their reconciliation flow directly from Theseus' refusal to heed Egeus' call for "the law, the law" (line 154). When Theseus said, after announcing the triple marriages, "Come, Hippolyta" (line 185), Hippolyta's reaction was very different from her reaction when he said, "Come, my Hippolyta" during the opening scene. She responded not by slapping the book of Athenian laws into Theseus' hands and exiting without him, but by taking first Egeus' hand and then Theseus', after which the three of them exited together.

If Hippolyta and Theseus are in harmony when they enter, the rest of act IV, scene i shows order and the awareness of order emerging in a clearly hierarchical pattern—beginning with the King and

Queen of the Fairies, followed by Theseus and Hippolyta, and finally by the four young lovers. A different pattern develops, however, if the reconciliation between Theseus and Hippolyta is delayed until Theseus affirms the lovers' pairings. Theseus' willingness to make that affirmation becomes, in effect, a condition for the reconciliation, and the movement from disorder to order does not proceed hierarchically, but rather from Oberon and Titania, to the four young lovers, to Theseus and Hippolyta. The Duke of Athens and the Queen of the Amazons—recent foes in actual battle—are the last to share in the concord that can result from the union of male and female.

The latest that the reconciliation between Theseus and Hippolyta can occur is the start of act V, which opens with Hippolyta saying, " 'Tis strange, my Theseus, what these lovers speak of." This is the first time during the play that she addresses Theseus by name, and her use of "my," conveying acceptance, even possessiveness, echoes Theseus' use of the same adjective during the opening scene: "Come, my Hippolyta," and "What cheer, my love?" The fact that Hippolyta (might well have) resisted the implications of that word during the opening scene makes her use of it now, immediately after the marriage ceremony, all the more telling. Perhaps equally telling is that the phrase "my Theseus" establishes a correspondence between the first words an audience hears Hippolyta speak to the man who has just become her husband and the first words Titania speaks when she awakes from her sleep and finds herself reconciled with her husband: "My Oberon, what visions have I seen" (IV.i.75).[12]

□   □   □

Hippolyta's open silence occurs during the opening scene of a play in which Shakespeare calls attention to and celebrates his own success in using language to engender dramatic illusion. To solve the problem posed by the fact that Pyramus and Thisby must meet by moonlight, Bottom suggests they "leave a casement of the great chamber window, where we play, open, and the moon may shine in at the casement" (III.i.48–50). Quince counters with a proposal to substitute figurative moonbeams for actual moonlight:

> Or else one must come in with a bush of thorns and a lantern, and say he comes to disfigure, or to present, the person of Moonshine.
>
> (lines 51–53)

Their laughable efforts highlight by contrast Shakespeare's success in coping with virtually the same problem. He deploys the resources of language in order to conjure up the illusionary darkness and moonlight in which much of *A Midsummer Night's Dream* takes place. We can better appreciate what Shakespeare achieves by means of words if we recall that most performances of the play in Shakespeare's time took place in daylight in an outdoor theater. Those who watched those first performances imposed on the daylight that their eyes registered the fictional darkness and moonlight that Shakespeare's language imprinted upon their minds.[13] They saw "not with the eyes, but with the mind" (I.i.234). By effectively using words to "present" moonlight during the play, Shakespeare gives Theseus' description of how a poet uses language a validity that Theseus himself did not intend:

> And as imagination bodies forth
> The forms of things unknown, the poet's pen
> Turns them to shapes, and gives to airy nothing
> A local habitation and a name.   (V.i.14–17)

Hippolyta's silence is open not because Shakespeare lacked the skill to give her words but because he did not exercise that skill, did not employ the power of his "poet's pen" to give her silence precisely fixed meanings and effects. He did not use the words at his command to provide her silence with "a local habitation and a name"—with specific "shapes." Until and unless her silence is given body during a performance, it remains one of those "things unknown." In effect, Shakespeare has assigned to those who perform *A Midsummer Night's Dream* the power to give Hippolyta's silence shape and local habitation. That power is not minor or peripheral, for the exercise of it determines the relationships among characters and the structural principle of the play. As the productions I have discussed illustrate, the exercise of that power can bring forth from Hippolyta's silence meanings and effects that differ, sometimes profoundly, yet remain compatible with the words that Shakespeare did pen.

Relinquishing the power to shape Hippolyta's silence entails risks. Like Quince, Bottom, and the others who rehearse and then perform the play of Pyramus and Thisby, actors and directors can, and have, and will run roughshod over the words a playwright puts down for them.[14] An open silence like Hippolyta's removes even the frail check that the dramatist's words impose upon their impulses and inclinations.

Balancing such risks are certain rewards. Because the words that came from Shakespeare's "poet's pen" establish the existence of Hippolyta's silence but do not specify its meanings and effects, those who perform and produce the play must do more than enact Shakespeare's intentions. Lacking the words necessary to know what Shakespeare intended, they must use their skills to determine what the meanings and effects of her silence will be. They must enact intentions that are theirs, not Shakespeare's. As they do, *A Midsummer Night's Dream* becomes their play as well as his and acquires a vitality it would not otherwise have.

Hippolyta's silence, in its openness, also offers another benefit. It helps to endow *A Midsummer Night's Dream* with the capacity to change significantly while retaining identity and coherence—to remain itself yet be "translated" not just from performance to performance and production to production but even from era to era across the centuries. To give but one example, *A Midsummer Night's Dream* can better and more revealingly accommodate and be adapted to the values and concerns brought to the fore by the feminist movement precisely because Hippolyta's silence allows for the possibility that she, like Hermia, does not submit to male authority. A version of the play that included words with which Hippolyta voiced her acceptance of Theseus' authority would not allow such a possibility. The freedom and flexibility generated by Hippolyta's silence increase the likelihood that, despite the changes in values and perceptions that come with time, *A Midsummer Night's Dream* will continue to find "a local habitation" that will allow audiences better to understand themselves and their culture.

2. Silence, Friendship, and *Twelfth Night*

The Folio of 1623 gives the full title of *Twelfth Night* as "*Twelfth Night, Or what you will*," and with that "*Or*" the play seems to announce its capacity to change and vary, to be "*what you will*." That capacity is largely the result of the silence imposed on Antonio during the play's final scene. Antonio's silence is open in the same sense that Hippolyta's is open, but his silence differs from hers in a significant way. Unlike hers, his is a silence that is unbroken, lasting. Hippolyta is silent during most of the opening scene of *A Midsummer Night's Dream*, but her silence eventually ends. When the audience next sees her—at the start of act IV, scene i—she breaks her silence by speaking to Theseus. In contrast, Antonio does not speak again after he asks Sebastian:

> How have you made division of yourself?
> An apple cleft in two is not more twin
> Than these two creatures. Which is Sebastian?   (V.i.214–16)

For the rest of the time that Antonio is onstage, he says nothing to anyone, including Sebastian, and—a fact of equal importance—no one, including Sebastian, says anything to Antonio or even about him for the rest of the play.

Sebastian himself never answers the questions that his loving friend Antonio asks with the last words an audience hears him speak. Sebastian's response is to turn from Antonio without speaking; he then finds himself looking upon the person who is, he soon learns, Viola. After Sebastian's entrance, neither Viola, who is Sebastian's sister, nor Olivia, who is his new wife, speaks a word to the man who saved his life and is his beloved friend. Viola's silence is all the more noteworthy because it was Antonio's willingness to take up her quarrel that first alerted her to the possibility that the brother whom she thought dead is still alive:

> He named Sebastian. I my brother know
> Yet living in my glass. Even such and so

In favor was my brother, and he went
Still in this fashion, color, ornament,
For him I imitate. O, if it prove,
Tempests are kind, and salt waves fresh in love!   (III.iv.359–64)

Olivia's silence toward Antonio contrasts with the words that Portia
speaks during the closing moments of *The Merchant of Venice* when
she meets another Antonio, who is her new husband's beloved
friend: "Sir, you are very welcome to our house" (V.i.139). To the
Antonio of *Twelfth Night*, Olivia offers no such welcome. Orsino,
who takes care during the play's last moments to order attendants
to pursue Malvolio "and entreat him to a peace" (V.i.369), utters
no words that eliminate or even mitigate the danger in which Antonio stands because his love for Sebastian has made him (as Orsino
points out) the prisoner of those "whom thou in terms so bloody
and so dear / Hast made thine enemies" (V.i.65–66).

Early during the final scene of *Twelfth Night*, Antonio, mistaking
Viola (as Cesario) for Sebastian, declares that Sebastian's "false
cunning"

(Not meaning to partake with me in danger)
Taught him to face me out of his acquaintance,
And grew a twenty years removèd thing
While one would wink; . . .   (V.i.80–84)

Antonio is wrong, of course, but the silence between Antonio and
Sebastian after Sebastian sees Viola establishes the possibility that
what is, at the moment it is spoken, an erroneous account of Sebastian's treatment of Antonio becomes an accurate description of how
Sebastian treats him after finding Viola alive. Sebastian says nothing
to Antonio, and that silence may arise from Sebastian's joy, from
forgetfulness or indifference toward Antonio, or even from a desire
to reject him. Whatever its source, Sebastian's silence toward Antonio can be tantamount, in effect if not intentionally, to treating his
friend as "a twenty years removèd thing."

The silence that envelops Antonio can also establish another correspondence between the early and late moments of the final scene.
Shortly after the scene starts, Feste tells Orsino that he fares "the
better for my foes, and the worse for my friends" (V.i.10–11). Antonio is both Sebastian's beloved friend and, as Antonio himself
declares, "on base and ground enough, / Orsino's enemy" (V.i.69–

70). However, insofar as neither Sebastian nor Orsino says anything to Antonio during the play's final moments, friend and foe treat him alike, and Antonio, in speaking to neither of them after Sebastian sees Viola, treats the two of them alike. His silence and theirs allow the play to pose the question of whether Antonio fares the better because of his enemy and the worse because of his friend.

Antonio's silence occurs during the concluding moments of *Twelfth Night*, moments that also reconcile and integrate various kinds of love that draw one person to another. Orsino, during these moments, announces that he is now willing to accept as a sister the woman whom he has sought for his wife:

> Olivia: My lord,[1] so please you, these things further thought on,
> To think me as well a sister as a wife,
> One day shall crown th'alliance on't, so please you,
> Here at my house and at my proper cost.
> Duke: Madam, I am most apt t'embrace your offer.   (V.i.306–10)

By agreeing to take Olivia as a sister, Orsino replaces, as it were, the brother whose death had prompted Olivia's resolution to live "like a cloistress . . . / And water once a day her chamber round / With eye-offending brine" (I.i.29–31). For her part, Olivia, married to the man who is (she learns) Sebastian, accepts as a sister the person she thought she had taken for a husband but is, in fact, her actual husband's sister. "A sister; you are she" (V.i.316), she tells Viola. The love for Orsino that Viola conceived and acted upon as his servant Cesario moves her to declare, "and I, most jocund, apt, and willingly, / To do you rest a thousand deaths would die" (lines 126–27). That love enables her to accept the marriage Orsino offers in terms that draw attention to the shift in their relationship, from master and servant to husband and wife:

> Your master quits you; and for your service done him,
> So much against the mettle of your sex,
> So far beneath your soft and tender breeding,
> And since you called me master for so long,
> Here is my hand; you shall from this time be
> Your master's mistress.   (lines 311–16)

The basis for Orsino's proposal of marriage to the person who is, he learns, Viola is the love he has developed for the servant and confidant whom he knew as Cesario. The shift from being Orsino's servant to being her "master's mistress" means that Viola succeeds where Malvolio fails. The steward who dreams,[2] even before finding Maria's letter, of becoming his mistress' master through marriage, never gets "to be Count Malvolio" (II.v.32).

The playtext of Twelfth Night requires that four characters—Viola, Olivia, Sebastian, and Orsino—discover as the play proceeds to its conclusion that they are bound to one another in complementary and interlocking relationships of love. Those loving relationships generate a festivity that they and the audience share. Antonio's open silence provides one means by which that festivity may or may not be modified during performance to achieve different emotional tones and to strike various balances among the play's interrelated themes of self-knowledge, excess, and the fluid complexity of personal relationships.[3] The last words spoken to Antonio are Sebastian's question "Fear'st thou that, Antonio?" (V.i.213), and the last words that Antonio speaks are another question, "Which is Sebastian?" The unbroken open silence that Shakespeare's playtext requires of Antonio raises the question of whether the love he feels for Sebastian is included among the modes of loving that join Viola, Orsino, Sebastian, and Olivia in a nexus that includes the love between man and woman, brother and sister, master and servant. Antonio's silence does not rule out the possibility that he and his love are included, but it is equally true that his silence does not dictate that he and his love must be included.

Malvolio's final exit, after vowing revenge, has a similar capacity either to increase the play's festivity by giving ludicrous final expression to Malvolio's vanity or to dampen that festivity by conveying the anguish inflicted on him by those whose "sportful malice" (V.i.355) has gone too far. In contrast with Antonio, Malvolio both speaks and is spoken to before making his final exit. Olivia, in what may be tantamount to an invitation to participate in the merriment, explicitly assures Malvolio of justice:

> . . . Prithee be content.
> This practice hath most shrewdly passed upon thee;
> But when we know the grounds and authors of it,
> Thou shalt be both the plaintiff and the judge
> Of thine own cause.   (V.i.341–45)

Malvolio's refusal to be included is just as explicit: "I'll be revenged on the whole pack of you" (V.i.367). No one extends such an invitation to Antonio who, far from threatening revenge, is himself vulnerable to the desire for vengeance implicit in Orsino's denunciation of him ("Notable pirate, thou salt-water thief" [V.i.63]) and in the officer's account of what Antonio did to the Illyrian fleet and to Orsino's nephew Titus:

> Orsino, this is that Antonio
> That took the Phoenix and her fraught from Candy;
> And this is he that did the Tiger board
> When your young nephew Titus lost his leg.   (V.i.54–57)

In his silence Antonio neither asks to be nor refuses to be included in the harmony engendered by the diverse kinds of love uniting Olivia, Orsino, Sebastian, and Viola.

□   □   □

Directors of *Twelfth Night* since the mid-1950s have responded in widely different ways to the challenge posed by Antonio's silence. One director's response was to dodge the challenge by arranging for Antonio to exit unnoticed while the audience's attention was being directed elsewhere.[4] Frank Rutledge, in his 1972 production for the Performing Arts Company of Michigan State University, took a different tack.[5] He had Antonio escape, in a manner clearly visible to the audience, from the officers guarding him while they and everyone else onstage watched, mesmerized, as Sebastian and Viola came face to face. By doing that, Rutledge made the moment of Sebastian's reunion with his sister coincide with the moment of his friend's escape from the danger that was a consequence of his love for Sebastian. Cut short in that way, Antonio's silence never became a prominent feature of the production.

Yakov Fried, in his 1955 movie of *Twelfth Night*, timed Antonio's escape from Illyria differently—in a way that sustained his silence much longer and developed the contrast between Malvolio and him.[6] In Fried's film, it was the officers guarding Malvolio who responded to Orsino's order to follow the departing Malvolio and "entreat him to a peace." Antonio reacted to the opportunity that their departure created by leaping upon a nearby horse and galloping to freedom. He did not so much as glance back at Sebastian, and since the camera had not focused on him after Sebastian turned from him and saw Viola, the audience had no sense that he felt any

anguish at being separated from his beloved friend. Just outside the
gates of the city, Antonio sped past an embittered Malvolio who
was trudging away from the city on foot. Thus, Malvolio's vengeful
withdrawal from Illyria became the occasion for Antonio's escape
from the threat of Illyrian vengeance.

In both Rutledge's production and Fried's movie, Antonio did
not participate in the loving relationships binding Olivia, Sebastian,
Viola, and Orsino, but that did not darken or undercut the festivity
that surrounded the fulfillment of those relationships. Why? Because the audiences of both productions were given no indication
that Antonio suffered as the result of his separation from Sebastian,
and because both productions established that the escape that made
his participation impossible also carried him out of danger. In addition, both escapes resulted from Antonio's initiative. In neither case
was his departure from Illyria a response to any failure to acknowledge him—deliberate or unintended—on Sebastian's part.

Clifford Williams' 1966 production for the Royal Shakespeare
Company demonstrated one way in which the silent Antonio can be
included in the love and harmony of the play's final moments.[7]
When Olivia discovered that the man who was her husband was not
Cesario but Sebastian, Orsino reassured her (and the other characters) by explaining, "Be not amazed; right noble is his blood"
(V.i.256). Sebastian and Olivia then crossed to where Antonio was
standing and embraced. The timing and the site of that embrace
linked Olivia's discovery that Sebastian, not Cesario, was her proper
husband with Antonio's discovery that it was not Sebastian but Cesario who had twice denied knowing him.

Williams' production makes it easy to conceive of other ways in
which a production might wordlessly but effectively include, in the
festivity of the play's final moments, Antonio and the love that he
and Sebastian share. Olivia and Sebastian could include Antonio in
one of their embraces, or they could turn from embracing one another to embrace him. Viola could embrace Antonio or could in
some other way acknowledge him as the man who saved her brother's life and is now his beloved friend. By a handshake or some
equivalent gesture, Orsino could make it unmistakably clear that he
no longer regards Antonio as an enemy and now accepts him as the
friend of the man who is the brother of the woman who will be his
wife. Another possibility is that Antonio could make his final exit

together with Sebastian and Olivia and Orsino and Viola; thus they would be signifying their willingness to give him a place in the new Illyrian society that is taking shape. However it is achieved, the inclusion of Antonio would have the effect of defining Illyria as a society capable of opening itself not just to strangers like Viola and Sebastian but also to an enemy like Antonio.

There is nothing in either Antonio's silence or the words that Shakespeare has assigned to other characters that rules out such inclusions, but there is nothing in what Shakespeare has written that compels them either. Most productions of *Twelfth Night* since 1970 have responded to the openness of Antonio's unbroken silence by establishing the fact of his exclusion and the pain he experiences because of it. Peter Gill's 1974 production for the Royal Shakespeare Company allowed for Antonio's inclusion but made it momentary and a point of contrast with what preceded and followed it.[8] On hearing the words "I am Viola" (V.i.245), Antonio crossed to downstage left and stood facing the audience. He chose not to watch during the ensuing moments, when Sebastian's identity as Olivia's husband and Viola's identity as Sebastian's sister became clear. Ignoring those around him as much as they ignored him, Antonio looked in silence at the audience until Orsino's final line announcing that Viola would be "Orsino's mistress and his fancy's queen" (V.i.377). As the stage emptied, with the minor characters taking the nearest exit, Orsino took hold of Viola and swung her joyfully in a circle; Viola then swung Sebastian, and Olivia and finally Antonio were caught up in the giddy swirl. They broke into two circles downstage before reuniting upstage in a single circle of five. That circle broke as the four lovers exited in separate pairs— Orsino and Viola moving off upstage right, Sebastian and Viola upstage left. They left Antonio behind, standing alone and with his back to the audience as, downstage, Feste began his concluding song.

Gill's handling of Antonio's silence suggested that Antonio's exclusion arises, at least in part, from his unwillingness or inability to accept that Sebastian is loved as a husband and a brother as well as a friend—that Sebastian loves and is loved by others besides Antonio. A sketch of Narcissus gazing into a pool dominated the set of Gill's production, emphasizing the motif of excessive self-love.[9] Antonio's silence allowed Gill to register the fact that Antonio's love

for Sebastian has elements of self-indulgence and self-absorption.
Those elements are implicit in the parallels between Antonio's love
for Sebastian and Orsino's for Olivia that Shakespeare establishes
by means of shared imagery. Antonio responds to what he thinks is
Sebastian's refusal to acknowledge their loving friendship by telling
the officers who arrest him:

> . . . This youth that you see here
> I snatched one half out of the jaws of death;
> Relieved him with such sanctity of love,
> And to his image, which methought did promise
> Most venerable worth, did I devotion.
> . . . .
> But, O, how vile an idol proves this god.   (III.iv.339–43, 345)

The same vocabulary of religious devotion runs through the words
that Orsino utters when Olivia makes it inescapably clear during the
final scene that she does not and will not return his love. Orsino
denounces her:

> . . . You uncivil lady,
> To whose ingrate and unauspicious altars
> My soul the faithfull'st off'rings have breathed out
> That e'er devotion tendered. . . .   (V.i.106–9)

Within the specific context of Gill's production, Antonio fell silent
and remained silent because he—like Orsino in his desire for Olivia,
like Olivia mourning her brother, and like Malvolio—was "sick of
self-love" (I.v.85). Orsino and Olivia progressed beyond that kind
of love during the final moments of Gill's production, but Malvolio
and Antonio did not.

John Barton's acclaimed 1969 production for the Royal Shakespeare Company also established the fact of Antonio's final exclusion, but in the context of this production the exclusion was significantly different.[10] The Antonio of Barton's production did not turn
away on learning that the friend whom he loved was also loved as a
husband and a brother, and Antonio's silence did not reflect dismay
at the discovery that he was not the only person whom Sebastian
loved. Nor did Barton use Antonio's silence and exclusion to suggest
that his love for Sebastian was unduly self-centered. Antonio's exclusion came about because, caught up in the wonder and joy of the

unfolding discoveries, everybody had forgotten him, particularly Sebastian. Barton's handling of Antonio's final exit emphasized the
differences in how he and Gill dealt with Antonio's silent exclusion.
Orsino and Viola kissed after he declared that she would be "his
fancy's queen," and a general exit followed. The two pairs of lovers
moved off without in any way acknowledging Antonio, who stood
silent and motionless until they were gone. He then crossed the stage
to the officers in whose custody he had entered, and he took back
from one of them the seaman's knife that they had seized when
arresting him. Rearmed with the weapon he had used on behalf of
the person who was, he thought, Sebastian, Antonio departed alone
and in a direction not taken by the lovers. His actions conveyed his
isolation and his sense of pain and loss, but at the same time they
also conveyed his self-assertive resolve in the face of the forgetfulness that had given rise to his exclusion. Before Feste began his
concluding song, Antonio was gone. He left Illyria saddened and
(perhaps) wiser but certainly not broken.

Two more recent productions—Robin Phillips' in 1980 for the
Stratford (Ontario) Shakespearean Festival[11] and John Gorrie's in
1979 for BBC-TV as part of the series entitled "The Shakespeare
Plays"[12]—prolonged Antonio's silence and stressed his exclusion by
delaying his exit until after Feste had begun the concluding song.[13]
In both productions Sebastian paid no attention to Antonio after
discovering Viola, and in both productions Antonio stood by silent
and unacknowledged, then departed during the second stanza of
Feste's song:

> But when I came to man's estate,
>> With hey, ho, the wind and the rain,
> 'Gainst knaves and thieves men shut their gate,
>> For the rain it raineth every day.   (V.i.382–85)

In Phillips' production, as Feste sang those words, Antonio crossed
the stage, passing behind the four lovers embracing at center stage.
He then exited using the same entrance through which he had been
brought on earlier in the scene as a prisoner. The manner of his exit
juxtaposed him and the lovers, who paid him no heed as he left.
That juxtaposition and Feste's reference in his song to "knaves and
thieves" brought into focus what might be called the negative and
positive aspects of the lovers' inattentiveness toward Antonio.

Caught up in his own happiness, Sebastian did not call on Antonio
to stay, nor did he even bid farewell to the man whom he had earlier
greeted with the words:

> Antonio, O my dear Antonio,
> How have the hours racked and tortured me
> Since I have lost thee!   (V.i.210–12)

On the other hand, Orsino, caught up (like Sebastian) in his own
happiness, also did not notice Antonio leaving and therefore had no
opportunity to order his officers to stop the man whom he had
earlier denounced ("Notable pirate, thou salt-water thief"). Forgotten by both his beloved friend and his declared enemy, Antonio
found himself free to leave Illyria.

In Gorrie's production—as in Fried's film—it was Antonio's
guards who followed Malvolio when Orsino commanded "entreat
him to a peace," but this Antonio, in contrast to the Antonio of
Fried's film, did not dash to freedom the instant he was left unguarded. Instead, he remained, even after the lovers departed following Orsino's declaration that Viola would be "his fancy's
queen." While singing " 'Gainst knaves and thieves men shut their
gate," Feste moved slowly across the set, then stopped as he finished
the line to face Antonio, whom the audience saw (for the first time
since Sebastian turned from him and saw Viola) sitting alone. The
camera focused on Antonio as he and the audience heard Feste singing the rest of the second stanza. Feste's movement and the camera
work combined to establish that Feste was directing the second
stanza specifically to Antonio. The same combination allowed Antonio and the audience to hear in Feste's reference to "thieves" an
echo of Orsino's earlier characterization of Antonio as "thou salt-
water thief." As the stanza ended, Antonio rose, with a slight smile
that mixed pain, insight, and resignation, and in what was tantamount to a confirmation of Feste's words, he left.

Within the specific context of Gorrie's production, what
prompted Antonio's departure was not his sense of danger, or even
the fact that Sebastian had become oblivious to him, but the impact
of Feste's words: " 'Gainst knaves and thieves men shut their gate."
They made explicit to Antonio the fact of exclusion implicit in the
silences of both his friend Sebastian and his enemy Orsino. Directed
to Antonio, the second stanza of Feste's concluding song became an

act of instruction, just as his previous songs to Orsino and Viola (II.iv) and to Sir Toby Belch and Sir Andrew Aguecheek (II.iii) had been. Unlike those earlier listeners, however, the Antonio of Gorrie's production understood and acted upon the truth articulated in the Fool's song.

Gorrie's production demonstrated that the second stanza of Feste's final song, with its account of how men treat those whom they regard as enemies, can raise again the issue of whether one fares, as Feste tells Orsino very early in the final scene, "the better for my foes, and the worse for my friends." When Orsino objects, saying, "Just the contrary: the better for thy friends" (V.i.12), Feste explains that his friends

> . . . praise me and make an ass of me. Now my foes tell me plainly I am an ass; so that by my foes, sir, I profit in the knowledge of myself, and by my friends I am abused; so that, conclusions to be as kisses, if your four negatives make your two affirmatives, why, then, the worse for my friends, and the better for my foes. (V.i.15–21)

The final scene of *Twelfth Night* is a series of encounters between those who are (or think they are) enemies, friends, lovers, and spouses. In some cases, those encounters yield self-knowledge, and in at least one case—Malvolio's encounters with Olivia and then with Feste—they do not. In Gorrie's production, Feste, as he sang the second stanza of his last song, came face to face with Antonio. That encounter completed a process by which the silent Antonio, the friend of one man and the enemy of another, came to know who he was in an Illyria that now included Sebastian as well as Orsino. Antonio remained an outsider.

□   □   □

Feste's comment that his friends make an ass of him whereas his foes tell him plainly he is an ass accurately describes Sir Toby Belch's treatment of Sir Andrew Aguecheek during the play. Throughout the first four acts, Toby makes an ass of Andrew while posing as his friend; during the final scene, Toby replies to Andrew's offer of assistance by telling him directly that he is (among other things) an ass:

Andrew: I'll help you, Sir Toby, because we'll be dressed together.

  Toby: Will you help? An ass-head and a coxcomb and a knave, a thin-
            faced knave, a gull?   (lines 196–99)

Andrew's response is to exit in silence.

Toby's words—potentially cruel in their accuracy—function as a
kind of pivot in the final scene. His denunciation of Andrew completes a pattern in which Antonio castigates the person he thinks is
his friend Sebastian, Olivia rebukes the cowardice of the person she
thinks is her husband, and Orsino denounces what he takes to be
the ingratitude of Olivia and the faithlessness of Cesario. Toby's
final words to Andrew also continue a pattern that originated with
Orsino's earlier meetings, first with his enemy Antonio and then
with his beloved Olivia. The final scene of *Twelfth Night* is struc-
tured as a series of encounters, the last of which is between two
enemies, Feste and Malvolio. Individuals come face to face with
others and, potentially, with themselves. They are given the opportunity to "profit in the knowledge of themselves."

Toby's denunciation of Andrew and Andrew's silent exit come
immediately before Sebastian enters and, after apologizing to Olivia
for hurting her kinsman, sees Antonio. The timing helps to focus
attention on correspondences between each pair of men. What Sir
Toby feigns is what Antonio and Sebastian share—friendship. Antonio, in friendship, gives Sebastian his purse when they arrive in
Illyria, whereas Toby, under the guise of friendship, urges Andrew
to "send for money, knight" (II.iii.172) and drains money from him.
"I have been dear to him," Toby tells Fabian, "some two thousand
strong or so" (III.ii.48–49). Toby denounces a man who thinks
Toby is his friend, and Antonio denounces the person he thinks is
his friend. Toby's final words to Andrew contrast both with the
words of welcome ("Antonio, O my dear Antonio") that Sebastian
speaks on seeing Antonio and with the silence toward Antonio that
Sebastian maintains after seeing Viola. Andrew's response to Toby's
words and Antonio's response to Sebastian's silence are identical:
each friend says nothing. Andrew's silence, although less sustained
than Antonio's, is equally open and, in its openness, is also capable
of altering the tone and meaning of the final scene.[14]

Andrew's silence can contribute to the laughter and festivity. In
Williams' 1966 production, Toby crossed to Andrew after rejecting
his help, then chased him in circles and eventually off the stage. The

effect was to convert a moment of potential cruelty and pain into a moment of slapstick. Toby's words and subsequent gestures made manifest, in laughable ways that even Andrew could no longer fail to see, the abuse that his seeming friend had been inflicting on him all along. Similar effects were created during Frank Hauser's 1976 production at the St. Georges Theatre in London, when Andrew exited with Sir Toby booting his behind.[15]

Robin Phillips, however, gave the same moments a stinging quality that stilled the audience's laughter. Immediately before offering to help Toby, Andrew daintily yet fearfully used his handkerchief to slap away the hand Viola held out to help him. That gesture increased the laughter, but it died when Toby angrily, bitterly slapped aside the helping hand that Andrew held out to him in friendship. In that stillness, Toby's words rejecting help knifed into Andrew, inflicting a wound deeper and more painful than the cut on his head. Stunned, he watched Toby limp off, then, not knowing what else to do, he trailed after him in silent, uncomprehending shock. After a pause long enough for the audience to register the sight of Andrew's pained exit in pursuit of Toby, Phillips had Olivia order Fabian and Feste to follow. The audience's laughter was silenced for a moment by what had happened to Andrew but began to build again when the audience, immediately after watching Andrew's exit, saw all onstage recoil in amazement as Sebastian entered, apologizing for having hurt Toby.

The productions directed by Gill and Gorrie invited their audiences to compare Andrew's silent exit with Antonio's. Each production used Andrew's exit to convey his pain, but each also muted that pain by having somebody assist and console him. In Gill's production, Fabian crossed the stage to help Andrew as he wandered, almost dazed, in the direction that Toby had taken. In Gorrie's production, Feste placed a reassuring hand on Andrew's shoulder as the two of them followed Toby, whom Fabian was assisting. After briefly including Antonio in their joyous circles, the pairs of lovers in Gill's production exited, leaving him alone. No one moved to assist him or to offer him companionship as Fabian had done earlier when Andrew found himself rejected by the man whom he had taken for a friend. In Gorrie's production, when Antonio rose and left at the end of Feste's second stanza, Feste did not extend a hand or go with him as he had earlier with Andrew. To Antonio, Feste offered neither sympathy nor companionship but something that, despite Toby's blunt words, Andrew had not been able to grasp: a fuller understanding of his situation and himself. Antonio's response was to depart—alone and unconsoled for the loss of his friend. In both productions, the concern shown for Andrew when Toby, ceasing his pretense of friendship, rejected him and his offer of help made Antonio's final isolation all the more pronounced and poignant.

John Barton's production, however, accented the similarities, rather than the contrasts, between the final exits that Andrew and Antonio make in silence. Antonio made his final exit after Sebastian, without in any way acknowledging him, had departed with Olivia as part of a general exit. The only figure in motion on a stage nearly free of people, Antonio crossed to where the officers who had been his guards stood. In a gesture that made clear that his departure was not prompted by any sense of danger, he reclaimed the knife the officers had seized when arresting him, then turned and made his exit. He left sadly cognizant of—but not shattered by—the fact that there was no longer any place in Illyria for him or for the love for Sebastian that had brought him there. Barton had already given Andrew's exit comparable prominence. Maria began helping Toby away immediately after he called Andrew "a thin-faced knave, a gull." There was a discernible pause and then, when Olivia ordered, "Get him to bed, and let his hurt be looked to" (line 200), Fabian and Feste obediently moved to catch up with Maria and Toby. No one, however, even acknowledged Andrew who, his head conspicuously gashed, stood silenced and immobilized by the ferocity of Toby's last words. After a sustained pause, he managed to offer Olivia an awkward, pathetic bow, then made a long, slow exit downstage right while all onstage stood motionless.[16] No one went with him. The direction he took was not that taken by Toby and those attending to him, and each step of Andrew's passage conveyed the sharpness of his pain and humiliation. This, however, was an Andrew who did not persist in following the man whom he had taken for a friend. Like Antonio, he found himself compelled to acknowledge that for him, there was no place in Illyria. He left Illyria alone and in pain, but the very fact that he chose to leave established the possible beginning of some degree of self-knowledge.

Terry Hands's 1979 production for the Royal Shakespeare Company altered the usual method of making an exit, and that, in turn,

allowed for exceptionally full development of the possible correspondences between the silences of Andrew and Antonio. Throughout the production, characters who exited sometimes did not disap-
pear from the audience's view but remained visible on the periphery
of the playing area. After refusing Andrew's help, Toby moved un-
steadily upstage left and seated himself there beneath one of the box
trees that lined both sides of the stage. For the rest of the scene he
sat with his back to the audience and to everybody onstage except
Maria and Fabian, who were looking after him.

Andrew's exit was reworked in a similar fashion.[17] After watching Toby take his place beneath the box tree upstage left, Andrew
gathered himself sufficiently to offer a feeble bow to Olivia, whose
wooer he had (with Toby's encouragement) thought himself to be.
Then, without receiving any assistance or even a show of concern
from her or anyone else, Andrew crossed and took a seat beneath
the box tree downstage of the one beneath which Toby had come to
rest. He used his handkerchief to cover both his face and his blood-
ied head and sat, elbows on knees, staring at the ground in pain and
humiliation for the rest of the scene. This was not an Andrew who
had persisted in following Toby in order to preserve a friendship
that all but he now knew was one-sided. But if this Andrew had
acquired some smattering of self-knowledge, it was not enough to
enable him to leave Illyria, to withdraw completely from the society
in which he had been ignored as a wooer and exploited as a friend.

The sight of Toby and Andrew sitting apart from one another
provided a sustained contrast to the succession of reunions that
began when Sebastian entered directly after Toby's denunciation of
Andrew. Husband was reunited with wife, friend with friend, and
brother with sister, but during the final moments of Hands's production, the reunion of Sebastian and Antonio dissolved into silence
and separation. As Sebastian came to understand that he had found
both a wife and a sister in Illyria, Antonio drifted away and eventually sat at a point far downstage and somewhat to the left of center.
Thus Hands made it difficult for the audience to watch the four
lovers discovering their relationships with one another without also
seeing both Antonio, who stared downward in dejection, and Andrew, who sat (upstage of him) with his handkerchief hiding his face
and head.

Antonio remained motionless where he sat until, following Orsino's declaration that Viola would be "his fancy's queen," the four lovers came together in a mutual embrace at center stage. Antonio then rose from his position downstage left. He did not, however, leave Illyria. Instead, he crossed the stage, passing conspicuously between the embracing lovers and the audience, and sat beneath a box tree placed center stage right. Antonio's crossing compelled the audience to register again the contrast between Antonio's isolation and his friend Sebastian's participation as husband and brother in the loving relationships that emerge during the play's final moments. By having Antonio sit beneath the box tree located center stage right, Hands reconfirmed Antonio's correspondence with Andrew, who remained sitting beneath the box tree located at approximately the same position on the left side of the stage.

Placed at corresponding points on opposite sides of the stage, Antonio and Andrew—each sitting alone—helped to frame the quartet of lovers embracing at center stage. The lovers were also framed by Feste, who sang his final song downstage center, and by Malvolio, who remained visible, far upstage center with his back to everyone—frozen as it were in the process of leaving. The frame was made even more complex by the presence of Toby and Maria. Toby remained seated under the box tree upstage left. Maria, who had walked away from him in stunned bewilderment after hearing Fabian announce that Toby had married her, sat alone under the corresponding tree upstage right.[18] Seeing the lovers framed so complexly encouraged the audience, as it listened to Feste's song about the changes time brings, to balance such antitheses as isolation and union, sadness and joy, knowledge and deception, relationships formed and relationships shattered—each defined and sharpened by the presence of its opposite.

□   □   □

The common response to conflicting diversity of the kind evident in the productions of *Twelfth Night* that I have discussed is to ask how faithful each director has been to Shakespeare's intentions. Even as it prompts such a question, *Twelfth Night* seems to warn against conceptions of fidelity to what has been written that, in their simplicity, distort the relationship among playwright, playtext, and the process of performance. The play's second title is "what you will," and the play offers the example of Malvolio converting the letter that he finds into the equivalent of a script. What he reads determines what he says, does, and wears when he is next in Olivia's presence. He enters during act III, scene iv, wearing, cross-gartered, the yellow stockings called for in the letter, and while Olivia is present, his speech is not spontaneous but consists mainly of lines memorized from the letter: " 'Be not afraid of greatness. . . . Some are born great. . . . Some achieve greatness. . . . And some have greatness thrust upon them' " (lines 35–41). Those whom Olivia sends to look after him he treats in a manner rigorously consistent with the directions given in the letter: "Be opposite with a kinsman, surly with servants" (II.v.137–38). Because the letter specifies that Malvolio should smile continually ("Therefore in my presence still smile, dear my sweet, I prithee," II.v.162–63), he insists on maintaining his smile even though he hears Olivia say, "Smil'st thou? I sent for thee upon a sad occasion" (III.iv.17).

Malvolio's conversion of the letter into a script that determines his performance in Olivia's presence can be a parody of the actor whose fidelity to what has been written for him is so single-minded that he acts without taking into account the responses of his fellow actors and his audience. The results of Malvolio's fidelity to the letter include actions—such as smiling constantly in Olivia's presence—that are wildly (and hilariously) inappropriate to their immediate context. He is, in fact, guilty of the charge that he levels against those whom he finds carousing late at night in Olivia's house: "Is there no respect of place, persons, nor time in you?" (II.iii.84–85). Malvolio exemplifies a mode of acting in which actors progress in almost mechanical fashion from scripted word to performed act—a mode that threatens to reduce the process of performance to little more than programmed repetition. Fidelity such as Malvolio's yields actions that are rigidly predetermined rather than adaptable to place, persons, and time.

The letter that Malvolio finds exercises over him a control far more rigid than that which the playtext for *Twelfth Night* exercises over those who perform the play. Precisely because they are moments when no words specify how actors are to act, the open silences of Antonio and Andrew give actors and directors both the freedom and the responsibility to adjust the play's emotional hues and thematic emphases to the contingencies of performance—to the place, the persons, and the time. Actors and directors are called upon to exercise that skill for which Viola praises Feste (whose flexibility stands in sharpest contrast to Malvolio's rigidity)[19]:

> He must observe their mood on whom he jests,
> The quality of persons, and the time;
> And like the haggard, check at every feather
> That comes before his eye.   (III.i.60–63)

It is Feste, speaking for all involved in the process of performance, who ends the play by affirming the importance of the audience: "But that's all one, our play is done, / And we'll strive to please you every day" (V.i.397–98).

In being rigorously faithful to what he reads even if it means disregarding those around him, Malvolio strives to fulfill exactly the intention of the person who, he thinks, wrote the letter, but the hand that wrote and delivered the letter is Maria's, not Olivia's. The intentions that Malvolio ends up fulfilling are not those of Olivia, the mistress whose master he had hoped to become, but of those people who, in Fabian's words,

> Set this device against Malvolio here,
> Upon some stubborn and uncourteous parts
> We had conceived against him. . . .   (V.i.350–52)

The movement from reading what is written to determining the writer's intentions is—*Twelfth Night* seems to caution—less direct, more fallible, and more hazardous than Malvolio allows. It may also be more complex than those who call for fidelity to Shakespeare's intentions are willing to allow. We have, it must be remembered, no Shakespearean playtext written in his hand, and we cannot be certain that any of those we do have came directly from his hand. Those which we have, have come to us through layers of intermediaries—among them compositors and printers, Shakespeare's fellow actors, and generations of editors—via a process that we do not fully comprehend.[20]

Twelfth Night provides another and more difficult lesson. Even if we could be absolutely certain that the playtext we have is Shakespeare's as he wrote it and as he intended it to endure, the fact remains that we could not use it to determine what the meanings and effects of Antonio's and Andrew's silences are or what they should be. The playtext establishes that both silences exist, but it also leaves them open to meanings and effects that, without contradicting anything in the playtext, can be sharply divergent and even contradictory. Within those open silences, actors and directors are free to settle upon and enact specific meanings and effects. The meanings and effects that emerge from those silences during a performance are not tangential to *Twelfth Night* or inconsequential, since they are critical to the play's thematic emphasis and its emotional tone, yet they cannot be judged as valid or invalid, appropriate or inappropriate, inspired or self-indulgent solely by reference to the words of the playtext. Such judgments must include within their primary field of reference the specific context of a given performance. Without the information that only performances can yield, our knowledge of the silences of Antonio and Andrew and, therefore, of *Twelfth Night* itself will be less than full.

3. Freedom, Silence, and *The Tempest*

The final Act of *The Tempest* is a single scene that includes a series of open silences involving Antonio, Miranda, and Ariel. Antonio says nothing when Prospero forgives him and reclaims the dukedom with the words:

> For you, most wicked sir, whom to call brother
> Would even infect my mouth, I do forgive
> Thy rankest fault—all of them; and require
> My dukedom of thee, which perforce I know
> Thou must restore.   (V.i.130–34)

In fact, Antonio, who speaks just once during the final scene, never says anything to Prospero. Miranda's last words are those she speaks when she looks upon Antonio, Alonso, Gonzalo, and other members of the courts of Naples and Milan:

>   O, wonder!
> How many goodly creatures are there here!
> How beauteous mankind is! O brave new world
> That has such people in't!   (lines 181–84)

She falls silent after Prospero responds, " 'Tis new to thee" (line 184), and during the rest of the play she says nothing to him or to anyone else. Ariel accepts in silence the freedom that he has long sought and that Prospero grants after calling upon him[1] to perform a last service by providing ideal sailing conditions:

>   . . . My Ariel, chick,
> That is thy charge. Then to the elements
> Be free, and fare thou well! . . .   (lines 316–18)

Ariel departs without uttering any words of affection and farewell. Ariel's silent exit completes a sequence that leaves Prospero, at the conclusion of *The Tempest*, facing the silences of his brother, his daughter, and his beloved servant.

When Antonio says nothing in response to Prospero's words extending forgiveness and reclaiming the dukedom, a silence that may be long or short envelops all onstage. Whatever its length, Shakespeare breaks that general silence by having Alonso call upon Prospero to "give us particulars of thy preservation" (line 135). The choice of Alonso is significant, for it juxtaposes Antonio's silence with the voice of the man who made it possible for him to usurp Prospero's dukedom. Alonso has already and without prompting explicitly asked for pardon and has returned to Prospero the dukedom that Prospero must "require" from Antonio. "Thy dukedom I resign," Alonso says, "and do entreat / Thou pardon me my wrongs" (lines 118–19). Antonio, in contrast, never says that he assents to relinquishing the dukedom, never verbally acknowledges his "wrongs," and never asks Prospero or anyone else for pardon.

Antonio's silence in response to Prospero also contrasts with the response of Sebastian, his coconspirator in the plot against Alonso, to Prospero. When Prospero warns Antonio and Sebastian that he can "justify you traitors," Sebastian does not remain silent but insists that "the devil speaks in him" (lines 128, 129). Later, when Prospero reveals Ferdinand and Miranda playing chess, Sebastian speaks again. This time, however, he declares, "A most high miracle!" (line 177). Sebastian's words, made more resonant by their contrast with Antonio's silence, show that his initial and explicit resistance to Prospero and his powers is changing into what could be reverence and, possibly, submission.

The only words Antonio speaks during the final scene are in response to Caliban's entrance with Trinculo and Stephano:

Sebastian:	Ha, ha!
	What things are these, my Lord Antonio?
	Will money buy 'em?
Antonio:	Very like. One of them
	Is a plain fish and no doubt marketable. (lines 263–66)

Like Antonio, Caliban has conspired with others to overthrow Prospero. He is, Prospero had earlier asserted,

A devil, a born devil, on whose nature
Nurture can never stick: on whom my pains

> Humanely taken, all, all lost, quite lost!
> And as with age his body uglier grows,
> So his mind cankers. . . .   (IV.i.188–92)

In response to Miranda's account of how she "took pains to make thee speak" and "endowed thy purposes / With words that made them known," Caliban had declared:

> You taught me language, and my profit on't
> Is, I know how to curse. The red plague rid you
> For learning me your language!   (I.ii.354, 357–58, 363–65)

During the closing moments of the play, however, Caliban employs the language that Miranda has taught him to make known purposes far different from any he has uttered before. Ordered to trim Prospero's cell handsomely, Caliban replies, "Ay, that I will; and I'll be wise hereafter, / And seek for grace" (lines 295–96). His words convey a willingness to obey, a penitence, and a desire to change,[2] and they accentuate the fact that Antonio, even when he does speak, never uses the language at his command to express similar sentiments.

Antonio is one of those of whom Prospero says,

> Though with their high wrongs I am struck to th'quick,
> Yet with my nobler reason 'gainst my fury
> Do I take part. The rarer action is
> In virtue than in vengeance. They being penitent,
> The sole drift of my purpose doth extend
> Not a frown further. Go, release them, Ariel.
> My charms I'll break, their senses I'll restore,
> And they shall be themselves.   (lines 25–32)

The open silence imposed on Antonio raises the issue of whether Antonio is "penitent" and what risks, if any, Prospero stands exposed to because he allows Antonio to be himself. One possibility is that Antonio in his silence feels a penitence so intense and profound that no words can convey it. That possibility is one that Antonio's silence allows but does not require, and Robin Phillips chose to develop it during his 1976 production of *The Tempest* at the Stratford (Ontario) Shakespeare Festival.[3]

The Antonio of that production sank penitently to his knees

without speaking when Prospero forgave him and reclaimed the dukedom. In a gesture that confirmed the forgiveness that he had just conveyed in words, Prospero took his brother's hands as he knelt in silence. Phillips also established that Antonio's silence signified penitent sorrow by means of his reactions to Miranda's lines expressing wonder at the "goodly creatures" whom she saw about her. She spoke those lines standing alone in approximately the same place that Antonio had stood when he knelt before Prospero. With the words "O brave new world / That has such people in't," she stepped toward Antonio and circled him in amazed curiosity. He, however, responded by moving away from her in remorse and crossing to the spot that she had just left. She followed, and although he kept his back to her, she continued to gaze at him even after Prospero said, " 'Tis new to thee." By thus juxtaposing Miranda's final words and Antonio's silence, Phillips allowed her naiveté to accentuate the feelings of guilt, sorrow, and even shame that had rendered Antonio speechless. Antonio's silent demeanor so clearly manifested those feelings that Gonzalo sought to ease them by directing specifically to Antonio the first words of his call to rejoice that good has flowed from the evil Antonio himself precipitated when he enlisted Alonso's support in usurping Prospero's dukedom:

> Was Milan thrust from Milan that his issue
> Should become kings of Naples? O, rejoice
> Beyond a common joy, and set it down
> With gold on lasting pillars: in one voyage
> Did Claribel her husband find at Tunis,
> And Ferdinand her brother found a wife
> Where he himself was lost; Prospero his dukedom
> In a poor isle; and all of us ourselves
> When no man was his own.   (lines 205–13)

The Antonio who says nothing to Prospero during the final scene of Phillips' production is a man who has "found" himself after having been "lost" while acting as Duke of Milan. Such a conception is certainly compatible with the terms that Prospero uses when he first tells Miranda about Antonio. Prospero informs her that by "neglecting worldly ends" he "awaked an evil nature" (I.ii.89, 93) in Antonio. He describes the brother to whom he gave "the manage of my state" as the victim of a profound self-deception:

. . . He being thus lorded,
Not only with what my revenue yielded
But what my power might else exact, like one
Who having unto truth, by telling of it,
Made such a sinner of his memory
To credit his own lie, he did believe
He was indeed the Duke, . . .   (I.ii.70, 97–103)

Prospero's words do not specify that Antonio is, always has been,
and must continue to be evil. They justify, even if they do not require, understanding Antonio's silence as the response of a man
who, no longer making "a sinner of his memory,"[4] is now in touch
with himself and most sincerely penitent.

Phillips linked Antonio in his silent remorse with Caliban. Miranda, who had moved toward Antonio in wonder, drew back in
fear when Caliban crawled toward her and her father after entering.
As Prospero ordered Caliban to "go, sirrah, to my cell," he held out
his hands to "this thing of darkness" (lines 292, 275) that he had
recently acknowledged to be his. Caliban crawled across to him and
knelt before him as Antonio had knelt earlier. Prospero took his
hand as he had earlier taken the hand of the man whom he had
acknowledged to be "brother mine, that entertained ambition, / Expelled remorse and nature" (lines 75–76). He tenderly put his arms
around the kneeling Caliban and held him as Caliban pledged to
obey and to "be wise hereafter, / And seek for grace." At the word
"grace," Caliban kissed the hem of Prospero's robes, certifying by
that gesture his now willing submission to the authority of the man
whom he had previously resisted and—like Antonio—had plotted
to overthrow. Caliban then rose and, walking rather than crawling,
crossed to Stephano and Trinculo before denouncing them and his
own stupidity in choosing to serve them:

. . . What a thrice-double ass
Was I to take this drunkard for a god
And worship this dull fool!   (lines 296–98)

In Phillips' production both Antonio and Caliban knelt to Prospero, who in turn took each of them by the hand. Those gestures
gave Prospero's "so potent art" (line 50) virtually unlimited effectiveness. Prospero says that Antonio has "expelled remorse and na-

ture," but the audience viewing Phillips' production subsequently saw that usurping brother kneel, after being released from Prospero's spell, in silent penitence and submission to the man who is both his brother and duke. Prospero calls Caliban "a born devil, on whose nature / Nurture cannot stick," but Phillips' audience saw Caliban, too, kneel before Prospero and heard him voice his resolve to "seek for grace." Phillips established that the "rough magic" (line 50) by which Prospero dims the noon sun and wakes the dead is also capable of extinguishing the evil rooted in the core of Caliban's and Antonio's being and of awaking their capacity for good. Thus, in the context of Phillips' production, Prospero's decision to cast off his magic and—without benefit of those powers by which he controlled and indeed transformed others—to resume his role as Duke of Milan was not one that placed him or those he loved at risk. The demonstrated penitence of Caliban and of Antonio established beyond doubt that both the island that Prospero is about to leave and the realms into which he will soon proceed are, for the foreseeable future, free of enemies and purged of evil. Having moved even the most hardened of evildoers to heartfelt penitence, Prospero's art had, at the end of Phillips' production, no further function in a world that had been brought to the verge of perfection. In abandoning his "so potent art," the Prospero of Phillips' production relinquished what he no longer needed.

Phillips used the silence with which Ariel accepts his freedom to emphasize that the price Prospero pays for rejoining mankind is the loss of his beloved Ariel. After Prospero promised "calm seas, auspicious gales, / And sail so expeditious that shall catch / Your royal fleet far off" (lines 314–16), all but Ariel and Prospero exited, leaving servant and master alone onstage. Holding out his hands, Ariel crossed toward his master, but Prospero, who had earlier taken Antonio's hands and Caliban's, turned away without taking Ariel's. That was not a gesture rejecting Ariel but a demonstration of Prospero's resolve, despite his own painful sense of loss, to allow his beloved servant the freedom that would mean their separation. As Prospero, facing the audience rather than Ariel, began speaking ("My Ariel, chick"), Ariel, facing the master who loved him, backed away, walking with the high, stiff steps he used throughout the performance; by the time Prospero said, "Be free," Ariel was gone. The words "Be free" did more than bestow freedom on Ariel. They also registered Prospero's acceptance and acknowledgment of Ariel's freedom. Prospero's final words to Ariel ("and fare thou well") conveyed a loving tenderness made all the more poignant by Prospero's isolation on the empty stage.

□   □   □

The speech in which Prospero parts with Ariel begins with Prospero's response to Alonso's wish "to hear the story of your life" (V.i.312) and appears as follows in the 1623 Folio:

> I'le deliver all,
> And promise you calme Seas, auspicious gales,
> And saile, so expeditious, that shall catch
> Your Royall fleete farre off: My *Ariel*; chicke
> That is thy charge: Then to the Elements
> Be free, and fare thou well: Please you draw neere.

The speech is deceptively, richly simple.[5] Consider, as one example of the theatrical possibilities it offers, the words "please you draw neere." To whom are they addressed? To Ariel? To one, or two, or several of those humans with whom Prospero has chosen to live out his future? To the theater audience?

The words "please you draw neere" are not an order or a command—not the language a person in authority uses to direct a subordinate. They are a request, even a plea, and should Prospero direct them to Ariel, the words may signify that their relationship is no longer that of a master and servant. If Prospero is addressing Ariel when he says, "please you draw neere," the timing is especially important. Spoken after Ariel has begun to depart, those words could be Prospero's attempt to elicit from Ariel some gesture more responsive to Prospero's love for "My *Ariel*; chicke" than Ariel is giving as he moves silently away. Hearing them, does Ariel turn back, perhaps to share an embrace with the master from whom he has long sought his freedom? Or is he, intent now on beginning his imminent freedom, indifferent to the last words he hears his former master speak? Perhaps, in his rush to freedom, Ariel does not even hear Prospero's plea. If Prospero asks Ariel to "draw neere" before Ariel begins to leave, what is Ariel's response? Does he freely choose to "draw neere" and perhaps embrace the man who no longer compels his obedience? Or does this spirit, whom Prospero released from imprisonment within "a cloven pine" (I.ii.277) but then confined in servitude to him, act out the freedom soon to be his by moving not toward Prospero but away from him and toward "the elements" that constitute his proper milieu?

Prospero's "please you draw neere" could also be directed to all of the humans who remain after Ariel has departed. So addressed, his words could be both a response to the loss of Ariel and an expression of Prospero's hope that human fellowship will in some measure offset that loss. Prospero might direct his words to a specific individual rather than to the group. Gonzalo is one possibility. Having Prospero ask him to "draw neere" would balance the loss of Ariel by directing attention to Prospero's reunion with the man whose charitable service years earlier had enabled Miranda and Prospero to survive. Miranda is another possibility. Spoken to her, "please you draw neere" could convey Prospero's effort to find solace for the loss of his beloved servant by seeking the closeness of the beloved daughter who is also lost to him—if only in the sense that he gave her to Ferdinand when he told him, "She is thine own" (IV.i.32). As *The Tempest* ends, Miranda stands on the threshold of a future that will increasingly separate her from the father who was once the sole focus of her attention and love as surely as Ariel's freedom will separate him from the man who answered his question, "Do you love me, master? No?" by saying, "Dearly, my delicate Ariel" (IV.i.48–49). Miranda may respond to her father's plea or, absorbed in a world no longer confined to the island and her father's company, she may not. Antonio is a third possibility. By asking him to "draw neere," Prospero could be seeking to find in their brotherhood a relationship that would ease the pain of losing both his beloved servant and his beloved daughter. Once asked, Antonio, in turn, could step toward his brother and perhaps embrace him, or he could stand off, exercising in either case his power to give or to withhold the consolation that Prospero seeks.

Prospero might also address "please you draw neere" to different combinations of people. He might ask Miranda and Antonio—the two people with whom Prospero shares blood ties—to come closer to him after Ariel's silent exit, and either or neither or both of them might grant his request. Ariel's departure to begin his freedom completes Prospero's renunciation of his powers, and he might then ask Ferdinand and Miranda to "draw neere," since they now embody the possibility of sustaining the unity of Milan and Naples that the exercise of Prospero's art has achieved. Or perhaps Prospero, aware that "every third thought shall be my grave" (line 311), could ask Gonzalo and Alonso, men of his own age, to "draw neere" now that he no longer has at his command the spirit who assisted him in performing an art potent enough to wake the dead.

If Prospero were to direct "please you draw neere" to members of the audience, the words would constitute his first acknowledgment of his need for their goodwill and help now that Ariel, his assistant, has departed silently into freedom. Should Prospero shift directly from saying farewell to Ariel to asking the audience to "draw neere," his words would function as a prelude to the Epilogue, thereby directing attention to the correspondences between Prospero, Ariel, and the audience. Prospero's last charge to Ariel is to provide "calm seas, auspicious gales, / And sail so expeditious," and Prospero's call for the audience's help in fulfilling his "project" is cast in similar terms:

> Gentle breath of yours my sails
> Must fill, or else my project fails,
> Which was to please. . . .   (Epi. lines 11–13)

With his final words Prospero asks the audience to grant to him what he has granted to Ariel—freedom: "As you from crimes would pardoned be, / Let your indulgence set me free" (Epi. lines 19–20).

The relationship between Prospero and Ariel was, for several reviewers, the focal point of John Barton's 1970 production of *The Tempest* for the Royal Shakespeare Company.[6] Their relationship was more complex than that between master and servant and consisted of what Elizabeth Knapp called "an ambiguous and unclarified attachment."[7] For Harold Hobson the key moment of the production was when Ariel asked whether Prospero loved him.[8] Barton used silences to make the moment particularly emphatic. Ariel, who had been moving away from Prospero in response to his command to assemble the spirits needed to perform the masque, stopped and turned to face Prospero, then, after a distinct pause, asked, "Do you love me, master?" (IV.i.48). When Prospero said nothing, Ariel asked a second question: "No?" (line 48). Only after another distinct pause did Prospero break his silence and answer Ariel's questions by saying, "Dearly, my delicate Ariel" (line 49).[9] That love made all the sharper the pain Prospero felt as, during the final moments of the play, he granted Ariel the freedom that would lead to their lasting separation. In Barton's production, "Please you draw near" came not after Ariel has been granted his freedom but before "My Ariel, chick, / That is thy charge" (V.i.316–17. The Prospero of that production spoke "Please you draw near" specifically to Ariel, who responded by crossing to his master. After hearing Prospero's final charge and the words granting him freedom, Ariel exited, while Prospero poignantly began quietly singing "Where the bee sucks" to himself.

The parting of Ariel and Prospero helped to convey a sense of Prospero's isolation as the production concluded. Anne Barton's note in the program for the production speaks of Prospero as a man "even more alone at the end of the play than at the beginning,"[10] and one reviewer, J. C. Trewin, characterized Prospero as "going into the loneliness of his restored dukedom."[11] At the end of Barton's production, Prospero faced a situation that offered him no consolation for having released his beloved daughter, Miranda, into the world beyond the island and his beloved servant, Ariel, into the elements. It was a world in which evil still existed—evil to which Prospero, having relinquished his magic powers, was more vulnerable than ever before during the play.

Antonio's silence was the most menacing expression of that evil. He did not, as he did in Phillips' production, drop to his knees in remorse and submission when Prospero required "my dukedom of thee, which perforce I know / Thou must restore." Standing alone, the Antonio of Barton's production responded by giving the badge of office to Prospero, and he bowed—but did not kneel—to his brother before walking away in silence. That bow suggested more a grudging acceptance of what, given Prospero's demonstrated power, was unavoidable than an acknowledgment of guilt and a resolve to do good in the future. Antonio surrendered his role as Duke of Milan, but his silence was testimony to the fact that his evil had been checked but not extirpated, defeated but not destroyed or redeemed.

As the scene progressed, the alliance between Antonio and Sebastian began to become manifest again. After returning the badge of office to Prospero, Antonio joined a Sebastian (upstage left) who had responded to the sight of Miranda and Ferdinand by delivering the words "a most high miracle" in a sneering fashion. Each an actual or would-be traitor to his own brother, Antonio and Sebastian remained paired through the rest of the scene, their menace

underscored by the timing of their movements. When Gonzalo exclaimed, "Look down, you gods, / And on this couple drop a
blessed crown!" (lines 201–2), Antonio and Sebastian—a couple of
conspirators whose desires for the thrones of Milan and Naples
respectively would be blocked by the marriage of Ferdinand and
Miranda—distanced themselves by stepping downstage left, away
from those who shared Gonzalo's sentiments. The pair remained
standing apart from those who rushed to congratulate Ferdinand
and Miranda as soon as Alonso had assented to their marriage with
the words "give me your hands" (line 213). Later, while the rest of
the court party gathered joyfully around the boatswain as he told
them that their ship was "tight and yare and bravely rigged as
when / We first put out to sea" (lines 224–25), Antonio and Sebastian circled ominously behind the group, stopping upstage right.
Immediately after Prospero told Ariel, "Thou shalt be free" (line
242), the audience saw Antonio and Sebastian cross to a spot downstage right. Antonio and Sebastian were not among those who departed with Miranda and Ferdinand into Prospero's cell. They remained onstage as Prospero parted with Ariel, the agent through
whom he had worked to frustrate their malevolent designs. Paired,
they highlighted Prospero's isolation, and their ominous presence
drove home his deepening vulnerability. After Ariel's final exit, Prospero sent them off before breaking his wand and turning to tell the
audience of his deliberately diminished powers:

> Now my charms are all o'erthrown
> And what strength I have's mine own,
> Which is most faint. . . .   (Epi. lines 1–3)

Barton employed Caliban to put final emphasis on Prospero's
vulnerability. As the members of the audience heard Prospero say,
"Now I want / Spirits to enforce, art to enchant" (Epi. lines 13–14),
they saw Caliban enter silently but menacingly from stage right. He
departed, harmlessly, when Prospero, catching sight of him, took up
again the wand that he had broken after parting with Ariel and
sending Antonio and Sebastian off. In Barton's vision, Caliban remained (despite his pledge to "be wise hereafter, / And seek for
grace") "a thing of darkness" still. With Antonio and Sebastian, he
embodied the enduring presence in man, no matter how savage or
how civilized, of a capacity for evil beyond the reforming reach even
of that art which Prospero had relinquished.

Clifford Williams' 1978 production of *The Tempest* for the Royal Shakespeare Company also used Antonio's silence to establish his unrepentant malevolence, but Williams cast that malevolence in terms clearly different from those used by Barton. Confronted by Prospero and called upon to "restore" the dukedom, Antonio broke away without yielding any badge of office or offering a bow, however perfunctory. Whereas Barton teamed Antonio and Sebastian during the play's final moments, Williams defined the enduring villainy signified by Antonio's silence by juxtaposing it with the change that came over Sebastian. When Prospero said that he knew but would not disclose the traitorous conspiracy between Antonio and Sebastian, Sebastian responded by saying of Prospero, "The devil speaks in him." However, when Prospero revealed Ferdinand and Miranda playing chess, Sebastian accepted the validity of Prospero's powers and submitted to them. He crossed himself as he exclaimed in heartfelt awe, "A most high miracle." Antonio, by contrast, turned his back to all onstage after hearing Prospero say, "I / Have lost my daughter" (lines 147–48). He kept his back turned as Alonso replied that he wished his "lost" son were alive and wedded to Prospero's "lost" daughter:

> O heavens, that they were living both in Naples,
> The King and Queen there! . . .   (lines 149–50)

One reason Antonio kept his back turned is that the marriage for which Alonso wishes would end the enmity between Naples and Milan that enabled Antonio to enlist Alonso's support in usurping Prospero's throne. As long as that enmity exists, support for another usurpation remains a possibility. The marriage that Alonso wishes had happened would narrow Antonio's chances of regaining the dukedom he has just returned to Prospero. Antonio's response to the subsequent appearance of Ferdinand and Miranda was to distance himself even farther from those involved in the reconciliation developing between Milan and Naples. He walked to a position downstage left and sat there alone, facing the audience. He did not change positions again until, with something less than enthusiasm, he followed those who entered Prospero's cell.

Williams also defined Antonio's evil by contrasting him with Caliban. Driven onstage by Ariel, Caliban dropped to his knees in guilt, fear, and awe, saying, "How fine my master is! I am afraid / He will chastise me" (V.i.262–63). He knelt beside a standing Antonio,

whose response to Prospero's presence had been unrepentant silence. The only words spoken by Antonio during the final scene
refer to Caliban. After speaking them, the Antonio of Williams'
production prodded the kneeling Caliban with his foot, as if dis-
dainfully curious about this creature—"a plain fish and no doubt
marketable"—whose words and gestures were expressions of distinctively human sentiments that Antonio did not share. Caliban
responded to Antonio's prodding foot by crossing the stage and
squatting near Prospero. Prospero, who had earlier acknowledged
Antonio as "flesh and blood, / You, brother mine" (lines 74–75),
then acknowledged Caliban as his own: "this thing of darkness I /
Acknowledge mine" (lines 275–76). The blocking of Caliban's
movements made the audience conscious that Prospero's "thing of
darkness" was willing—as his "brother" was not—to voice a resolve to "be wise hereafter, / And seek for grace." By contrasting
Antonio with both Sebastian and Caliban, Williams confined to Antonio the malevolence manifested by his silence. Thus isolated, it
was less threatening than in Barton's production, which compelled
its audiences to recognize in Sebastian and in Caliban manifestations of the same ineradicable capacity for evil signaled by Antonio's silence.

Barton and Williams also employed Miranda in ways that reveal
differences in how each conceived of the malevolence both saw in
Antonio's silence. The Miranda of Barton's production reacted to
her first sight of men other than Ferdinand and her father by leaving
Ferdinand and walking toward Antonio and Sebastian. She knelt
before them as she spoke the last words that Shakespeare assigned
to her during the play:

> O, wonder!
> How many goodly creatures are there here!
> How beauteous mankind is! O brave new world
> That has such people in't!   (lines 181–84)

In that specific context, her words and gestures arose from an innocence that left her unable to distinguish between the appearance of
goodness and the fact of human evil. Miranda's innocence made all
the more menacing the evil embodied in the two men whose presence filled her with wonder.

The Miranda of Williams' production also responded to her initial sight of a group of men by stepping away from Ferdinand. Her

first two sentences ("O, wonder! / How many goodly creatures are there here!") she spoke while standing in front of Sebastian and studying him intensely, but this was a Sebastian who had, upon seeing her with Ferdinand, accepted the validity of Prospero's powers by saying, "A most high miracle." From Sebastian she crossed to Alonso, the king whose sense of guilt had already prompted him—in contrast to the silent Antonio—to "resign" Prospero's dukedom and explicitly ask for pardon. Standing before him, she spoke her next sentence: "How beauteous mankind is!" Turning from him, she crossed the stage again; she stopped before Gonzalo and looked at him as she declared, "O brave new world / That has such people in't!" Gonzalo sank to his knees and kissed her hand.

As Miranda moved from Sebastian to Alonso to Gonzalo, she said nothing to Antonio. He was not one of the "goodly creatures" who stirred her wonder. He sat downstage left, facing the audience. By focusing Miranda's wonder on characters other than Antonio, Williams avoided undercutting her innocence as Barton had. Her innocence stirred her to single out and respond first to two men, each guilty of past evil, whose capacity for goodness Prospero's art had very recently awakened. The last of the "goodly creatures" on whom Miranda specifically focused was Gonzalo, the man whose "charity" and "gentleness" Prospero had earlier praised when telling Miranda how the two of them had survived the plot that overthrew him:

> Some food we had, and some fresh water, that
> A noble Neapolitan, Gonzalo,
> Out of his charity, who being then appointed
> Master of this design, did give us, with
> Rich garments, linens, stuffs, and necessaries
> Which since have steaded much. So, of his gentleness,
> Knowing I loved my books, he furnished me
> From mine own library, with volumes that
> I prize above my dukedom. (I.ii.160–68)

Miranda's response to her father's account had been to wish, "Would I might / But ever see that man!" (lines 168–69). During the final scene of Williams' production, that wish was fulfilled in a way that defined the quality of her innocence. It was the presence of Gonzalo that stirred her to exclaim, without knowing his identity, "O brave new world / That has such people in't!" In contrast to the

Miranda of Barton's production, this Miranda has an innocence that brings her not to Antonio but to Gonzalo, a man who is indeed "goodly." In Williams' production the moment when Miranda sees Gonzalo brought together an old man whose goodness has survived a world dominated by evil and a young woman whose innocence enables her to single him out as she enters a world in which that domination has been broken.

" 'Tis new to thee," Shakespeare has Prospero say on hearing his daughter's words of wonder, and Miranda says nothing in reply, beginning a silence that endures for the rest of the play. Her silence may be a reaction to what could be the paternal rebuke implicit in Prospero's words—if indeed she hears them—and that reaction could range from acquiescence to indifference to defiance without contradicting the words of Shakespeare's playtext. If Miranda's silence conveys her indifference or even her defiance of Prospero in a production that also presents her wonder as a response specifically to a silently malevolent Antonio, the audience's sense of future danger for both her and her father will increase. However, the indifference or defiance of a Miranda whose wonder is a response to Gonzalo will increase the audience's sense of Miranda's growing independence from her father without suggesting that he or she is likely to be in future jeopardy. If Miranda's silence signifies acquiescence to her father's words, any sense the audience might have of a threat posed by an unrepentant Antonio will decrease and the bond between father and daughter will remain firm.

Miranda's silence might instead (or even simultaneously) convey her continuing wonder and deepening absorption in the "new world" that Prospero has opened to her—a world that is no longer limited to the island and to the human company of no one but her father. It may be that Miranda does not even hear Prospero say, " 'Tis new to thee," or if she does, she may in fact pay no attention to his words. What is clear is that, smitten with wonder, the daughter whom Prospero repeatedly called upon to pay attention to him during act I, scene ii,[12] is now moving into that "new world" without saying anything to him. Prospero is no longer the sole or even the primary focus of his daughter's attention, and her silence toward him can endow the words he uses to mislead Alonso with a poignantly ironic truthfulness: "I / Have lost my daughter."

In the productions of Barton, Williams, and Phillips, Miranda's silence was accompanied by actions that allowed audiences to register Prospero's sense of loss but did not suggest any tension or split between father and daughter. During Barton's production, which strongly established Prospero's final loneliness, father and daughter embraced as he said,

> . . . and so to Naples,
> Where I have hope to see the nuptial
> Of these our dear-beloved solemnizèd.   (lines 307–9)

Prospero crossed to Miranda and Ferdinand at the same moment during Williams' production. Earlier, Miranda and Prospero had held hands while Gonzalo called upon everyone to rejoice at the mysteriously benevolent ways of Providence:

> Was Milan thrust from Milan that his issue
> Should become kings of Naples? O, rejoice
> Beyond a common joy, . . .   (lines 205–7)

Phillips did not pair Prospero and the silent Miranda in so clear-cut a fashion, but he muted any possibility of discord between them by having Miranda speak her lines of wonder to an Antonio who had earlier knelt in silent repentance before Prospero and was moved to shame by her words. The Miranda of John Gorrie's 1979 production of *The Tempest*, produced for television as part of "The Shakespeare Plays,"[13] remained near or beside Prospero virtually all the while she was silent. After Prospero promised "sail so expeditious that shall catch / Your royal fleet far off," she was (with Ferdinand) the last to depart into the cave that was Prospero's cell. Before leaving, she looked long and lovingly at her father.

Gorrie did not make Antonio's silence as prominent as Phillips, Barton, and Williams did, and he left it ambiguous. When Prospero asked for his dukedom in Gorrie's production, Antonio did not kneel or bow or hand over any badge of office. He simply turned and walked away, and the camera quickly shifted the audience's attention away from him by focusing on Alonso, the next person to speak. Antonio's movements during the rest of the scene did not definitely establish—as they had in Barton's and Williams' productions—his continuing malevolence. Prospero moved toward Antonio and Sebastian before saying,

> . . . But, howsoev'r you have
> Been justled from your senses, know for certain
> That I am Prospero, and that very duke
> Which was thrust forth of Milan, who most strangely

Upon this shore, where you were wracked, was landed
To be the lord on't. . . .   (V.i.157–62)

By having Prospero direct his words specifically to them, Gorrie
allowed for the possibility that Antonio's silence arose, in some
measure, from confusion and disbelief. Antonio stood beside Miranda, at the entrance to Prospero's cell, when she spoke her lines of
wonder, and she looked at him when she began speaking. As she
continued, however, her gaze widened to include others from the
court who were ranged around her. Her words became, then, a
response not to Antonio specifically but to men in numbers and
variety that she had never before encountered. For the most part
Gorrie kept Antonio, once he had turned away from Prospero, relatively inconspicuous on the periphery of the action. The members of
the audience saw him, at the edge of the television picture, silently
look away. In the center of the picture, they saw Ferdinand kneel to
his father and heard him say, "Though the seas threaten, they are
merciful. / I have cursed them without cause" (lines 178–79). Antonio also looked away briefly when Alonso, taking Miranda and Ferdinand by the hand, declared: "Let grief and sorrow still embrace
his heart / That doth not wish you joy" (lines 214–15). Again, the
camera focused not on Antonio but on the betrothed pair and
Alonso, and the audience could not be certain whether Antonio's
silent gesture signified remorse or a hostile unwillingness to wish
Ferdinand and Miranda well.

Taking advantage of the camera's ability to direct an audience's
attention to specific details, Gorrie contrasted Miranda's last, loving
look at Prospero with the look that Ariel gave him before departing
to begin his freedom. When Prospero said, "My Ariel, chick," Ariel
materialized behind Prospero's right shoulder, but Prospero did not
look at him as he said, "That is thy charge. Then to the elements /
Be free, and fare thou well!" Prospero's face, photographed by the
camera with an intimacy not possible in the theater, registered his
pain and loss. When he heard the words with which Prospero
granted him freedom, Ariel, before wordlessly disappearing into the
elements, fixed upon his master a final look that conveyed neither
hostility nor gratitude. Cedric Messina described it as "a cold, flat,
hard look without feeling."[14] It fused indifference and curiosity in a
way that seemed nonhuman, and in doing so, it defined the absence
in the spirit Ariel of anything like the human capacity to love.[15] That

capacity was manifest in Miranda's last look at her father and was the source of Prospero's pain when he said farewell to his beloved servant. At the moment of freedom, this Ariel gave no sign of reciprocating Prospero's love—of having any affection for or emotional attachment to the man who had first freed him from the pine and then made him his servant. He did not hold out his hand to Prospero or sigh or keep looking toward Prospero while backing away. Once Ariel was gone, Prospero, after a sustained pause, removed his hat and, speaking to the camera and the silent audience beyond it, said, "Please you draw near," as if seeking from the audience the affection that Ariel had not given him. With that maneuver, Gorrie's production brought the silences of Antonio, Miranda, and Ariel toward Prospero into alignment with the audience's silence. Miranda's silence obviously included continuing and deep love for her father, while Ariel's made it clear that for Prospero he felt nothing—literally nothing. Antonio's silence left the members of the television audience knowing only that they did not fully know his feelings. By asking the television audience to "draw near," Prospero began a process, continued in the Epilogue, that called upon those watching to plumb their own silences in order to clarify and express their feelings toward him and toward the play itself.

□   □   □

Ariel's silent departure into freedom completes a pattern in which Prospero confines and then releases during the play many of those who come under the power of his "so potent art." Ariel, whom Prospero found confined within "a cloven pine," is released first into Prospero's service and, ultimately, into the freedom of the elements. After being confined within a rock as punishment for trying to rape Miranda, Caliban exults in the freedom he thinks he has gained by taking Stephano as his new master:

> No more dams I'll make for fish,
>   Nor fetch in firing
>   At requiring.
> Nor scrape trenchering, nor wash dish.
> 'Ban, 'Ban, Ca-Caliban
> Has a new master: get a new man.
> Freedom, high-day! high-day, freedom! freedom, high-day, freedom!
>   (II.ii.175–82)

The mariners whom Ariel, responsive to Prospero's commands, "clapped under hatches" find themselves released from that confinement and "straightway at liberty" (V.i.231, 235). Early during the final act, Ariel reports to Prospero that Alonso and his followers are

> Confined together
> In the same fashion as you gave in charge,
> Just as you left them—all prisoners, sir,
> In the line grove which weather-fends your cell.
> They cannot budge until your release. . . .   (lines 7–11)

Prospero not only orders their release but also pledges, "My charms I'll break, their senses I'll restore, / And they shall be themselves." Released from the line grove, they are brought into Prospero's presence where, "spell-stopped" (line 61), they stand powerless to move. As "the charm dissolves apace" (line 64), however, all of them, including the silent Antonio, find themselves released from that spell and, as Prospero had pledged, free to "be themselves."

Their freedom is all the greater because of Prospero's resolve to relinquish the powers by which he has previously controlled them: "But this rough magic / I here abjure" (lines 50–51). The powers Prospero ceases to exercise are greater than those which Shakespeare grants to any other character in his plays; they approach those that Shakespeare himself wields as a playwright. Prospero can bedim "the noontide sun" (line 42), as Shakespeare did each time he imposed night on the daylight stage of the Elizabethan public theater during the performance of such plays as *Macbeth* and *A Midsummer Night's Dream*. Prospero can summon storms, as Shakespeare himself does during *King Lear* and at the start of *The Tempest*. Prospero can awaken the dead, and Shakespeare does that each time a person out of the past—Theseus, Caesar, Cleopatra, Hamlet, Macbeth, Henry V, Richard III—comes to life as one of his characters, talking and striding across the stage for the duration of the performance. Prospero can make those who are subject to his "so potent art" move or stand paralyzed, speak or be dumb. He can, in short, control their actions—what they say and do—just as Shakespeare has it in his power to control the actions of those who perform his plays.

Although Prospero's powers are extraordinary—the highest that Renaissance man could properly possess—they are not without limits, which he must respect as he employs those powers to implement the moral and political design he has in mind. Some of those limits arise from the fact that although Prospero can darken the sun and awake the dead, he must, as he explains to Miranda, work in accord with time:

> . . . by my prescience
> I find my zenith doth depend upon
> A most auspicious star, whose influence
> If now I court not, but omit, my fortunes
> Will ever after droop. . . .   (I.ii.180–84)

Other limits exist because Prospero must work through and ultimately with others to give his design shape and substance. Prospero can control the actions of those who are subject to his "so potent art," but even at the zenith of his power he cannot control their minds and hearts.[16] He can make Caliban and Ariel his servants, but he cannot extinguish their desire to be free from the servitude that he has imposed upon them. Prospero can confer freedom on Ariel, but he cannot compel that spirit to reciprocate his love. Although Prospero has the power to bring Miranda and Ferdinand together, he cannot compel them to fall in love, yet love between them is an essential element in his design to regain his dukedom and to dissolve the longstanding enmity between Naples and Milan by uniting their ruling families in marriage. Nor can Prospero compel Alonso to respond to Prospero's disclosure that "I / Have lost my daughter" by wishing that Ferdinand and Miranda were "living both in Naples, / The King and Queen there." Without Alonso's freely voiced wish for such a royal union, however, Prospero's plan for reconciling Naples and Milan has little chance of achieving enduring success. Prospero can nurture and tutor Miranda,[17] but when he introduces her to mankind, he cannot ensure that his relationship with her will hold or that she will know those "goodly creatures" for who and what they are. Prospero can "require" the silent Antonio to return the dukedom that he usurped, but he cannot force Antonio to be sincerely and everlastingly penitent. Prospero's magic is "rough" not only in the sense that it inflicts pain but also in the sense that its effects are approximate and its results are not entirely his to control.[18]

Prospero's decision, early during the final scene, to cease being a mage who acts upon men reflects both Prospero's need to involve others in implementing his design and his acknowledgment of the benefits such collective involvement makes possible. An order imposed single-handedly on indifferent or recalcitrant human beings is one that, at best, cannot endure much beyond the remaining years of Prospero's life. An order in whose implementation some, if not all, come willingly but not necessarily consciously to participate has a chance to endure much further into the future—to delay the moment, which Prospero says must come, when order disintegrates, when

> The cloud-capped tow'rs, the gorgeous palaces,
> The solemn temples, the great globe itself,
> Yea, all which it inherit, shall dissolve,
> And, like this insubstantial pageant faded,
> Leave not a rack behind. . . .   (IV.i.152–56)

In surrendering his magic, Prospero chooses to be a man among men, to work, even as Duke of Milan, with his fellow humans rather than upon them. That choice, which the freeing of Ariel makes final, entails risks and losses that are greater or smaller depending on the meanings and effects that emerge from the open silences of Antonio and Miranda.

Shakespeare has the power to determine what the characters in his plays do and say, think and feel. Prospero cannot compel Ferdinand and Miranda to love one another, but Shakespeare can, and he does by giving each of them words that decisively establish the mutuality of their love:

> *Miranda:*   I am your wife, if you will marry me;
>   If not, I'll die your maid. To be your fellow
>   You may deny me; but I'll be your servant,
>   Whether you will or no.
> *Ferdinand:*   My mistress, dearest,
>   And I thus humble ever.
> *Miranda:*   My husband then?
> *Ferdinand:* Ay, with a heart as willing
>   As bondage e'er of freedom. Here's my hand.
> *Miranda:*   And mine, with my heart in't; . . .   (III.i.83–90)

Prospero must hope that Alonso will freely wish for a marriage between his "lost" son and Prospero's "lost" daughter, but Shakespeare assigns to Alonso words that compel him to express that wish:

> O heavens, that they were living both in Naples,
> The King and Queen there! That they were, I wish

> Myself were mudded in that oozy bed
> Where my son lies. . . .   (V.i.149–52)

However, at three moments during the last scene of *The Tempest*—each of them potentially crucial and each marked by an open silence—Shakespeare does not exercise the power that is his as a playwright. He does not use the words at his command to dictate whether Antonio is or is not penitent, and he does not dictate whether Miranda does or does not break with Prospero as she enters a world that she may or may not accurately perceive. Finally, Shakespeare does not specify whether Ariel, as he goes into freedom, does or does not show any affection for his master.

The open silences of Antonio, Miranda, and Ariel widen the issue of freedom within *The Tempest* to include all who are involved in performing the play. They are free to determine which specific meanings and effects will emerge from those silences, and their freedom is not peripheral. It bears directly on major concerns of the play. If Antonio's silence is evidence of heartfelt penitence, *The Tempest* conveys a conception of man's capacity to triumph over personal and political evil. A different, decidedly less optimistic vision comes into focus if Antonio's silence signifies a malignity that has been checked but not destroyed or replaced by a desire to do good. Miranda's silence after her final words of wonder allows for the possibility that she rejects her father as she moves into a world she finds dazzling but whose dangers she does not perceive. Her silence also allows, however, for other alternatives, among them the possibility that the bond between father and daughter, although changed, remains intact as she begins to participate in a world that is "new" not only in the sense that she is looking on it for the first time but also because, remade by Prospero's exercise of his "rough magic," it has been brought to the verge of perfection. A *Tempest* that presents Ariel's silent departure after being granted freedom as a renunciation of Prospero differs significantly from one in which Ariel's silence suggests the mixture of joy and pain that Ariel himself feels as he and his master separate—Ariel moving into the freedom of the elements and Prospero rejoining the world of men.

The freedom of the actors, directors, and others involved in producing and performing *The Tempest* makes Shakespeare himself subject—in effect, if not by design—to risks analogous to those Prospero faces once he renounces his "rough magic" and leaves those formerly subject to his power free to "be themselves." Just as Prospero remains vulnerable to the possibilities that Alonso will reject the marriage of their offspring and that Antonio will continue to be malevolent and that Miranda will break with him, so Shakespeare faces the possibility that those to whom he extends freedom will abuse it. Such abuses have occurred and will continue to occur. The most disturbing are those which violate the open silences from which that freedom arises. For example, Terence Kilburn, in his 1978 production of *The Tempest* at the Meadow Brook Theatre in Rochester, Michigan, violated Antonio's silence by having him speak lines that Shakespeare assigned to Alonso:

> This is as strange a maze as e'er men trod,
> And there is in this business more than nature
> Was ever conduct of. . . .   (V.i.242–44)

According to John Russell Brown, the directors of some productions have filled the silence that Shakespeare assigns to Ariel by having him laugh or sing as he leaves Prospero.[19] Barton's decision to have Prospero softly sing "Where the bee sucks" as Ariel makes his final exit bespeaks a similar refusal to let Ariel's silence be silence.

Balancing such risks is the extraordinary flexibility that freedom generates. Without a loss of its identity or a violation of what Shakespeare wrote, *The Tempest* can accommodate and convey strikingly different conceptions of mankind's ability to counter evil and to bring into being an order that is both moral and lasting. Depending on the precise meanings and effects that the trio of open silences yields in performance, the play can convey unchecked optimism: man is capable of extirpating individual and collective evil and replacing it with good. At the other extreme, the play can convey guarded, pragmatic skepticism: man, even at the zenith of his powers, is capable of doing little more than checking, temporarily, the evil that festers in individuals and that corrupts the ties of blood, passion, need, and power binding them to one another.[20]

The freedom that flows from the play's open silences has additional effects. As a playwright, Shakespeare must rely on others to transform into theatrical fact the design he has conceived—to give *The Tempest* shape and substance through performance. That design is as much dramatic and aesthetic as it is moral and political, and like Prospero Shakespeare faces the problem of how best to induce others to act in ways that will bring that design to fulfillment. The masque performed for Ferdinand and Miranda suggests one alternative. Prospero explains that those performing it are

> Spirits, which by mine art
> I have from their confines called to enact
> My present fancies.   (IV.i.120–22)

He regards them as instruments for making his own imaginings visible and audible.[21] *The Tempest*, however, requires that those who enact it have a different status. Its open silences ensure that the specific conception of man's effectiveness in the face of evil enacted during a performance will, in important respects, arise from decisions made not by Shakespeare but by directors, actors, and others involved in the process of performance. The "fancies" they "enact" will be theirs too and not Shakespeare's alone. The design of *The Tempest* is not, then, one that imposes itself on those who contribute to the performance. It is, rather, a design that summons them to act as free and human beings whose actions help to fashion the very design in whose fulfillment they participate.

The Epilogue extends that summons to include the audience of *The Tempest*. "Now 'tis true," Prospero tells those who have silently watched him confine others and set them free, "I must be here confined by you, / Or sent to Naples" (lines 3–5). Earlier, Prospero had insisted that those watching the masque must silently behold the enactment of his "present fancies." "No tongue! All eyes! Be silent." (IV.i.59), he warns Miranda and Ferdinand as the masque begins, and during it he repeats the instructions:

> Sweet now, silence!
> Juno and Ceres whisper seriously.
> There's something else to do. Hush and be mute,
> Or else our spell is marred.   (lines 124–27)

At the end of *The Tempest*, however, Prospero calls upon those in the audience to cheer and applaud. If they do, the sounds they make "release" him from the "spell" that, by their silence, they exercise over him both as an actor seeking his audience's approval and as a mage who has renounced his "so potent art" in order to rejoin his fellow men:

>   . . . Let me not,
> Since I have my dukedom got

> And pardoned the deceiver, dwell
> In this bare island by your spell;
> But release me from my bands
> With the help of your good hands.
> Gentle breath of yours my sails
> Must fill, or else my project fails,
> Which was to please. . . .   (lines 5–13)

In a certain respect members of the audience find themselves asked to take on Ariel's role as Prospero's servant, providing with their "gentle breath" the "auspicious gales" that were part of Prospero's final charge to Ariel. However, the "project," which may fail if the audience, withholding all sounds of approval, chooses to remain silent, is not only Prospero's but also the actor's playing him and Shakespeare's as well. Each time *The Tempest* moves to conclusion, actors, director, playwright, and all others involved in performing the play find themselves at risk, dependent for success or failure on an audience free to give or withhold approval. If the members of the audience give their approval, *The Tempest* becomes not just Prospero's "project" but theirs too—not just Shakespeare's play and the performers' play and the director's play but the audience's as well. The result can be a moment of full and free human community embracing playwright, characters, director, actors, designers, and audience, but such a moment occurs just as the performance that brings it into being is ending. The last words an audience hears during *The Tempest* are Prospero's asking for freedom for himself and, through him, for all those whose efforts and talents give the play its being. Each time *The Tempest* ends, those who are its audience have the opportunity to end their silence and sound their approval—to set free all who have served them during the course of the play.

4. The Final Silences of *Measure for Measure*

Measure for Measure provides the most challenging and complex example of Shakespeare's use of open silence. During the final moments of the play six characters fall silent. One of them is Angelo who, after being compelled to marry Mariana, speaks just once. With those words, the last he speaks, he asks for the imposition of a lasting silence: "I crave death more willingly than mercy; / 'Tis my deserving, and I do entreat it" (V.i.472–73). Barnardine, a convicted murderer who had earlier refused to be executed (IV.iii.33–61), is brought on immediately after Angelo says he craves death. The contrast between the two characters deepens when Barnardine silently accepts from the Duke the life-giving mercy that Angelo has just explicitly rejected. Claudio (like Barnardine, with whom Shakespeare has him enter) says nothing all the while he is on stage during the final scene—not to the Duke whose maneuvers have saved his life, not to his sister, Isabella, not even to his beloved Juliet. Juliet also enters with Barnardine and Claudio, and her presence during the final scene is also characterized by unbroken silence. Even her reunion with Claudio does not prompt her to speak. Mariana and Isabella slip resolutely into silence after each of them calls upon the Duke to extend to Angelo the mercy that Angelo himself subsequently rejects with the last words he speaks. Isabella maintains her silence not only when she sees alive the brother whom the Duke has twice told her is dead but also when the Duke himself twice proposes marriage to her. The silences of Angelo, Barnardine, Claudio, Juliet, Mariana, and Isabella are made all the more striking by the sustained contrast with Lucio's irrepressible garrulousness. His flamboyant and repeated failure to hold his peace, even after the Duke commands him to be quiet, accentuates the silences in which the other six characters wrap themselves as the play concludes.

Each of those six silences is open, and each of them can alter an audience's sense of the moral vision of *Measure for Measure*. As the implications and impacts of those silences vary from production to production, the play's perspective upon a host of issues shifts accordingly. Those issues, several of which continue to trouble and divide societies to this day, include the role of deception in the act of governing, the proper exercise and the limits of civil power, the relationship between mercy and human systems of justice, the morality of capital punishment, the wisdom of using law to control sexual behavior, the conflicting desires to engage in and to withdraw from a sordid world, and the interplay between legal authority and erotic love in the institution of marriage. The openness of each of these separate silences deepens and becomes more extensive because of the groupings that emerge from them.

Consider that during the final scene four men appear on stage who are or come under the sentence of death. One of them, Barnardine, has killed a man; another, Angelo, has tried to kill a man; the other two, Claudio and Lucio, are "guilty" of fathering a child out of wedlock. All are spared, but three of them say nothing. Only Lucio responds verbally to the Duke's words of life-giving mercy. "Upon mine honor," the Duke tells him,

> thou shalt marry her.
> Thy slanders I forgive, and therewithal
> Remit thy other forfeits. Take him to prison,
> And see our pleasure herein executed.   (lines 513–16)

Lucio's reply to the Duke expresses something other than gratitude: "Marrying a punk, my lord, is pressing to death, whipping, and hanging" (lines 517–18). None of the four men reprieved from the death sentence, not even the one among them who speaks after being saved, utters a word of gratitude for the life he has been given. Lucio's spoken response can sharpen the audience's awareness of the silence—the absence of words—by which the other three respond to the words the Duke speaks to put aside the sentences of death previously pronounced upon them. The interplay of words spoken and silences maintained during the final moments of the play underscores the power of language in this play. The Duke, Angelo, or whoever is the voice of Viennese law can, by phrasing words into sentences, take or bestow human life. "Mortality and mercy in Vienna / Live in thy tongue and heart" (I.i.44–45), the Duke tells Angelo on appointing him deputy.

The silence that the words of *Measure for Measure* impose on

Barnardine, a convicted murderer whose guilt is "most manifest, and not denied by himself" (IV.ii.135), has the potential to confirm, cast into doubt, or totally undercut the Duke's mercy toward him. Robin Phillips, in his production of *Measure for Measure* at the Stratford Festival in 1975, acknowledged the problematic qualities of Barnardine's silence and used entrances and exits to isolate and diminish their impact.¹ The playtext of *Measure for Measure* specifies that Barnardine enter with the Provost, Claudio, and Juliet immediately after Angelo declares that death is "my deserving, and I do entreat it." In Phillips' production, Barnardine was brought on with the Provost and Claudio but without Juliet.² The exclusion of Juliet muted the contrast between Barnardine's silence here and Juliet's earlier declaration of penitence for having had intercourse with Claudio: "I do repent me as it is an evil, / And take the shame with joy" (II.iii.35–36). Excluding Juliet from the entrance also had the effect of presenting as a group three men who received life from the Duke without speaking a word: Barnardine, Claudio, and Angelo. That grouping of the speechless recipients of the Duke's mercy heightened the contrast between Angelo's desire to die and the earlier refusals of Barnardine and Claudio to accept death. Presenting the three men as a group also sharpened the audience's sense of the discrepancy in the crimes that prompted the death sentences from which the Duke had reprieved them. Barnardine stood condemned for taking human life, Claudio for begetting human life, and Angelo for killing a man who remains alive.

Earlier, in defending his decision to have Claudio executed, Angelo had argued that the act of illicitly begetting a human life was morally equivalent to the act of taking a human life:

> . . . It were as good
> To pardon him that hath from nature stol'n
> A man already made, as to remit
> Their saucy sweetness that do coin heaven's image
> In stamps that are forbid: 'tis all as easy
> Falsely to take away a life true made,
> As to put mettle in restrainèd means
> To make a false one.   (II.iv.42–49)

Phillips' grouping of Barnardine, Claudio, and Angelo helped the audience to see that the Duke's mercifulness during the play's final moments confirms that disturbing equation. The Duke treats as equally "good" a murderer, a would-be murderer, and the father of an illegitimate child: he spares them all. Angelo, in pursuing rigorous justice, and the Duke, in dispensing all-inclusive mercy, both act according to systems of values that regard murder and fornication as morally equivalent. For Angelo, both are acts that merit death. For the Duke, both are acts that call forth mercy.

By having the Duke forgive the "earthly faults" of a Barnardine who had earlier spat in his face, Phillips established the selflessness of the Duke's mercy while making all the more disturbing the silence with which Barnardine accepted it. However, by having Friar Peter take Barnardine away before the Duke turned to ask, "What muffled fellow's that?" (line 482), Phillips isolated the Duke's act of mercy toward Barnardine from those acts of mercy, soon to follow, by which life is granted to Angelo, Claudio, and Lucio (whose slanders against the Duke are metaphorically equivalent to spitting in his face). Thus, Phillips did not allow the first and perhaps least deserving beneficiary of the Duke's mercy to remain onstage as a silent, visible reminder of how freely, and perhaps how imprudently, the Duke dispenses mercy.

In Keith Hack's 1974 production for the Royal Shakespeare Company, Barnardine was played as "a belching, bare-bummed loon."[3] Summoned from his cell to be executed (IV.ii), that grossly fat Barnardine proceeded to frustrate the Duke's design to use his head to deceive Angelo and save Claudio. Refusing to accept that his time to die had come, Barnardine bared his buttocks to all onstage and in the theater before defiantly returning, through the stage trapdoor, to his cell. During the final scene Barnardine entered— with Claudio and Juliet—through that same trapdoor, but the Duke's lines forgiving him were dropped entirely, and he remained visible for the rest of the scene: the silent, huge embodiment of the impulses toward rebellious defiance and carnal fulfillment[4] still present in Vienna despite the Duke's effort to impose his conception of order upon the city and its people. Barnardine's continuing presence defined, in effect, the limits—practical and moral—of the power of a Duke whom Edward Bond's program note characterized as "a vain face-saving hypocrite."[5]

The Barnardine of Barry Kyle's 1978 production for the Royal Shakespeare Company was naked when he was called from his cell. Speaking with the accent of an educated Englishman, he refused to be executed, then strode with resolute dignity back to his cell. When brought on during the final scene, however, Barnardine was no longer naked but wore a white garment of the same color as the monk's garb in which the Duke was attired—a visual and nontextual detail that suggested either a change in Barnardine's attitude or the successful assertion of the authority he had earlier defied. As the Duke said, "But for those earthly faults, I quit them all," he took Barnardine's hand, a gesture that linked that act of forgiveness to two other moments during the scene. Earlier, with the words "give we our hand" (line 13), the Duke had seemed to approve Angelo's conduct as his deputy by taking his hand, and almost immediately after taking Barnardine's hand as a gesture of forgiveness, the Duke proposed to Isabella by offering her his hand and asking for hers: "Give me your hand and say you will be mine" (line 488). This Barnardine, like the Barnardine of Hack's 1974 production, remained onstage until the conclusion of the play. Kyle directed the audience's attention to him one more time by having the Duke speak lines 480–82 to him as part of the final address, in which he counsels Claudio to "restore" Juliet and counsels Angelo to "love" Mariana. "And pray thee," the Duke then told Barnardine,

> take this mercy to provide
> For better times to come. Friar, advise him:
> I leave him to your hand. . . .[6]

All in all, the context established during Kyle's production made Barnardine's potentially disturbing silence convey the appropriateness of having the Duke spare his life. The naked man who earlier had resolutely voiced an impatient refusal to accept death and had then strode off in defiance did not stride off self-assertively during the final moments of the play. Instead, he remained onstage— clothed, patient, silent. Barnardine's silent presence affirmed the Duke's power and mercy rather than (as in Hack's production) suggesting their limits.

Desmond Davis' 1978 television production of *Measure for Measure* for "The Shakespeare Plays" series muted Barnardine's character and eliminated some of the potentially problematic aspects of his final silence. In refusing to die, Barnardine was firm without being outrageous. He did not spit on the Duke nor bare his buttocks, and he was modestly, if raggedly, clothed. Because he remained in his cell during this scene, he did not have an opportunity to convey his resolve to continue living by returning self-assertively to the cell from which he had been summoned. Instead, he terminated the exchange with the Duke more passively—by rolling over so that his back was turned to the Duke and resuming his sleep. This Barnardine ignored the Duke more than he defied him.

During the final scene of Davis' production Barnardine and Claudio were brought on together; Juliet's entrance was delayed, as in Kyle's production, until immediately after Lucio's exit. Claudio and Barnardine were both hooded as if for execution, a detail that suggested the effective imposition on Barnardine of that authority he had earlier frustrated. Barnardine was then unhooded as the Duke had been earlier. Barnardine's unhooding linked the surprise felt by the assembled citizens of Vienna when he was pardoned with their previous surprise at finding the Duke beneath the friar's hood and their subsequent surprise at finding Claudio beneath the hood of a condemned man. Once unhooded, Barnardine, dazed, was pushed without noticeable resistance to his knees, and he remained in that position, without trying to turn away, while the Duke, in another exercise of his authority, spoke the words with which he gave him life. Thus tamed, Barnardine rose and bowed his head slightly in a nod of assent, then drifted into the crowd (and off camera) with Friar Peter[7] as the Duke turned away asking, "What muffl'd fellow's that?" (line 482). The audience's final glimpse of Barnardine affirmed his inclusion in the new order established by the Duke. He could be spotted, briefly, among the train of characters who, following the Duke and Isabella, exited through the applauding crowd and past the camera.

□   □   □

A second grouping that emerges from the silences of the final moments of *Measure for Measure* consists of those who say nothing when confronted with the fact or the prospect of marriage.

Angelo and Mariana exchange no words after the Duke reveals himself and orders their marriage. Although they are onstage together during the final scene, Juliet and Claudio say nothing to one another or to anyone else, and Isabella says nothing in reply to either of the Duke's proposals of marriage. Thus, *Measure for Measure*—a play that concludes with multiple marriages either performed or made possible—ends without any verbal expression of reciprocal love, and that in turn generates a field of possible effects and meanings as wide and complex as those arising from the silences of those who receive life from the Duke. The range of possibilities comes into view if we consider just two of many alternatives. The first is that the silences of those facing marriage at the end of the play are an expression of their mute, accepting wonder at what has come to pass. The second is that their silences testify to a resistance that wordlessly but effectively drives home the fact that at least two of the marriages result far more from the Duke's exercise of his legal authority than from the imperatives of shared erotic love.

Angelo and Lucio are both beneficiaries of acts of mercy that spare their lives, but they are sentenced to live out those lives as married men. Lucio, as he is led off to have his sentence of marriage executed, equates the state of matrimony that awaits him with the more lethal sentences he has been spared: "Marrying a punk, my lord, is pressing to death, whipping, and hanging." The words with which he enters into matrimony resonate against the silence of Angelo, who, earlier, was taken off wordlessly to be married to Mariana. Brought back onstage as "this new-married man" (line 396), Angelo says nothing for the rest of the play to the woman who has been made his wife. Thus, the only couple whose marriage during the play is required by Shakespeare's playtext never exchange words once they are made husband and wife. The timing and content of the only words that Angelo does speak after being married are also troublesomely suggestive. Angelo tells the Duke, "I crave death more willingly than mercy," shortly after the woman who has been made his wife in compliance with the Duke's orders has pleaded for her new husband's life with the words, "I crave no other, nor no better man" (line 422). The repetition of "crave" underscores that what Mariana wants is precisely what Angelo has no desire to be: a living man who is her husband. What Angelo expressly asks for with the last words he utters is death, but what he receives from the Duke is life, and it is life with a woman to whom he never again speaks.

The silence that Angelo maintains toward Mariana from the moment he realizes that she must be his wife becomes total; after saying that death is preferable to married life, Angelo speaks to no one for the remainder of the play. He remains silent even when Claudio is brought forth living and he "perceives he's safe" (line 490). "Methinks," the Duke continues, "I see a quick'ning in his eye" (line 491). The Duke's words in and of themselves do not require that what he says he thinks he sees in Angelo's eyes be there. For one thing, the Duke's phrasing is decidedly tentative, cautious: "Methinks I see." In addition, Angelo himself never voices the "quick'n-ing"—the awakening of his desire to live—that the Duke thinks he sees. Finally, most (if not all) members of a theater audience cannot, given their distance from the stage and the actors, actually see for themselves what is (or is not) in Angelo's eyes. Thus, the "quick'n-ing" that the Duke says he thinks he sees must be validated by an appropriate and clearly visible gesture on the part of a silent Angelo. He might, for example, take Mariana's hand or put his arm around her or kiss her. Without such a gesture of confirmation, however, the possibility increases that Angelo's "quick'ning" exists only in the mind and eyes of a Duke whose capacity to say what he knows is not the truth and to overestimate the effectiveness of his own designs[8] has been well established.

After declaring that he thinks he sees a "quick'ning" in Angelo's eyes, the Duke charges him: "Look that you love your wife; her worth, worth yours" (line 493). In the final lines he speaks to Mar-iana and Angelo, the Duke rephrases that charge: "Joy to you, Mar-iana; love her, Angelo; / I have confessed her and I know her virtue" (lines 521–22). The combination of Angelo's continuing silence and the Duke's calls for him to love his wife raises but does not resolve the issue of whether Angelo does now or ever will reciprocate Mar-iana's love for him. The more often the Duke calls and the more persistently Angelo stays silent, the less certain we can be that An-gelo feels the love that in a comedy we would expect a newly mar-ried husband and wife to share. The combination of the Duke's calls for love and Angelo's enduring silence also raises the issue of the limits to the power that the Duke exercises during these final mo-ments. He can compel his subjects to marry but is it consistent with comedic values that he should? And can he compel Angelo to love the woman whom he has been sentenced to take as his wife? Is love—as distinct from the institution of marriage—subject to ducal dictate?

By its contrast with Lucio's outspoken words equating marriage with death and the Duke's twice-repeated call for Angelo to love his wife, the silence Angelo maintains first toward his new wife and then toward everyone can direct attention to a disconcerting parallel between the beginning and the conclusion of *Measure for Measure*. In the early scenes Angelo, as the highest officer of Vienna, con-demns Claudio to death in an application of Viennese law that makes impossible the union in marriage of the only man and woman in the play who are required by Shakespeare's words to love one another: Claudio and Juliet. The play concludes with the Duke himself utilizing Viennese law to impose marriages on two pairs of men and women—Lucio and Kate Overdone, Angelo and Mariana—whose affections are not undoubtedly reciprocal. One can see *Measure for Measure* as a play that opens with the law being invoked to punish fornication by death and that closes with the law being utilized to punish fornication by marriage.

Comparisons with *A Midsummer Night's Dream* and *As You Like It* also bring into focus some unsettling aspects of the silences at the end of *Measure for Measure*. All three plays conclude with multiple marriages or betrothals, but only in *Measure for Measure* are any of them the result of an exercise of legal authority. In *As You Like It*, two of the four marriages are "conjured" into being by Rosalind's "magic," which operates in isolation from the authority of Duke Senior, her father. His ducal authority is employed only to marry those pairs of "country copulatives" (V.iv.53–54) who, impelled by Rosalind's "magic" or by mutual desires, come before him to be wed. Among them is Phebe who, because of her promise to marry Silvius if she should ever refuse to wed Ganymede, finds herself obliged to become the wife of a man whose love she has rejected throughout the play. In contrast to the silent Angelo, however, she makes explicit her acceptance of her spouse: "I will not," she tells Silvius, "eat my word, now thou art mine; / Thy faith my fancy to thee doth combine" (V.iv.143–44).

At the start of *A Midsummer Night's Dream*, Duke Theseus attempts to impose upon Hermia a marital pairing consistent with the Athenian law upholding her father Egeus' right to marry his daughter to Demetrius, the man he has chosen for her. Ultimately, however, Theseus accepts, at the cost of setting aside the law he initially upheld, the pairings among the four young lovers that have inexplicably formed after their night in the woods. Those pairings—Hermia with Lysander, Helena with Demetrius—are based on mutual attraction rather than paternal preference or Athenian law. Theseus not only accepts but also formally and officially validates the pairings by combining the weddings of the four young lovers with his own wedding to Hippolyta. Theseus puts law aside in order to allow the four young lovers to marry, whereas Duke Vincentio employs law toward the end of *Measure for Measure* as an instrument to bring about marriages.

In his 1974 production of *Measure for Measure* for the Royal Shakespeare Company, Keith Hack responded to the "openness" of the silence with which Angelo accepts marriage and life by both lengthening that silence and simplifying it. In Shakespeare's playtext Angelo speaks his final words (expressing his craving for death) in response to Escalus' expression of sorrow that

> . . . one so learned and so wise
> As you, Lord Angelo, have still appeared,
> Should slip so grossly, both in the heat of blood
> And lack of tempered judgment afterward.   (lines 466–69)

In Hack's production, that exchange was moved forward nearly 100 lines and placed immediately after Angelo's request that the newly revealed Duke speedily impose the death sentence: "Immediate sentence, then, and sequent death / Is all the grace I beg" (lines 369–70). That repositioning meant that the Angelo of Hack's production did not—as he does in Shakespeare's playtext—continue to call for death even after he is married to Mariana and after both she (as his wife) and Isabella plead for his life.

Hack simplified Angelo's silence in another way—by having Angelo and Mariana embrace one another, crying and on their knees, as the Duke, speaking lines that were significantly different from Shakespeare's, called in the same breath for Angelo to be both married to Mariana and executed with dispatch:

Duke: Say, was thou ere contracted to this woman?
Angelo: I was, my lord.
Duke: You should be married to her instantly.
          The very mercy of the law cries out
          "An Angelo for Claudio, death for death!"
          Waste still pays waste, and pleasure answers pleasure,
          Like doth quit like, and Measure still for Measure.[9]

Thus, the Duke in Hack's production called for the death of an Angelo whose gestures forcefully and unequivocally conveyed both his acceptance of Mariana and his desire to live. Mariana followed the Duke as he moved away, clutching at him as she pleaded for Angelo's life:

Mariana: O, my most gracious lord,
          I hope you will not mock me with a husband.
  Duke: It is your husband mocked you with a husband.

Mariana: O my dear lord,
      I crave no other, nor no better man.

However, Hack's production omitted the offstage marriage between Mariana and Angelo that, according to Shakespeare's playtext, precedes Mariana's lines in which she pleads for the Duke to spare him. Thus, in that production, Mariana craved the life of a man who was not yet legally married to her and who did not continue to crave death even after she and Isabella pleaded for his life. Once Claudio was revealed as being alive, Mariana returned to Angelo, and they remained side by side, holding hands. When the Duke spoke his final words to them ("Joy to you, Mariana; love her, Angelo; / I have confessed her and know her virtue"), they came forward together, as a couple, to accept the applause of an audience who had seen in their gestures evidence that Angelo's silence expressed his full acceptance of Mariana as the wife-to-be with whom he would live out a life that he now intensely wanted.

David Giles's 1969 production of the play for the Stratford (Ontario) Shakespeare Festival also gave the silence between Angelo and Mariana a positive cast, but without distorting Shakespeare's playtext. Brought in after their marriage, Angelo and Mariana remained together and unguarded on the second step of the stage, on the periphery of the action. When Mariana heard the Duke sentence Angelo "to the very block / Where Claudio stooped to death" (lines 410–11), she proceeded to the deck of the stage to plead for her husband. As the Duke repeated the sentence ("Away with him to death," line 425), she moved to the center of the stage, stopping on the word "death." She then turned to look toward Angelo, directing to him the words, "O my good lord!" (line 426). He and the guards who were leading him off turned back on hearing her, after which she asked Isabella to "take my part" (line 427). Mariana and Angelo remained separated while the Duke heard Isabella plead for him, inquired how "Claudio was beheaded / At an unusual hour" (lines 453–54), pardoned Barnardine, and revealed that Claudio was still living. After proposing to Isabella, the Duke took Mariana across the stage and presented her directly to Angelo with the words, "Look that you love your wife; her worth, worth yours." Angelo remained with his wife, and that, together with his silence, suggested that his craving for death had subsided. Giles affirmed the bond between Angelo and Mariana more directly by pairing them during the Duke's final speech with Juliet and Claudio. That pair of lovers walked toward the center of the stage from the steps on the left of the stage as the Duke said, "She, Claudio, that you wronged, look you restore" (line 520). When the Duke directed his next words to Angelo and Mariana ("Joy to you, Mariana; love her, Angelo; / I have confessed her and know her virtue"), they also walked together toward the center of the stage from the steps on the right.

Angelo's silence was given much less prominence in the Royal Shakespeare Company's 1978 production of *Measure for Measure*, directed by Barry Kyle. After Claudio was revealed, Angelo and Mariana moved together when the Duke charged him, "Look that you love your wife." They remained together, holding hands, on the periphery of the action for the rest of the scene, before exiting together at what were, in that production, the Duke's last words, "So, bring us to our palace."

Desmond Davis, in his television production, used the gesture of holding hands to give the silence between Angelo and Mariana overtones that were more ambiguous and less positive. At the Duke's command, the couple left to be married and walked through the crowd holding hands in a formal manner—arms held chest-high, her hand atop his without their fingers interlocking. They returned in the same way, and never once did the audience see Angelo smile, nor did they witness between the newlyweds any physical contact such as an embrace or a touch that was any less stiff or more intimate than their hand-holding. Often when the camera showed Angelo—for example, when he said he craved death—it also showed Lucio in the immediate background, as if linking Angelo, now married, with the character who subsequently denounced as the equivalent of pressing to death, whipping, and hanging the state of matrimony to which he too would later be sentenced.

Robin Phillips in his 1975 production for the Stratford Shakespearean Festival established a context that, without doing violence to Shakespeare's playtext, allowed Angelo's silence to convey his resistance to the marriage imposed upon him. Angelo's silence also conveyed the force of the sexual desire (what Escalus calls "the heat of blood," line 468) that consumed the chastity that he, like Isabella, deeply prized. The Angelo of Phillips' production stayed apart from Mariana even after Claudio was revealed. The Duke's twice-repeated call for him to "love" his wife was addressed to a man whom the audience never saw paired with her except when, under guard, they were taken off to be married and then brought back. Phillips also used the play's final exits to establish the distance between Mariana and Angelo that his silence toward her can imply and to define parallels between him and Isabella. After the Duke spoke the last lines ("So, bring us to our palace, where we'll show / What's yet behind, that's meet you all should know," lines 533–34), the stage emptied, except for Isabella and Angelo, the two characters whose self-knowledge had been most rigorously tested by the events of the play. They stared silently at one another across the stage and then, following a prolonged pause, Angelo, using the exit through which the others (including Mariana) had already departed, left the stage, moving briskly but alone.

The only sexual pairing in the play that Shakespeare's playtext unambiguously establishes as being both reciprocal and fruitful is that of Claudio and Juliet, and they are also enveloped in silence during the final scene. They say nothing, not even to one another, after they enter, and theirs, too, is a silence whose meanings and effects elude purely literary analysis and therefore must be established in performance.

Hack, in his 1974 production, followed the playtext of *Measure for Measure* by having Claudio and Juliet enter together and with Barnardine immediately after Angelo had said that he craved death. By having them enter through the trapdoor—an entry used before only by Barnardine—Hack presented them as a trio sharing correspondences that set them apart from other characters. None of the three speaks after entering, and all are known violators of Viennese law—Barnardine by murdering a man, Claudio and Juliet by conceiving a child out of wedlock. Juliet's previously expressed repentance for her "crime" contrasts with Barnardine's silence, and although Barnardine and Claudio have committed different offenses, both (in contrast to Angelo) have refused to accept the death to which each has been sentenced. After Claudio had been revealed, he and Juliet stood together inconspicuously on the perimeter of the subsequent action, then came forward and took a bow together as the Duke spoke the only words addressed directly to either of them during the scene: "She, Claudio, that you wronged, look you restore."

Phillips, by contrast, altered the conventional entrances by having Juliet enter not with Claudio and Barnardine but with the newly married Angelo and Mariana (at line 395). The decision had the effect of encouraging the audience to compare the couple who had been parted by law early in the play with the couple who never exchange words after they are married by law during the play's final scene. In each case, the sexual relationship between the pair was consummated in secret and prior to the formalities of matrimony, then was humiliatingly revealed to full public scrutiny. Viennese law, which Angelo employed as punishment for the fornication between Claudio and Juliet by sentencing Claudio to a death that would have canceled any possibility of marriage between the lovers, is the instrument by which the Duke, responding to the sexual union between Angelo and Mariana, yokes them in a marriage that may be devoid of mutual affection.

In Phillips' production, Claudio entered with Barnardine, and that set up a further contrast. After Claudio's unhooding, he and Juliet—unmarried lovers—walked to each other and embraced without speaking, then remained together, standing on the fringe of the ensuing events. In contrast, Angelo, who had entered paired with Mariana as her lawful husband, silently kept a distance between himself and his spouse. The timing of Juliet's entrance also meant that, carrying life in her womb, she was present as both the still chaste Isabella and the no longer virginal Mariana called upon the Duke to let Angelo live. Juliet's speechless presence helped to reveal a crucial but unarticulated link between her and the Duke: each of them has the power to give life—he by means of the words sparing Angelo that the other women present call upon him to speak, she by means of the silent (wordless) processes of gestation.

Juliet's procreative powers were made visually explicit in Davis' production of the play for television. She entered carrying an infant, and her entrance came immediately after Lucio was taken off to be married. That repositioning set up a three-way contrast between Juliet's silence, Lucio's talkativeness, and the wail that announced the infant's presence even before it was visible. Davis' relocation of Juliet's entrance also gave to the reunion of the two lovers who had been taken from one another at the start of the play greater prominence than would be possible if she had entered with Barnardine and Claudio. Babe in arms, Juliet entered from the rear of the crowd and proceeded on her own down the lane they formed for her. As she approached the foot of the slightly raised platform on which the Duke sat, Claudio stepped toward her and they embraced. Their embrace also marked the meeting of a father freshly saved from death with his child newly born to life, and that moment made visible the conjunction of two different expressions of mankind's power to give life, the one biological and natural, the other political and cultural.

In the Royal Shakespeare Company's 1978 production, Kyle, like Davis, had Juliet enter directly after Lucio's exit, but she carried no infant, and the Duke's role in bringing the separated lovers together was far more pronounced. The Duke escorted Juliet by the hand down the stage, while Claudio, leaving Isabella with whom he had been kneeling downstage, rose and rushed toward her. While all onstage watched wordlessly, the lovers embraced joyously and sensuously. After a sustained pause, the Duke broke the silence by addressing to Claudio the first line of the play's concluding speech: "She, Claudio, that you wronged, look you restore."

By giving Juliet a separate entrance, Davis and Kyle both isolated the reunion of the lovers, thus heightening its theatrical impact and establishing it as a parallel to the earlier reunion between brother and sister. Both reunions are marked by silence: neither the lovers nor the siblings speak to one another. The silence that Isabella and Claudio maintain when they are brought face to face comes into revealing focus if their reunion is set against the moment in *Twelfth Night* when Viola, like Isabella, finds herself looking upon a brother she thought was dead:

Sebastian: Do I stand there? I never had a brother;
Nor can there be that deity in my nature
Of here and everywhere. I had a sister,
Whom the blind waves and surges have devoured.
Of charity, what kin are you to me?
What countryman? What name? What parentage?

Viola: Of Messaline; Sebastian was my father;
Such a Sebastian was my brother too;
So went he suited to his watery tomb.
If spirits can assume both form and suit,
You come to fright us.

Sebastian: A spirit I am indeed,
But am in that dimension grossly clad
Which from the womb I did participate.
Were you a woman, as the rest goes even,
I should my tears let fall upon your cheek
And say, "Thrice welcome, drowned Viola!"

. . . .

> *Viola:*   If nothing lets to make us happy both
> But this my masculine usurped attire,
> Do not embrace me till each circumstance
> Of place, time, fortune do cohere and jump
> That I am Viola; . . .   (V.i.218–33, 241–45)

The tone of the words they exchange is questioning, tentative. Sebastian and Viola are baffled and amazed, but—in contrast to Claudio and Isabella—they do not remain silent in one another's presence.

The potential ambivalence of the silence between Isabella and Claudio becomes evident if one recalls their only conversation together. Before leaving her brother's prison cell, Isabella vowed to speak "no word to save thee" (III.i.147) and concluded by declaring,

> Thy sin's not accidental, but a trade;
> Mercy to thee would prove itself a bawd,
> 'Tis best that thou diest quickly.   (III.i.150–52)

Thus, the last words an audience hears Isabella speak to Claudio are those with which she denies his fitness to receive the mercy that she, looking on in silence, sees the Duke extend to him during the final scene. The silence between Claudio and Isabella may be tantamount to a retraction of the bitter words they had earlier exchanged, or—to pose another possibility—that silence may signify a continuing rupture in their relationship.

The silence between Claudio and Isabella coincides with the silence with which she responds to the Duke's initial proposal of marriage. The lines in which the Duke presents and pardons Claudio are also those in which he reveals himself as Isabella's suitor:

> If he be like your brother, for his sake
> Is he pardoned, and for your lovely sake—
> Give me your hand and say you will be mine—
> He is my brother too. . . .[10]   (lines 486–89)

The roles of husband and brother come close to converging at this point, and that conjunction seems particularly appropriate given Claudio's earlier declaration to Isabella concerning how he would face death:

> . . . If I must die,
> I will encounter darkness as a bride,
> And hug it in mine arms.   (III.i.83–85)

The newly unmuffled man will be spared insofar as he is "like" the brother whom Isabella thought dead, and the Duke's proposal of marriage, if Isabella accepts it, will make that man the Duke's brother as well as hers.

Isabella's silence here is all the more striking because the Duke phrases his marriage proposal as a call for her to assent with words as well as with a gesture: "Give me your hand and *say* you will be mine" (emphasis added). The Duke's request (or command) can be set against Mariana's earlier call for Isabella to join her in seeking mercy for Angelo: "Sweet Isabel, do yet but kneel by me, / Hold up your hands, say nothing, I'll speak all" (lines 433–34). Offered that chance to be silent, Isabella chooses to speak on Angelo's behalf, yet when called upon to voice her acceptance of the Duke, she says nothing. The Duke, whose declared wish to become a husband has been met with silence, breaks that silence by turning to Angelo, who has been made a husband by ducal command, and calling upon him to "love your wife." The Duke's shift from Isabella to Angelo helps to emphasize that both respond to the marriages they face with silence. Isabella says nothing to the man who would make her his wife, just as Angelo says nothing to the woman who has been made his wife.

□   □   □

The Duke's words pardoning Claudio, proposing to Isabella, and instructing Angelo to love his wife are embedded within as many as five silences: Isabella's toward the Duke, Angelo's toward Mariana, Claudio's toward both Isabella and Juliet, and, if he remains visible, Barnardine's. Each of these silences is open to a range of meanings and effects, and the interplay among the silences generates a cumulative openness that is even more challenging. The result is a theatrical moment strikingly rich in possibilities. By means of gestures, movements, and other nonverbal details of performance, all productions of *Measure for Measure* tap that richness, giving those individual silences and the relationships among them definition and coherence. In so doing, every production aligns in different ways the erotic, sibling, and marital bonds that can come into conjunction at this extraordinarily challenging moment in the play.

The directors of the specific productions being considered here responded to the complexity of that moment by narrowing, and thus simplifying, the confluence of silences in different ways and to different degrees. Keith Hack, in his 1974 production, simplified most drastically the possibilities inherent in that moment. As the Duke of that production brought Claudio and Isabella face to face for the first time since their encounter in Claudio's prison cell, he said, "If he be like your brother, for his sake / Is he pardoned." However, the line in which the Duke proposed to Isabella was dropped, thus concentrating attention upon the reunion, in silence, of the sister and brother. Isabella crossed to Claudio and kissed him. Claudio's response to that gesture was a chilling stare as he silently rejected the sister who had refused to sacrifice her virginity to save him but had been willing, a few moments before, to plead in tears for the life of the man who, she thought, had had her brother executed. As Isabella watched silently in dismay, Claudio stepped away to be with Juliet. His silence in embracing Juliet contrasted with both the silence with which he responded to Isabella's kiss and the silence with which she watched her brother walk away from her and toward his lover. By omitting the Duke's proposal of marriage, Hack made Isabella's silence toward the Duke insignificant. That, in turn, permitted Hack to use the concurrent silences between Isabella and Claudio and between him and Juliet to convey the final rupture of familial ties and the triumph of the erotic bond that unites Claudio and Juliet—the only pair who have loved each other from the start of the play and who have expressed that mutual love in sexual acts that have engendered new life. The Duke broke those silences by addressing himself to another pair of silent characters, Angelo and Mariana—the only other couple in the play whose relationship has been consummated sexually: "Well, Angelo, your evil quits you well. / Look that you love your wife; her worth, worth yours." As he spoke, Mariana crossed to Angelo (a movement that paralleled Isabella's earlier crossing to Claudio), but Angelo did not move away from her. They stood together, paired like Claudio and Juliet in a silence that affirmed the bonds between them, while Isabella, who had refused to have sexual intercourse with Angelo in order to save Claudio, stood alone and silent.

Two other directors—Barry Kyle and Desmond Davis—narrowed the silences in a different way, by delaying Juliet's entrance until after Lucio's final exit. That enabled both directors to postpone the silence between Juliet and Claudio, thereby intensifying the audience's concentration on the silences between Isabella and Claudio and between her and the Duke. In Kyle's 1978 production, the Duke, after unmuffling Claudio, knelt between him and his sister while addressing to Isabella the words sparing her brother and asking for her hand. The Duke's act of kneeling linked that moment to others earlier in the scene when Isabella had knelt to him—first to plead (falsely) against Angelo for violating her chastity and then to plead in earnest for the Duke to spare Angelo's life. When the Duke finished speaking his words of pardon and proposal, Isabella crossed past him to Claudio and caressed her brother's face for a moment before recrossing to the Duke and raising him from his knees. The gestures and blocking in Kyle's production emphasized Isabella's status as the person who has the power to make Claudio and the Duke brothers, to make true the words with which the Duke concludes his proposal of marriage: "He is my brother too." In the specific context of that production, the silence that Isabella maintained established the possibility of reconciling fraternal and marital bonds—of merging the family into which she was born with the new family that the Duke asks her to help bring into being. In her surprise, she spoke neither to the brother whom she was stunned to find alive nor to the friar-turned-Duke whose expressed desire to make her his wife was equally stunning. The hands with which she silently stroked her dazed brother's face were also the hands she silently extended to raise the wooing Duke from his knees. That gesture, although it was not an explicit rejection of his proposal, was not an unambiguous acceptance of it either. Kyle's production concluded the conjunction of silences that the moment generates by affirming the bond between brother and sister, which was shattered in Hack's production. As the Duke turned to address Angelo, his words breaking the silences, Isabella moved with her brother to a point downstage center, where she knelt with him, staring into and stroking his face. That downstage tableau of the reunited brother and sister functioned as a "frame" through which the audience watched as, upstage, the Duke proceeded to deal with Lucio.

Davis intensified the impact of the sibling bond in a different way and set it sharply against the marital bond offered by the Duke. As soon as the Provost (not, as in Kyle's production, the Duke) removed the hood from Claudio's head, Isabella rushed to embrace her brother. As the television camera showed them in close-up clinging to one another, the audience heard the Duke's voice intrude to propose a marriage that would make Claudio his brother too. The camera continued to focus on Isabella, rather than the Duke, giving weight to her response to what she was hearing. Her arm still around Claudio's neck, as if to emphasize that he was *her* brother, Isabella stared blankly toward the man proposing marriage to her from a distance. In contrast to Kyle's kneeling Duke, this Duke, as he spoke of marriage, remained seated on the throne placed on the rostrum at the foot of which Isabella and her brother stood paired together. The Duke's "but fitter time for that" quickly followed, breaking in upon Isabella's silence and sounding like an embarrassed, even defensive reaction to her blank expression, her silence, and her evident love for Claudio. The camera followed the Duke when he turned away, and as Claudio and Isabella disappeared from the audience's view, the Duke urged the silent Angelo to give to his wife the love that the silent Isabella, his own would-be wife, had shown no sign of extending to him.

In his 1975 production, Phillips also made the silences between Isabella and Claudio and between her and the Duke the center of the audience's attention, but he did so without excluding Juliet and in a way that made visible in still another fashion the conflict between Isabella's role as sister and the role of wife that the Duke asks her to assume. The Duke stood between Claudio and Isabella—as much a barrier as a bridge—while holding out his hand and asking for hers. As Isabella stared silently at her brother, the Duke circled her until, stung by her failure to extend her hand to take his, he turned away, hands clasped behind his back, to announce to Angelo the pardon that he had previously made Mariana and Isabella plead for on their knees. As he did, Isabella crossed to Claudio, who stood with Juliet. That sequence of movements and gestures conveyed an alignment of erotic and familial bonds different from that established in Kyle's production. By crossing from the Duke to Claudio and Juliet, Isabella signified her approval, as Claudio's sister, of the erotic bond uniting her brother and his beloved, and at the same time she excluded the Duke from the merging of an old and a new family implicit in her actions. By remaining silent and not giving her hand to the Duke, she chose not to make Claudio the Duke's "brother too."

The presence of both Claudio and Juliet gave visible expression to another facet of Isabella's silence toward the Duke. The couple kept before the audience the example of an erotic pairing based on something other than deception like that which the Duke, Isabella, and Mariana practiced with such skill in order to bring about the sexual coupling and then the marriage between Angelo and Mariana—who, in Phillips' production, remained apart from each other all the time they were on stage after being married.

The woman whom the Duke asks to be his wife has herself been subjected to his powers of deception. Twice before proposing marriage, the Duke lies to Isabella with cold-blooded precision about the death of her brother. As Friar Lodowick, he tells her false "news" of Claudio's execution as part of his scheme "to make her heavenly comforts of despair":

Isabella:	Hath yet the deputy sent my brother's pardon?
Duke:	He hath released him, Isabel, from the world;
	His head is off and sent to Angelo.
Isabella:	Nay, but it is not so.
Duke:	It is no other. Show your wisdom, daughter,
	In your close patience. (IV.iii.107, 111–16)

Shakespeare's playtext emphasizes the anguish that the Duke's deception, however well-intentioned, has caused Isabella. Twice in subsequent lines, the Duke must interrupt what he is saying and urge her to stop crying, and even the usually flippant Lucio responds sympathetically to her pain: "O pretty Isabella, I am pale at mine heart to see thine eyes so red; thou must be patient" (lines 151). The audience's sense of Isabella's grief can be sharpened in performance. The Isabella of Kyle's production sank to her knees on hearing of Claudio's death, then slowly, somewhat angrily, removed her veil and cincture before leaning wearily against the Duke. In Davis' production, the camera gave added impact to Isabella's anguish by moving in for a close-up shot of her tears and then allowing the audience to see her walking slowly and solitarily away into the dawn mist while, in the foreground, the Duke and Lucio continued talking.

During the final scene the Duke lies to Isabella a second time:

Your brother's death, I know, sits at your heart,
And you may marvel why I obscured myself,
Laboring to save his life, and would not rather

> Make rash remonstrance of my hidden power
> Than let him so be lost. O most kind maid,
> It was the swift celerity of his death,
> Which I did think with slower foot came on,
> That brained my purpose; but peace be with him.
> That life is better life past fearing death,
> Than that which lives to fear. Make it your comfort,
> So happy is your brother.   (lines 385–95)

Those words, spoken after the Duke has shed his disguise as a friar
and revealed his identity, are untrue. The more intensely Isabella
grieves in response to what the Duke tells her is the fact of her
brother's death, the more likely it is that the audience will find the
Duke's sustained deception of her distasteful, cruel, or even inhu-
man.[11] The more pronounced her anguish, the more moving will be
her capacity to plead for the life of the man she thinks has killed her
brother, and the more willing an audience will be to accept any
shock or dismay or hesitation she shows when the Duke first proposes to her. Isabella begins her speech on Angelo's behalf—sometimes after a prolonged hesitation[12]—by calling upon the Duke to
act as if her brother's death were the fiction he knows it to be:

> Most bounteous sir,
> Look, if it please you, on this man condemned
> As if my brother lived. . . .   (lines 439–41)

The words with which Isabella concludes that speech are the last she
utters during the play, and, significantly, they specify a realm of
human experience that lies beyond the Duke's authority: "Thoughts
are no subjects, / Intents but merely thoughts" (lines 449–50).

In Phillips' production, Isabella's silence in response to the
Duke's initial marriage proposal—her refusal to express her
thoughts—was tantamount to another assertion of the limits of ducal prerogative and power. That refusal also pointed to the contra-
diction between the love that presumably motivated the Duke to
propose marriage and the anguish that he inflicted upon her by lying
twice about her brother's death. Her silence also served as an indict-
ment, appropriately wordless, of the Duke's tendency to abuse or
even to corrupt language by employing his powers of speech to deceive rather than to enlighten. In addition, her silence conveyed her

recognition that she had compromised herself by participating in that abuse of speech. Her speeches earlier in the final scene denouncing Angelo for subjecting "my chaste body / To his concupiscible intemperate lust" (lines 97–98) are, after all, as false as they are eloquent. The context established by Phillips' production enabled him to employ Isabella's first silence to pose—if not to answer—the question of whether the Duke's exercise of his powers, particularly with respect to Isabella, had been moral, humane, or loving.

David Giles's 1969 production at Stratford, Ontario, invested the silences surrounding the Duke's first proposal with still another set of effects and meanings. Barnardine's silence was cut short by having him exit with Friar Peter at line 482, before the Duke asked, "What muffled fellow's that?" After Claudio was unhooded, he and Isabella embraced at center stage, then crossed together to Juliet, standing at the left on the first step. As the Duke said, "Give me your hand and say you will be mine," he stepped toward the trio. He and Isabella joined hands while Claudio and Juliet, the only couple in the play whose love is from the first undoubtedly reciprocal, stood together with them. Isabella's silent but unambiguous assent and the proximity of the two couples established correspondences between erotic and familial love different from those in the other productions under discussion. By giving her hand to the Duke, Isabella made Claudio his "brother too," and as the two couples stood together—one newly united, the other reunited—their pairings made visible the possibility of renewing a family that seemed to have no future when Claudio the brother was arrested for a crime punishable by death on the same day that Isabella the sister "should the cloister enter" (I.ii.172).

Isabella's silence in response to the Duke's second proposal of marriage exists within a network of silences less complex than that of which her silence in response to his first proposal is a part, but her second silence is nevertheless open in performance to a range of meanings and effects that have the potential of being all the more resonant because they come so near the conclusion of the play. Giles enhanced the impact of Isabella's final silence by relocating the last two lines of Shakespeare's playtext, placing them after the Duke's call for Angelo to forgive the Provost. When the Duke said, "So, bring us to our palace, where we'll show / What's yet behind that's meet you all should know" (lines 533–34), the other characters ex-

ited, leaving the Duke standing upstage center and Isabella seated
on a bench downstage center. The last words the audience heard
were:

> . . . Dear Isabel,
> I have a motion much imports your good,
> Whereto if you'll a willing ear incline,
> What's mine is yours, and what is yours is mine.   (lines 529–32)

Isabella's wordless response to that second proposal was as elo-
quently affirmative as her response to the first. She rose after the
Duke finished speaking, paused briefly but noticeably, then went
swiftly toward him. They embraced and kissed, their affectionate
gestures made all the more prominent by their isolation on the
stage; then they exited together. Isabella's movement toward the
Duke reciprocated his earlier movement toward her with his first
proposal, and the kiss they shared manifested a kind of love different from, yet linked to, the love expressed in the embrace that Isabella and Claudio had shared earlier in the scene. Her free and considered acceptance of the Duke—in private and for a second time—
capped and endorsed the order the Duke had effected. At the same
time, her acceptance muted any distaste the audience might have felt
for the manipulations and deceptions he had practiced upon her,
and others, in the process of establishing that order.

Hack's production, on the other hand, prompted the audience to
feel a distaste for the Duke, his methods, and the order he established. Hack dropped the Duke's first proposal of marriage to Isabella, and his production concluded (as did Giles's) with the words
"What is yours is mine." As he spoke those final words, however,
the Duke embraced Isabella, enfolding her stiff, resisting body
within the vast golden robes of his office. Earlier in the scene, after
the Duke had abandoned his disguise as a friar, those robes had
been stripped from Angelo. Now, those same robes of state helped
to establish that in embracing Isabella and taking her for himself,
the Duke was succeeding where Angelo had failed.

The Isabella on whom the Duke imposed himself was wearing
the brownish-orange dress worn by Mariana in previous scenes;
Mariana appeared during the final scene in the severe yet ornate
black dress that Isabella had worn throughout the play.[13] That exchange of dresses extended the pattern of entrapment in the play.
Isabella found herself snared by the Duke just as Angelo found him-

self snared by Mariana. The switch in dresses had the additional effect of momentarily involving the audience in a visual deception akin to that practiced upon Angelo. Those watching the production were forced to rework the visual clues by which they had previously identified and to some extent "measured" Isabella and Mariana.

The exchange of dresses was one of several Brechtian devices employed during the performance to make the audience aware that the events unfolding during the final scene and the order emerging from them were, on one level, a contrivance of the Duke and, on a second level, a contrivance of the performers and playwright. Scaffolding and other apparatus usually kept out of sight were visible when the audience entered the theater and remained so throughout the performance. The entire final act was played under a banner reading "*Deus ex machina*," which dropped into view as the Duke entered and greeted Angelo and Escalus: "My very worthy cousin, fairly met. / Our old and faithful friend, we are glad to see you" (lines 1–2). As the Duke, in the final speech of the play, addressed Escalus, Claudio, Juliet, Angelo, Mariana, and other characters, he beckoned them forward, individually and in pairs, to take their curtain calls. The applause that the theater audience gave them echoed earlier moments during the scene when the Viennese citizenry, assembled as an onstage audience, broke into applause. The most chilling of such moments came when they began to clap rhythmically and ominously as the Duke, with Mariana and Angelo kneeling and embracing tearfully at his feet, called for Angelo's execution: " 'An Angelo for Claudio, death for death!' " (line 405).

A series of gestures emphatically established that the anguish that moved Mariana, Isabella, and Angelo to tears during the scene was provoked, perhaps even gratuitously exacerbated, by a Duke whose manipulations of his subjects and their emotions came to have an unsavory quality, particularly with respect to the women. When Isabella first called out for "justice, O royal Duke . . . justice, justice, justice, justice!" (lines 20–25), he carefully turned her around to face the theater audience before saying, "Relate your wrongs" (line 26). The Duke also turned Mariana to face the theater audience when she came before him, and after she unveiled herself, he turned her in a full circle, in smiling self-satisfaction, showing her face to all onstage and in the theater, before allowing her to proceed, tearfully, with her charges against Angelo. The embrace to which the Duke forced Isabella to submit at the conclusion of Hack's production was, therefore, the culmination of a series of actions by which he repeatedly turned and manipulated the bodies as well as the emotions of those "poor informal women" (line 234), one of whom he sentenced his deputy to marry, the other of whom he literally took for himself as he spoke the production's final words, "what is yours is mine." In that context, Isabella's speechlessness conveyed her horrified, even hysterical helplessness before the willful authority of the Duke, who had exercised his power to impose on her and on Vienna an order whose moral foundations were seen to be self-serving, if not perverse.

Though produced for television, Davis' production, like Hack's, gave the final scene a specifically theatrical quality. A rostrumlike platform on which a throne had been placed provided what Davis himself termed "the bare bones of an Elizabethan theater,"[14] and the courtiers and people of Vienna, assembled in daylight in the city square, constituted an audience who broke into applause on several occasions. Their applause, however, was never threatening as in Hack's production but was genial, even festive.[15] Davis presented the final scene as a play (within a play) staged by and starring the Duke,[16] but this Duke, in contrast to the Duke of Hack's production, employed his power to deceive and manipulate people less as a means of indulging his own vanity and desires than as a way of making clear to all Vienna that humanity and life itself are best served when justice is tempered by mercy.

The Duke's participation in his own "play" marked a significant change in his character. Toward the end of Shakespeare's opening scene, immediately before the Duke seems to leave Vienna, he says:

> I'll privily away; I love the people,
> But do not like to stage me to their eyes;
> Though it do well, I do not relish well
> Their loud applause and aves vehement,
> Nor do I think the man of safe discretion
> That does affect it. . . .   (I.i.67–72)

Hack's Duke turned smiling and bowed slightly to the theater audience while speaking those lines, by his gestures inverting the literal meaning of his words. What he said he did not like was what, in fact, he deeply relished. Davis' Duke spoke the same words with sincerity, addressing them directly, almost intimately, to Angelo amid the background noise of the crowded throne room. Very shortly after, the Duke made his exit swiftly and somewhat uncomfortably through the ranks of applauding courtiers, his gaze fixed rigidly ahead.

The Duke's entrance at the beginning of the final scene in Davis' production was not done at all "privily" but was a carefully arranged public spectacle. The Duke entered on horseback, waving in response to the applause of a crowd that had gathered in the square on his orders.[17] The first of his two exits during the final scene closely paralleled the exit the audience saw him make during the opening scene. After delegating to Angelo and Escalus the task of rooting out the conspiracy, the Duke strode off through his subjects who, like the courtiers in the opening scene, applauded as he, again, passed without looking to either side. The audience sensed in his departure the same distaste for "loud applause and aves vehement" that he had expressed before leaving his court in act I, scene i.

The parallel, however, had limits that are themselves significant. A few moments after that departure the Duke returned wearing the disguise he had earlier assumed in order to hide himself from his subjects. Once Lucio had unhooded him, however, he stepped out of his friar's robes, mounted the rostrum, and, reclaiming the throne from Angelo, proceeded to perform in full public gaze the very duties of finding and punishing evil that he had previously seemed to reject. As he carried out his ducal tasks, he seemed at times not displeased with the surprised gasps stirred in the throng by such feats as the unhooding of Claudio and his reunion with Juliet. The Duke did not relish or "affect" their applause, but neither did he shrink from it. What the audience and his subjects saw in the play's closing moments was a man who had moved closer to being able to reconcile his taste for privacy with those demands of office requiring him to act effectively before the eyes of the people.

The interplay between public roles and private preferences in Davis's production had an important bearing on the Duke's proposals of marriage to Isabella. In contrast to the "proposal" made to her in private by Angelo, both of the Duke's proposals were made in public, revealing to all present personal feelings the Duke had hidden so deeply that no sign of them had been given previously either to Isabella or to the audience. His first proposal was made with a self-protective formality; the Duke remained on his throne while asking for Isabella's hand. Proposing the second time, he made himself, despite her nonacceptance of his first proposal, even more vulnerable as his people watched. Leaving his throne, he stepped closer to her and, no longer relying on words alone, he held out his hand to her rather than asking that she give him hers. His words and that gesture proved all the more moving because they were, in effect, his response to her earlier silence and her unwillingness to give him her hand. For several seconds (six by my count) Isabella stood expressionless, motionless, silent—her stillness intensified by the hush of the crowd. Then, with the beginnings of a smile, she accepted the hand the Duke was holding out to her. Amid a storm of applause the couple swept off hand in hand through the crowd, followed by the other major characters. Isabella's pronounced hesitation before taking the Duke's hand contrasted directly with the swiftness with which, in response to Mariana, she knelt to plead for the life of Angelo, the first man to propose sexual union with her. That contrast helped to define her silent acceptance of the Duke's hand as being an act of forgiveness for the pain he had inflicted upon her as much as an act of love. By accepting the Duke as her husband when asked a second time, Isabella in effect extended to him a mercy tempered with love that matched the justice tempered with mercy he had extended to others.

Kyle's production, however, established a context in which Isabella's final silence became more an expression of her power. The entire final scene was played on a white forestage outside the three-sided box formed by contiguous black walls that represented urban Vienna and within which all other scenes had been set. The forestage had been used just once before the final act. After Pompey, Mistress Overdone, and her prostitutes were taken off to prison, the Duke stepped forward onto the white forestage and defined the demands that the office of duke makes upon the man who holds it:

> He who the sword of heaven will bear
> Should be as holy as severe;
> Pattern in himself to know,
> Grace to stand, and virtue go;
> More or less to others paying
> Than by self-offenses weighing.   (III.ii.244–49)

The responsibilities that the Duke articulated were those that Angelo failed to meet, and they were also responsibilities that set the man holding ducal office apart from other men—a loneliness that, in Kyle's production, was given visual expression through the

Duke's isolation on the forestage. The final scene, set on that same forestage, marked the completion of the Duke's efforts, by applying "craft against vice" (III.ii.260), to set right the wrongs generated by Angelo's failure.

In Kyle's production, Isabella, silently crossing from her brother to the Duke, had raised the Duke from his knees after his first proposal, and he had proceeded to assure Angelo of his safety and to mete out justice to Lucio. While he did, Isabella accompanied Claudio to a point downstage center and knelt there with him, stroking his face. When Juliet entered, via the same rear entrance through which Lucio had just been taken off, the Duke escorted her toward the center of the stage as Claudio, leaving Isabella kneeling alone, went toward her. The lovers embraced at center stage. The movements of the different characters established parallels that made visible a conception of the relationship between erotic and familial love different from those of Phillips, Giles, Hack, and Davis. Just as Isabella crossed from Claudio to the Duke, so Claudio crossed from his sister to embrace Juliet. Just as Isabella's act of crossing to the Duke and raising him from his knees held open the possibility that, through her, Claudio might become his "brother too," so the Duke's act of bringing Juliet downstage (as Isabella had earlier brought Claudio) emphasized—in a way Davis' production did not—his role in completing the process of bringing together again two lovers from whose earlier union new human life had sprung. Erotic and familial love were seen as distinct yet complementary.

The embrace between Juliet and Claudio intensified the audience's sense of Isabella's isolation as she knelt downstage, and that embrace continued while the Duke addressed various characters. That final speech begins with what can be construed as the Duke's command for Claudio to marry Juliet ("She, Claudio, whom you wronged, look you restore"), and the last sentences he addresses to a specific individual are those in which he proposes again to Isabella. Even after hearing that second proposal, Isabella remained kneeling—isolated and silent. A long pause followed while the Duke waited for her to reply. He ended the silence by speaking to all others assembled around him the final words of the play: "So, bring us to our palace, where we'll show / What's yet behind, that's meet you all should know." The Duke waited, looking at Isabella, as his subjects, in response to his command, exited from the white forestage, passing through doors in the black walls of urban Vienna.

Their departures left him increasingly alone, and his gradual isolation upstage paralleled Isabella's downstage, thus visually linking
his isolation in office with her double isolation—as the sister of a
brother who has committed himself to another woman, and as a
woman who had earlier sought to become a religious sister, shun-
ning the presence of men among "the votarists of Saint Clare"
(I.iv.5). Isabella rose and, as she went toward the exits used by the
others, she walked past the waiting Duke. Then she stopped and
looked back to him. He walked toward her, and they exited side by
side in a pairing that diminished, even if it did not end, their respec-
tive isolations. In Kyle's production the pairing of Isabella and the
Duke was a mutual decision: she chose the Duke for her spouse as
much as he chose her for his. Within the specific context created by
that production, the silence that Shakespeare's playtext imposes
upon Isabella did not reflect either her helplessness (as in Hack's
production) or her almost reflexive acceptance of the Duke. Her
silence arose from and expressed the power she came to have and to
exercise during the final scene. That power made Isabella, as she and
the Duke left the stage together, his equal.

Phillips, in his 1975 production, also made Isabella's final silence
an expression of her power and will, but she exercised them in ways
that infused the play's final moments with still another cluster of
meanings and effects. Proposing for the second time, the Duke stood
with arms outstretched toward Isabella—a gesture that tied that
moment to the earlier moment during the scene when Isabella,
falsely denouncing Angelo, had knelt with her arms outstretched to
the Duke. On hearing the Duke's second proposal Isabella remained—as she had on hearing his first—both motionless and silent. After an excruciatingly long wait, during which the Duke's
happy anticipation changed to embarrassed anger, he lowered his
arms and, tersely stressing the first word, said, "So, bring us to our
palace"(line 533). He exited quickly with the others, perhaps even
leading them, and Isabella and Angelo were left looking across the
stage at one another for several long moments. That tableau im-
pressed upon the audience one last time the symmetry between
those two characters, both of whom had had their once-certain conceptions of virtue and of their own identities challenged by what
they had experienced.

After Angelo's departure through the exit used by the others, the
stage gradually darkened, and Isabella stood alone in a small pool

of light that further emphasized her isolation.[18] Carefully, she removed the severe wire-rimmed glasses that she had worn throughout the play. Then, with a slowness suggesting both deliberation and
a touch of weariness, she took off her religious headdress and veil,
at which point the theater was plunged into darkness. Those last
gestures conveyed her recognition, as much pained as joyous, that
she was now so enmeshed in worldly concerns that returning to the
serenity of the convent was no longer possible. Having deliberately
rejected the roles of wife and "sister," the Isabella of Phillips' production stood alone at the play's conclusion, but alone in an isolation she had freely and knowingly chosen for herself.

□   □   □

The five productions of *Measure for Measure* I have discussed demonstrate that the silences that occur during the play's final moments
are open—individually and in combination—to a wide variety of
meanings and effects. An assessment of the specific meanings and
effects generated during a particular production requires that we
judge how well or how poorly a director and a group of performers
have used the freedom that open silences allow. In reaching those
judgments, literary analysis has a clear but ultimately limited role.
The fundamental norm of literary analysis is fidelity to the words
that make up the Shakespearean playtext and, at a more sophisti-
cated level, to meanings and patterns of meanings that those words
yield. That norm permits us to make some definite judgments about
Hack's 1974 production of *Measure for Measure* for the Royal
Shakespeare Company. We realize that Hack substituted words of
his choice for those in the playtext, converting, for example, Shakespeare's "Haste still pays haste, and leisure answers leisure" (line
406) into something decidedly different: "Waste still pays waste,
and pleasure answers pleasure." Hack omitted the offstage marriage
between Angelo and Mariana, and he repositioned the lines in
which Angelo craves death so that they preceded rather than followed (and thus contradicted) the appeals for his life made by Mariana and Isabella. Hack also dropped entirely lines as important as
those in which the Duke spares Barnardine's life and those in which
he first proposes to Isabella. Those cuts, among others, allowed
Hack to avoid the question he would otherwise have had to answer:
why a Duke who is presented as selfishly willful and a "public

fraud" grants life to Barnardine and finds it necessary to propose twice to an Isabella who is powerless to defy his wishes.

Hack's production is a clear and distressing example of how, to avoid the complexities posed by the words Shakespeare wrote, a director has refashioned them so that they conform to and confirm, rather than challenge, his own conceptions. Rather than engage in the creative collaboration between playwright, director, and performers that open silences help to foster, Hack preferred to make the production a vehicle for transmitting insights and attitudes that he shared, not with Shakespeare but with another playwright, Edward Bond. In a note addressed to Hack and published in the program, Bond set forth what seems to have been the controlling vision of the production:

> Angelo is a lying, self-deceiving fraud, the Duke a vain face-saving hypocrite, and the saintly Isabella a sex hysteric. That is a total arraignment of conventional authority and the morality used to explain and excuse it. I also think that Lucio is a prototype of the fool in Lear, and that he tells the truth about the Duke. That is, he describes the Duke as another Angelo, a public fraud. . . . There is no political problem that the Duke can solve, no reason for him to dress up a fake holy-father, nothing for *him* to put right in the city. The city is happier and more peaceful without him. The problem is *in him*, *Angelo*, *Isabella*, and those who support them. It's not just the ending of the play that's a charade, the whole political set-up is.

However, our success in using even such an unsophisticated mode of literary analysis to make judgments about Hack's production underscores the difficulties we face when using the same kind of analysis to judge the other four productions under consideration. None of them is absolutely faithful to the words of Shakespeare's playtext. Three of the directors, for example, reposition Juliet's entrance during the final scene. Shakespeare calls for her to enter after line 473 when three other characters also enter; the words of the Folio text are "*Enter Barnardine and Provost, Claudio, Julietta.*" Both Davis and Kyle had Juliet enter far later in the scene, immediately after Lucio is taken off to be married to the whore who has borne his child. In Phillips' production, Juliet entered earlier, during line 395, and with the newly married Angelo and Mariana (as well as Friar Peter and the Provost). Giles did not shift Juliet's entrance, but he did reposition what Shakespeare wrote as the final lines of the play. The Duke in that production said, "So, bring us to our palace, where we'll show / What's yet behind, that's meet you all should know" before proposing marriage to Isabella a second time.

Even if those four productions had not deviated in the slightest from the words of Shakespeare's playtext for *Measure for Measure*, the fact remains that we still could not use fidelity to the playtext as the measure by which to judge how each production utilized the open silences of the play's final moments. Why? Because an open silence is characterized by the absence of words spoken by or in reference to the silent character(s). There are, then, no words of Shakespeare's to which open silences can be "faithful." The productions directed by Giles, Kyle, Davis, and Phillips endowed those silences with different, even contradictory meanings and effects. I prefer Phillips' production to the other three, principally because it did more than convert Isabella's final silences into either outright acceptance or outright rejection of the Duke's marriage proposal. I cannot, however, defend my preference by arguing that Phillips remained truer to the words of Shakespeare's playtext and to the patterns of thought and feeling they yield than did Kyle, Davis, and Giles, each of whom had Isabella accept the Duke as her husband and leave the stage paired with him. Indeed, there is nothing in the playtext of *Measure for Measure* that rules out Hack's presentation of some of the final silences: a Barnardine who remains defiant and unsubdued, a Claudio who spurns his sister and embraces Juliet instead, an Angelo who accepts Mariana as his wife and is eager to live. The playtext even allows the possibility of a Duke who imposes himself on a helpless and unwilling Isabella after having given her, with his first proposal of marriage, an opportunity—perhaps out of his own vanity—to accept him freely.

The six open silences of the final scene of *Measure for Measure* and the groupings that can emerge as a result of the links among them give the play an extraordinary freedom, a capacity for contingency and change unmatched by any other Shakespearean play with the possible exception of *King Lear*. We cannot even be certain what kind of play *Measure for Measure* is. During the first two acts, it heads toward tragedy, but then veers away and ends in a fashion that Northrop Frye and Suzanne Langer have told us is typical of comedy—with deaths avoided and with marriages performed, proposed, or imminent.[19] We cannot doubt the presence of such comedic elements, but the open silences shared by those spared from death and those confronted by marriage allow us to question whether the presence of such elements in *Measure for Measure* affirms or undercuts those values essential to comedy that prize human life and celebrate its capacity to persist and to renew itself through sexual energies that lead to marriages based on mutual love. As a murderer, Barnardine is the antithesis of the comedic values that emphasize preserving and continuing human life. Sparing him from death can mean that he is free to kill again. The Duke uses his legal authority to force Lucio to marry a woman whom he certainly does not love, and Angelo's silence can mean that he must live out the life given to him as the husband of a woman whom he has been forced by law to marry and does not love. Isabella may silently refuse to become the Duke's wife. Such a refusal would undercut the values of comedy, particularly if it involved her resolve to return to the convent, to a realm that excludes the sexual energies necessary for the renewal of human life. *Measure for Measure* may be a comedy, but it does not have to be. The open silences that abound during its final moments ensure that its generic identity is not fixed and cannot be definitively specified.

Measure for Measure must always pose problems for those who equate the play with the words that Shakespeare wrote, who seek to make the play conform to the words that are a major part of it. Those words establish the presence of open silences that require the play, during its final moments, to move beyond and float free of its verbal elements. As it ends, *Measure for Measure* defies easy categorization as a comedy and mutely but insistently asserts its identity as drama, as "a piece of pure theatrical art, dependent upon nothing except the conditions of theatre for its effect and meaning."[20]

5. Open Silences and the Ending(s) of *King Lear*

Stage traditions, editorial practices, and habits of interpretation have combined in ways that drastically narrow, if they do not obliterate, awareness of the presence and the ramifications of open silences during the final moments of *King Lear*. The first of what can be as many as three silences is mandated by both of the authoritative playtexts of *King Lear* that have come down to us from Shakespeare's era—the Quarto of 1608 and the Folio of 1623.[1] That silence occurs during moments that are among the most moving in all of Shakespeare—those which come immediately after Lear seems at last to accept the finality of Cordelia's death. "Thou'lt come no more," he says in the Folio, "Never, never, never, never, never."[2] Lear then makes a request found in both the Quarto and the Folio. In the Folio, Lear says, "Pray you undo this Button. Thanke you Sir"; in the Quarto, he says, "pray you undo this button; thanke you sir." The words that each playtext assigns to Lear are simple, and their syntax is straightforward. The Quarto and the Folio establish a silence between the instant when Lear finishes asking that "this" button be undone and the instant when he begins voicing his gratitude for that action. Whatever its duration, that silence leaves open for definition during performance details that can crucially shape the audience's sense of how Lear dies and, therefore, of how the play ends.

That silence also generates a series of questions for which neither the words of the Quarto nor the words of the Folio provide answers. Is it a particular person whom Lear asks to undo "this" button, thus singling that person out from those around him as the one to whom Lear appeals? Or does Lear address his request more generally to some or even all of those around him, a possibility that requires that whoever undoes the button be someone who feels more strongly than anyone else a desire or obligation to assist the king? The "you" to whom Lear explicitly directs his request in both the Folio and the Quarto can be either plural or singular. If Lear does ask a particular person, is it (to cite but three possibilities) Kent? or Edgar? or Albany? If Lear makes a general request, who singles himself out by stepping forward, undoing the button, and receiving thanks from the dying king? Is it—to cite the same trio of possibilities—Kent, Edgar, or Albany? And whose button is it that Lear wants undone, his own or Cordelia's?

In performance the button that is undone is traditionally Lear's, and among the meanings and effects that that stage tradition helps to generate are those that Marvin Rosenberg has described in *The Masks of* King Lear:

> *Pray you undo this button* may refer to Cordelia's dress; but almost universally it is taken to reflect the constricting of Lear's throat, a last attack of *this mother*, ironically reverberative of a child's appeal to a mother. The release from his last garment—symbolically, from life— recalls visually his first divestment and both visually and verbally the culmination of that undressing before Edgar in the storm—is there a deep, unspoken impulse to go naked again? go naked, to death, as he came?[3]

The tradition of having "this" button be Lear's requires that Lear shift his attention away from Cordelia and to himself after declaring that she will "come no more." When that tradition is combined with the words of the Quarto, the shift in Lear's focus becomes his last. In the Quarto, "thanke you sir" are the last words Lear utters before fainting ("o, o, o, o"). Reviving momentarily, he calls with his final words for his own death: "Breake hart, I prethe breake."[4] Thus the combination of stage tradition and the Quarto links his fainting, his expressed desire to die, and his death to his heartrending recognition that Cordelia will "come no more, never, never, never." He dies unwilling and unable to live without the company of the beloved daughter whom he had banished from his presence during the opening scene:

> Thou hast her, France; let her be thine, for we
> Have no such daughter, nor shall ever see
> That face of hers again. . . . .   (I.i.262–64)

Decidedly different possibilities emerge, however, when the stage tradition that Lear's button is undone is combined with the words of the Folio playtext rather than with those of the Quarto. Lear's focus shifts to himself once he realizes that Cordelia will "never" come again, but in the Folio that shift in focus is not final. After thanking whoever undoes his button, Lear turns his attention back to Cordelia and calls on those around him, or perhaps just the person who has undone his button, to look at her with an intensity that matches his own:

> Do you see this? Looke on her? Looke her lips,
> Looke there, looke there.

The Folio then states, "*He dies.*" Thus, what are Lear's final words in the Folio establish the possibility that he dies looking on the face of Cordelia (whom he had once pledged not to see "again ever") and believing that she lives. The Quarto, in contrast, specifies that Lear dies convinced Cordelia is dead. The illusion that the Folio allows Lear may be of comfort to him and even to those (members of the audience as well as characters in the play) who, in watching him suffer, have suffered themselves. However, that illusion is also one final, poignant demonstration of Lear's habit of imposing on the world around him his vision of what is and what will be. During the play's opening scene, that habit prompted Lear to disown the very daughter whose death he will not now accept. He insists now, as he did then, on looking for something from "her lips." As he would not then accept her silence in love, so he will not now accept her silence in death.

The tradition of having the button that is undone be Lear's is consistent with the request Lear makes and the thanks he gives in both the Quarto and the Folio, but there is nothing in what either playtext assigns for him to say that requires the button be his. In neither playtext does Lear say, "Pray you undo my button," a choice of words that would preserve the meter while making clear that the button must be his. The combination of "this button" and the silence specified by each playtext leaves open the possibility that it is Cordelia's button, not his own, that Lear wants undone. If it is Cordelia's button, different sets of possibilities arise. Lear's attention does not shift to himself but remains fixed on Cordelia even after he declares that she will "come no more." By asking at that moment for her button to be undone, Lear could be making a last gesture of tenderness to her before, in the Quarto, he faints from grief. That grief ultimately prompts him, when revived, to call upon his own heart to break, thus allowing him to escape the pain of having lost Cordelia and to join in death the daughter, earlier disowned, whose corpse remains the focus of his attention.

What the Quarto may establish as an act of tenderness, confirming Lear's recognition that the dead Cordelia will "never" again be with him, becomes in the Folio an act of tenderness that, once it is performed, gives way to another refusal to accept the fact of Cordelia's death. Lear, looking on "her lips," sees signs that persuade him, even as he himself approaches death, that she lives still. The Folio also allows, as an alternative, the possibility that Lear's call to undo Cordelia's button is a denial of his recognition that she will "never" come again—an effort to give her more room to breathe, to make her "come" once more into life. The Folio gives him as his dying statement words that suggest that he believes he has succeeded in reviving her: "Looke her lips, / Looke there, looke there."

According to Richard David, Trevor Nunn's 1976 production of *King Lear* for the Royal Shakespeare Company made that possibility an actuality. Lear settled on his knees at the very front of the apron,

> facing the audience and with Cordelia's body stretched in front of him. The phases of his grief were delicately distinguished, from the frantic eagerness of "Cordelia, Cordelia, stay a little," with kisses rained upon the body to resuscitate it, to the five "Never"s, the dull hopelessness of the first two changing, frighteningly, in the last three to bitter realism as the full certainty of the word seized him. And all the while the hands were restlessly busy applying this test, that remedy. The request, "Prithee undo this button," was one of these efforts to revive Cordelia, for the button was at her throat rather than at Lear's. . . . The way in which the reading led directly to the miraculous exaltation of Lear's last "Do you see this . . .", spoken straight out to the audience, should have convinced anyone not blinded by tears that this, if not the only right way to play Lear's death, is a superbly right way.[5]

If it is Cordelia's button that Lear wants undone, then his act of asking someone else to do it establishes that he has been moved, by a combination of his own feebleness and the sight of Cordelia's lifeless body, to abandon that vision of self-sufficiency ("We two alone," V.iii.9) in which he had sought comfort when he and Cordelia were led off to prison. In such a context, such questions as whether Lear asks for assistance from a specific person and who it is that aids him become significant. Suppose, as one possibility, that Lear specifically asks Kent to undo Cordelia's button. Hearing Lear seek help from the one person whose love for him approaches Cordelia's, the audience realizes, even if Lear does not, the appropriateness of that choice. Should Lear direct his request generally to those around him, then as Kent alone responds and proceeds to undo Cordelia's button, the audience sees another demonstration of the loving service that not only affirms the bond between Kent and Lear but also distinguishes Kent from all those who look on but do not act, most particularly Edgar and Albany. As Kent undoes Cordelia's button, he is serving, as he did during the opening scene, both Lear and Cordelia. In that scene he sought to serve Lear by insisting that he "see better" (I.i.158) Cordelia's love; now Kent serves by performing, on Lear's behalf, an action that can be either a final gesture of loving tenderness toward Cordelia or (as the Folio allows) a final effort to keep death from claiming her. If it is the latter, then Kent's service proves as futile now as it did on that earlier occasion. The father who would not see Cordelia's love during the opening scene will not or cannot (in the Folio) see that she is dead.

The moment takes on a different significance if Lear singles Edgar out and asks him specifically to undo Cordelia's button. Such a choice has its own appropriateness, for Edgar, as the audience knows even if Lear does not, has proved as faithful to the father who disowned him as Cordelia was to Lear. If Edgar is not specifically asked but steps forward on hearing Lear's request and undoes Cordelia's button, the audience sees the virtues that enabled him to minister to his father prompt him to attend to Cordelia in response to her father's words. Whether or not Lear specifically asks Edgar, Edgar's act of undoing Cordelia's button brings the two of them together, thus emphasizing visually the correspondence between the faithful daughter and the faithful son. The Folio allows an additional possibility if it is Edgar who responds to Lear's request. The audience watches the son who earlier reported that he watched his father die "'twixt two extremes of passion, joy and grief" (V.iii.199) move to assist a father who tries to find signs of life in the daughter whom he has just seen hanged. By having Lear's final words be "Looke there, looke there," the Folio allows for the possibility that Lear dies, as Gloucester did, between the extremes of joy and grief. Having Edgar undo Cordelia's button would make visible the "aesthetic parallel" between Lear and Gloucester that Judah Stampfer has described:

> Gloucester died between extremes of joy and grief, at the knowledge that his son was miraculously preserved, Lear between extremes of illusion and truth, ecstasy and blackest despair, at the knowledge that his daughter was needlessly butchered.[6]

Edgar's act of undoing Cordelia's button can bring into final focus not only the correspondences between the two faithful children, but also the correspondence between the two erring fathers.

Different meanings and effects emerge if it is specifically Albany whom Lear calls upon to undo Cordelia's button. By asking Albany for help, Lear singles out from those around him the man who is his son-in-law, thus implicitly invoking the bonds arising from blood and marriage that have been repeatedly violated and repeatedly affirmed during the play. Alternatively, Albany himself can be the agent for bringing those bonds to the attention of the audience if, in response to a request from Lear that is general rather than specific, he moves to assist Lear and Cordelia, thus distinguishing himself, as Lear's son-in-law, from those who do not move. Whether Albany acts in response to a specific or a general request from Lear, his gesture of undoing Cordelia's button can be a final affirmation that the bonds of blood and marriage endure. By such a gesture Albany acts out the values, arising from such bonds, that had earlier prompted him to denounce Goneril and Regan as "tigers, not daughters" (IV.ii.40). As Albany undoes Cordelia's button, the audience sees Lear's faithful son-in-law—whose wife proved as faithless to him as to her father—attending to Lear's faithful daughter.

Paralleling the stage tradition that specifies that Lear is calling for his own button to be undone is another that specifies that it is Kent who undoes "this button" (whether it be Lear's or Cordelia's).[7] The effect of the second tradition is, like that of the first, to conceal and downgrade possibilities that both playtexts of *King Lear* allow. As we have seen, Albany or Edgar rather than Kent could undo Lear's button or Cordelia's. If Kent undoes Lear's button, the audience watches Kent perform an act of loving service that affirms the bond between master and servant. The precise nature of that affirmation varies somewhat depending on whether Lear specifically asks Kent to undo his button. If Lear does, then Lear himself recognizes and invokes that bond at precisely the moment when he is convinced that death has separated him from Cordelia. In his anguish, Lear turns from the corpse of his beloved and faithful daughter and asks for help from his loving and faithful servant. If Lear's request is general, then Kent, by being the one who responds to Lear's words, affirms the bond between master and servant by acting out again a love for and fidelity to Lear as exemplary as Cordelia's. The Quarto, because it assigns to Lear the words "breake heart, I prethe breake," adds an additional dimension to the affirmation of the love and fidelity that can bind servant and master as well as father and child. Just as Lear, with those words, insists on following Cordelia into death, so Kent declines the share of the kingdom Albany offers in order to follow his master into death: "I have a journey sir, shortly to go, / My maister cals, and I must not say no."[8] Servant follows master as father follows daughter.

By specifying that Kent undo Lear's button, stage traditions lend the weight of what becomes a kind of authority to meanings and effects like those just described,[9] but they do so at the cost of obscuring meanings and effects—equally compatible with both playtexts of *King Lear*—that become clear if someone other than Kent undoes Lear's button. It could, for example, be Edgar, and if it is, the audience sees Edgar ministering to the man who had earlier cared for him in his near-nakedness as Poor Tom. The reciprocity implicit in having Edgar undo Lear's button can include a visually striking element of repetition if it was Edgar, disguised as Poor Tom, who obeyed Lear's earlier command on the heath during the storm: "Off, off, you lendings! Come, unbutton here!" (III.iv.103).[10] Should it be Edgar who undoes Lear's button during the final moments of the play, the two plots of *King Lear* converge in a way that aligns familial and political ties as sources of acts of loving kindness. The audience watches a subject minister to his king as he had earlier ministered to his own father. In addition, the parallels between Cordelia and Edgar—each a child faithful to a rejecting father—are made more visible. Having Edgar undo Lear's button also brings to the audience's attention the correspondence between Gloucester and Lear. That correspondence could become particularly prominent if, when pretending to revive Gloucester after the supposed suicide during act IV, scene vi, Edgar undid his father's button as he now undoes Lear's. In the Quarto the correspondence between the two erring fathers has another aspect: with his words "breake hart, I prethe breake," Lear expresses a resolve to die akin to that which drove Gloucester to and then over what he thought was the edge of a Dover cliff.

However, without violating the words of either the Quarto or the Folio, it could just as well be Albany who undoes Lear's button. He would express through that gesture affection and compassion for Lear exceeding the affection and compassion Goneril and Regan had for their own father. Such a gesture would also be consistent with Albany's earlier expressions of dismay at the mistreatment of Lear and would show Albany taking the kind of action proper to a son or daughter. The act of undoing Lear's button would pair Albany, Lear's son-in-law, with Cordelia on the one hand and Edgar on the other, both of whom ministered to their fathers. By permitting such pairings, the play allows for (but does not require) effects and meanings that demonstrate that the human capacity to act with loving kindness does not arise exclusively from the blood ties that bind parent and child. Having Albany undo Lear's button can also heighten what might be called political resonances that are muted if either Kent or Edgar undoes the king's button. In both the Quarto and the Folio, Albany returns to Lear the "absolute power" that Lear himself divided and gave away during the opening scene (here quoted from the Folio):

> . . . For us we will resigne,
> During the life of this old Majesty,
> To him our absolute power. . . .

Albany's words, spoken immediately before the speech in which Lear asks that the button be undone, take on additional force and undeniable sincerity if it is he who, with the final constricting of Lear's throat, silently undoes Lear's button in an effort to prolong "the life of this old Majesty."

The particular alternatives considered here—six in all—are not the only possibilities generated by the open silence that occurs after Lear asks that "this" button be undone. It need not be Albany, Edgar, or Kent who undoes Lear's button or Cordelia's. It could be an anonymous soldier or attendant, and this would show that those beyond the immediate circle of Lear's family and court have been moved by his plight and by Cordelia's. Robin Phillips' 1979 and 1980 productions at Stratford, Ontario, presented a related but different possibility.[11] Kent undid Lear's button with help from an unidentified soldier, thus linking in a single act of kindness Lear's faithful servant and someone from the army that has just triumphed over those who fought on behalf of Cordelia and Lear. It is also possible that Lear asks a specific person to undo "this" button, but that someone else, unasked, actually undoes it. Another possibility is that several or even all of those around Lear move toward him in response to his words, and one of them reaches him (or Cordelia) faster than the others. The response to Lear's request may be swift, or it may be slower, more thoughtful, perhaps even tentative. Michael Warren has pointed out still another possibility: no one acts in response to Lear's words, no button is undone, and Lear is in a world of his own imagining (especially in the Folio, since he may look at Cordelia as he speaks his last two lines).[12] What needs to be emphasized is that by not specifying who undoes "this" button, how it is unbuttoned, and even if a button is actually undone, the Quarto and the Folio allow alternatives—each consistent with Lear's request and the silence that follows it—far more numerous than those permitted by the stage traditions that specify that it is Kent who undoes Lear's button.

Although the number of alternatives allowed is considerably greater than those stage traditions acknowledge, it is not unlimited, for both the Quarto and the Folio establish a range of alternatives by clearly excluding certain possibilities. Since all of Lear's children are dead by this point in the play, it must be someone not of his blood who undoes the button. In both playtexts, Lear thanks someone whom he calls "Sir." Thus, the person who undoes his button must be masculine, which rules out all of the women (if any) who are attendants of Cordelia, Goneril, or Regan. The man cannot be the loyal Gloucester, since he is dead, and neither the Folio nor the Quarto allows the possibility that Edmund's desire to do "some good . . . / Despite of mine own nature" (V.iii.244–45) prompts him to heed Lear's request. In both, Edmund's death is announced before Lear asks that "this" button be undone. If it is Lear's button that is undone, then the man who undoes it—whoever he is during a given performance—gives Lear in his final moments something of the "kind nursery" (I.i.124) that, at the start of the play, he says he looked for from Cordelia. Alternatively, if it is Cordelia's button that is undone, then her father watches a man give to her the "kind nursery" that he had hoped to receive from her.

□   □   □

Once Lear is dead, matters of state become the focus of concern in both the Quarto and the Folio. Albany orders the bodies of Lear and Cordelia removed, then (in the Folio) goes on to say:

> . . . our present businesse
> Is generall woe: Friends of my soule, you twaine,
> Rule in this Realme, and the gor'd state sustaine.[13]

By calling on Edgar and Kent ("Friends of my soule") to rule, Albany makes his second attempt during the final moments of the play to pass power to someone else. The first occurred when Albany, on hearing that Edmund is dead, declared that he would hand power to Lear. "For us," Albany announces,

> we will resigne,
> During the life of this old Majesty
> To him our absolute power. . . .

By pledging to return to Lear power that has become—with the deaths of Cornwall, Goneril, and Regan—"absolute," Albany seeks to restore the political order that Lear himself fractured during the opening scene, when he divested himself of the royal power that was his alone, divided it, and gave it to others.

Albany's renunciation of "absolute power" is, one must note, conditional and temporary. He specifies that he relinquishes it only while Lear lives—"During the life of this old Majesty." Lear, however, dies almost immediately after Albany returns power to him, and as Lear dies, Albany, who might well have undone Lear's button in an effort to prolong his life, says nothing. His silence stands in marked contrast to the concern for the dying king that Kent and Edgar voice:

Edgar: He faints, my Lord, my Lord.
  Kent: Breake heart, I prythee breake.[14]
Edgar: Looke up my Lord.

> Kent: Vex not his ghost, O let him passe, he hates him,
>   That would upon the wracke of this tough world
>   Stretch him out longer.
> Edgar: He is gon indeed.
> Kent: The wonder is, he hath endur'd so long,
>   He but usurpt his life.

With Lear's death, Albany finds himself again the possessor of the "absolute power" that he had sought to return to Lear and the unchallenged ruler of a kingdom that is no longer divided. His response to that development is to call—as Lear did during the opening scene—for others ("you twaine") to take his place and "rule in this Realme." Albany seeks to renounce the power and responsibilities that have come to him, and as he does, the audience witnesses what could be a repetition, as the play ends, of that process witnessed earlier when Lear, determined to shed the burdens of "rule, / Interest of territory, cares of state" (I.i.49–50), divided his kingdom in two.

Kent refuses, as Cordelia did during the opening scene, the share of the kingdom offered to him. In the Quarto Kent tells Albany, "I have a journey sir, shortly to go, / My maister cals, and I must not say no." In the Folio, Kent declines the offer using very similar words: "I have a journey Sir, shortly to go, / My Master calls me, I must not say no." By speaking the words assigned to him in either playtext, Kent, who insisted on speaking during the opening scene in what proved to be both a futile and a dangerous effort to keep Lear from dividing the kingdom, ensures that he himself will not participate in a second division of royal authority like the first. About Edgar and Albany we have no comparable certainty.

What is Edgar's response to the opportunities presented by Albany's words renouncing power and Kent's words refusing to be one of the "twaine" who will rule in Albany's place? And how is that response made? *How* Edgar responds is not the same in the Quarto and the Folio. The Folio, by assigning the final words of the play to Edgar, makes his response a verbal one. The words of the final lines of the Quarto are identical to those of the Folio, with one exception. Where the Folio has "hath," the Quarto has "have." In the Quarto, however, it is Albany, not Edgar, who speaks the final lines:

> The waight of this sad time we must obey,
> Speake what we feele, not what we ought to say,

> The oldest have borne most, we that are yong,
> Shall never see so much, nor live so long.

By assigning those lines to Albany, the Quarto establishes for Edgar a way of responding that is decidedly different from the verbal one given him in the Folio. In the Quarto, Edgar's response to the words by which Albany and then Kent open his way to the throne of England is to say nothing, to use no words. Instead of speaking, as the Folio calls for him to do, Edgar remains silent.

Working within an assumption that has governed the editing of Shakespeare's plays since the eighteenth century, modern editors of *King Lear* find themselves compelled to decide whether to follow the Folio or the Quarto—to have Edgar speak or to have him be silent while Albany speaks. The assumption that compels such a decision is that both the Quarto and the Folio are corrupted versions of the single manuscript, now lost, that Shakespeare himself wrote and from which each of them derives. That assumption has come under sharp attack since 1978,[15] but it and the editorial practices that follow from it have determined the form of the editions of *King Lear* that are most widely used even today. In those editions an editor has decided which of the playtexts of *King Lear* more closely accords with how Shakespeare's original manuscript presented the final lines of the play. In choosing to follow one, the editor effectively dismisses the alternative posed by the playtext not chosen. To follow the Folio is to have Edgar speak words that obliterate the silence the Quarto assigns to him and the meanings and effects that can flow from it. Conversely, to follow the Quarto is to impose on Edgar a silence that obliterates the meanings and effects that arise from having Edgar speak the words given him in the Folio.

King Lear ends differently in each playtext, and what is lost by presenting one ending or the other as definitive is the awareness that each way of concluding the play poses alternatives that, although different, have their own coherence and integrity.[16] Edgar's silence in the Quarto links him with Cordelia and Albany with Lear, thus aligning the play's final moments with its opening scene in a specific way not possible in the Folio. Having offered Edgar a share of the kingdom, Albany looks for words from him just as Lear had looked for words from Cordelia when he called upon her to "speak" in order "to draw / A third more opulent than your sisters." In the Quarto (but not in the Folio), Albany hears nothing from Edgar just as Lear initially heard nothing from Cordelia and then heard her say, "Nothing" (I.i.85–86, 87).

The Quarto, in requiring silence of Edgar, does not specify that he must accept the powers and responsibilities that Albany seeks to evade, nor does it specify that Edgar must refuse to accept them. Edgar's silence is open, and the meanings and effects that arise from it during a particular performance will determine the audience's sense of what political order, if any, exists to sustain the state as the play ends. If in his silence Edgar wordlessly but clearly accepts Albany's offer to "rule in this kingdome," the play concludes with a definite political order centered on Edgar. Albany succeeds—as Lear did during the opening scene—in relinquishing the burden of rule, but he does so in a way that seems to avoid the evil consequences of Lear's abdication. With the abdication of Albany, who came to share in Lear's royal power because of Goneril's willingness to speak, the kingdom passes intact to a silent Edgar. That development does not cancel out the audience's sense of the injustice of Cordelia's death, but it may nevertheless mitigate the dreadful starkness that is one facet of the play's final moments. Undivided royal power passes into the hands of a single person who, like Cordelia, remained faithful to his father and who—like Cordelia during the opening scene—will not "speak and purpose not" (I.i.225) in order to gain power. After Edgar's silent acceptance of the royal burdens that Albany has relinquished, *King Lear* ends by establishing a union of morality, loving compassion, and political authority—a union made all the more appropriate if it was Edgar who, at Lear's request, undid Lear's button or Cordelia's.

What can be Edgar's silent acceptance of royal responsibility establishes a context within which Albany's lines concluding the Quarto take on specific pertinence. Albany's reference to obeying "the waight of this sad time" would then set Edgar's silent and perhaps reluctant assent to rule against the lust for power that drove Goneril and Regan and brought Edgar's brother Edmund within a single murder (Albany's) of gaining the crown that Albany ultimately decides to pass freely to an Edgar who had not sought it. Within such a context, Edgar's silent act of obeying the time would also stand in contrast to Goneril's and Regan's willingness to obey Lear's command to speak in order to gain a portion of his kingdom. What Edgar accepts from Albany in silence is what Goneril and Regan gained by speaking. It is also what Cordelia, disobeying Lear, would not speak to obtain. Albany's observation about the need to "speake what we feele, not what we ought to say" would draw attention to Edgar's silence—a silence that would not only testify to his moral integrity but could also mark a change in how he responds to what happens to and around him. Edgar has been prone to extract *sententiae* from events ("The lamentable change is from the best; / The worst returns to laughter," IV.i.5–6), but now, without speaking a word, he obeys the temporal flow of events that have brought him to the point where he is the one who must "rule in this kingdome, and the goard state sustaine." In the context established by Edgar's silent obedience, Albany's last words can be an example of speaking "what we feele, not what we ought to say." To the man who silently assumes the burdens of rule that he himself was unwilling to take on, Albany speaks words that offer, in place of expected congratulations, reassurance and consolation: "The oldest have borne most, we that are yong, / Shall never see so much, nor live so long." The use of "have" (the Folio has "hath") makes "The oldest" plural in reference. What Edgar has agreed to bear will not, Albany says, match what has already been borne by those who were oldest—Gloucester as well as Lear, Edgar's father as well as the king whom Edgar succeeds.

By specifying that Edgar must respond in silence to Albany's offer of power, the Quarto also allows for a radically different possibility—that Edgar wordlessly but clearly refuses to take Albany's place as Lear's successor and ruler of England. If Edgar declines, the correspondences between Cordelia and him take on a slightly different configuration. Each of them remains faithful to an erring father and each chooses not to say what is expected in order to gain part or all of a kingdom. Edgar's silent refusal to rule establishes a different context for Albany's words concluding the play. They may signify that Albany, faced with Kent's explicit and Edgar's wordless refusal to rule, is himself now willing to obey "the waight of this sad time" and assume the royal responsibilities that he has twice shunned.[17] The words Albany then speaks are not those that "ought" to be said by a new ruler assuming power. Instead, they express his view that neither he nor others who are "yong" will have to bear the horrors that "the oldest have borne."

If Albany's words express his willingness to rule, *King Lear* ends with a political order that is centered on Albany rather than on Edgar. Such an order would also unite compassion, authority, and morality. In addition, since Albany is the last living member of the royal family that Lear gathered around himself during the opening scene, Albany's succession to the throne would endow that order with a degree of continuity that would be absent if Edgar were to become ruler of England. The possibility that Albany is eventually willing to rule means that *King Lear* can end with men avoiding rather than repeating the example of the opening scene, when Lear succeeded in acting out his desire to relinquish kingly responsibilities so that he might "unburdened crawl towards death" (I.i.41). The consequences of Lear's success include excruciating personal suffering, war, and a series of deaths—those of Cornwall, Regan, Goneril, and Edmund—that leaves Albany possessing both "absolute power" and undisputed title to the throne. Twice he rejects them, first returning them to Lear, then offering them to Kent and Edgar. Twice his intentions are frustrated, first by Lear's death, then by the refusals of Kent and Edgar. In the Quarto, Edgar's open silence allows for the possibility that ultimately Albany brings himself to accept the crown that Lear gave away and that Albany himself sought to avoid. From the horrors unleashed by Lear's abdication something has perhaps been learned, something that may temper the starkly nihilistic elements of the play's final moments, which confront the audience with the possibility, if not the fact, "that we inhabit an imbecile universe."[18] Implicit in Albany's acceptance of the crown that he shirked are his recognition of and submission to what Lear at the start of the play would neither recognize nor submit to: all that time thrusts upon them men must endure in patience and to the utmost of their capacities.

Although Edgar's silence in the Quarto *King Lear* permits an ending in which Albany becomes king, it does not require such an ending. The words Albany speaks in response to Edgar's silent refusal could equally well be a call for Edgar to reconsider and accept the crown. Since Albany would be calling on Edgar to do what Albany himself is trying to avoid having to do—obey "the waight of this sad time"—such a call would not be without irony. By insisting on the need to "speake what we feele, not what we ought to say," Albany could emphasize both the fact of Edgar's silence and the sincerity of the plea he is now making, a plea that he concludes by assuring Edgar that for him the future holds nothing comparable to what "the oldest have borne."

If the final words in the Quarto are a direct appeal from Albany that Edgar assume the kingship, Edgar's response is to continue to say nothing. By that silence Edgar either accepts what he had previously refused or continues to refuse it. Should Edgar, obeying "the waight of this sad time," wordlessly assent to Albany's plea, the audience would see that his actions expressed the willingness to endure life's burdens in the patience that he had sought to inculcate in his father by means of the mock suicide. Returned to consciousness at what he thinks is the foot of the cliff from which he has jumped, Gloucester hears a man he does not know is Edgar tell him, "Thy life's a miracle" (IV.vi.55), and Gloucester resolves to accept all that life brings:

> . . . Henceforth I'll bear
> Affliction till it do cry out itself
> "Enough, enough, and die." . . .   (IV.vi.75–77)

Edgar's response, "Bear free and patient thoughts" (IV.vi.80), can foreshadow an ending for *King Lear* in which Edgar silently and with a patience free of despair agrees to bear responsibility for the kingdom.

Edgar's silence as he accepts that burden would make more pronounced the contrast between him and Albany, who has for the third time—all of them during the final moments of *King Lear*—used words to convey his unwillingness to accept the royal responsibility that time has thrust upon him. Edgar's silence would also deepen an audience's sense of his reluctance, thus sharpening the contrast between him and those who, thirsting for power, were willing to say whatever was necessary or to kill whoever stood in the way. Edgar's silence in the Quarto allows *King Lear* to end by affirming the moral integrity of the man who, out of duty rather than desire, patiently undertakes to "rule in this kingdome, and the goard state sustaine."

However, Edgar's response to Albany's final appeal to him to rule in his place could be to persist in silently refusing. In such a case, *King Lear* would end with no one willing to be the center of a new political order, and the play's final moments would be a reenactment, but in more extreme form, of the dissolution of power acted out during the opening scene. When Lear announced his resolve to cease ruling England, there was no lack of people willing to take on the burdens he was determined to relinquish. Goneril and Regan quickly spoke the words necessary to win for themselves and their husbands shares of the authority that Lear had renounced. In contrast, when Albany renounces his "absolute power," Kent refuses with words and Edgar may refuse with silence to accept what Albany seeks to give them. Lear, during the opening scene, made clear who would exercise the royal functions that had been his alone, by specifically assigning them "jointly" to Albany and Cornwall:

> I do invest you jointly with my power,
> Preeminence, and all the large effects
> That troop with majesty. . . .
> . . . .
>   . . . The sway,
> Revenue, execution of the rest,
> Belovèd sons, be yours; which to confirm
> This coronet part between you.   (I.i.130–33, 136–39)

The audience watches as power is diffused, passing from one person to two, but Lear limits that diffusion by specifying who now shares authority. No such limit operates at the conclusion of *King Lear* if, after hearing Albany make a last appeal, the audience sees Edgar silently refuse to assume the royal powers that Albany will not exercise. The lust for power so pronounced in Goneril and Regan at the start of the play can thus become, by the end of the play, an aversion to power. The impact of events can be so shattering that the best of those who survive—Kent, Edgar, and Albany—are unwilling to bear responsibility for sustaining the state. The attempt to establish a clear political order fails.

The political vacuum that results allows *King Lear* to end in a way that intensifies the idea of a universe devoid of moral order that the deaths of Lear and Cordelia force the audience to confront. Her death in particular testifies to the fact that events do not always fall out in a way that permits men to say, as Edgar did after mortally wounding Edmund, "The gods are just" (V.iii.171). In the Quarto, Edgar ultimately falls silent in the presence of Cordelia's corpse and Lear's. If, as the Quarto allows, Albany, Kent, and Edgar refuse to rule, there is no final alliance of moral goodness with power and political authority. The play ends by extinguishing the possibility that men can establish, by and for themselves, an order that is just and moral.

In contrast to the Quarto, the Folio playtext of *King Lear* assigns the final words of the play to Edgar, and most editions used today

for teaching, studying, and performing the play follow the Folio.[19]
Whereas the Quarto requires that Edgar say nothing in response to
Albany's call for Kent and him to rule, the Folio specifies that Edgar
respond by saying:

> The waight of this sad time we must obey,
> Speake what we feele, not what we ought to say:
> The oldest hath borne most, we that are yong,
> Shall never see so much, nor live so long.

The Folio seems, on first glance, to rule out the range of alternative
meanings made possible by the silence that the Quarto imposes on
Edgar as the play concludes. The prevailing tendency among critics
and scholars is to say that with the words the Folio gives him to
speak, Edgar expresses a resigned willingness to accept the crown in
obedience to what time dictates.[20]

Edgar's spoken acceptance of royal responsibility would signal
the emergence of a political order like that which the Quarto permits to come into being if, during the silence mandated for him in
that playtext, Edgar wordlessly accepts the crown. In both cases,
royal power, which Lear renounced during the open scene and
which Albany twice shuns during the final scene, would ultimately
pass to a man who (in contrast to Goneril, Regan, Cornwall, and
Edmund) has not sought it. Thus, the Folio *King Lear* could end—
as could the Quarto—by positing the emergence of a political order
uniting goodness and authority that would mitigate, without necessarily eradicating, the nihilistic implications of the manner in which
Lear and (especially) Cordelia die.

Edgar's words about the need to "speake what we feele" can
direct an audience's attention to his own act of speaking (the last in
the play) and can link it to both Cordelia's refusal to "speak and
purpose not" and Kent's repeated insistence on speaking with painful, even dangerous, bluntness—before Lear during the opening
scene and before Cornwall and Regan during act II, scene ii. The
lines that Edgar speaks at the conclusion of the Folio *King Lear* can
also register a change in him. Absent from what he says after seeing
Cordelia dead in her father's arms and after watching Lear die is the
kind of certainty that enabled him, earlier during the final scene, to
see in his victory over Edmund proof that "the gods are just, and of
our pleasant vices / Make instruments to plague us" (V.iii.171–72).
What Edgar says is not what a man who has just assumed kingly

power "ought to say." For example, he does not, as Albany did moments before, promise justice:

> . . . All Friends shall
> Taste the wages of their vertue, and all Foes
> The cup of their deservings. . . .

He does not proclaim the start of a new era as did Henry Tudor at the end of *Richard III*: "Now civil wounds are stopped, peace lives again: / That she may long live here, God say amen!" (V.v.40–41). He does not pledge to perform appropriately royal actions, as Malcolm promised at the conclusion of *Macbeth*:

> . . . What's more to do
> Which would be planted newly with the time—
> As calling home our exiled friends abroad
> That fled the snares of watchful tyranny,
> Producing forth the cruel ministers
> Of this dead butcher and his fiend-like queen
> Who (as 'tis thought) by self and violent hands
> Took off her life—this, and what needful else
> That calls upon us, by the grace of Grace
> We will perform in measure, time, and place.   (V.viii.64–73)

Instead of saying what a new king "ought to say," Edgar compares what "the oldest hath borne" with what a younger generation will "see" and endure during their lives. His use of the singular form "hath" rather than the Quarto's "have" allows these final lines to be, more specifically, a form of self-consolation resulting from a comparison of what Lear has borne with what Edgar as king, speaking in the royal "we," will bear.

The final lines of *King Lear* in the Folio can undoubtedly make explicit Edgar's decision to "rule in this Realme," but they need not do so. In fact, like Hippolyta's lines at the start of *A Midsummer Night's Dream*, the more closely they are scrutinized, the less clear they prove to be. "The waight of this sad time we must obey" may convey Edgar's less-than-enthusiastic consent to assume responsibility for "the gor'd state," but the same words could equally well be Edgar's call for Albany to accept, rather than evade, the responsibilities that time, with Lear's death, has thrust upon him as the sole survivor of those among whom Lear initially divided the "Realme." Such a call would be consistent with the values that prompted Edgar to utter the last words that he spoke to his father when Gloucester again wanted to die in order to be free of life's burdens:

> . . . Men must endure
> Their going hence, even as their coming hither;
> Ripeness is all. . . .   (V.ii.9–11)

The rest of Edgar's speech at the conclusion of the Folio *Lear* is similarly consistent with the possibility that he is urging Albany, as he earlier urged Gloucester, to accept what life imposes. He is, Edgar could explain, speaking what he feels, not what, having been offered the throne, he "ought to say." If so, he, like Cordelia during the opening scene, would not be speaking what one ought to say in order to gain power. Alternatively, "Speake what we feele, not what we ought to say" could be Edgar's invitation for Albany to withdraw what Edgar could regard as his pro forma offer to relinquish "absolute power." Edgar could conclude (what might be) his appeal to Albany by observing, reassuringly, that the burdens that await Albany as king and also await those "that are yong" will not match those borne by Lear specifically and by the older generation of which Lear was the embodiment. By calling on Albany to keep what he is intent on giving away, Edgar would be trying to prevent someone whose power has become "absolute" from making an error whose consequences would further injure a state already "gor'd." If Edgar were to make such an effort with the last words the audience hears, he would be repeating the effort Kent made during the opening scene, when he urged Lear not to give his royal powers to others:

> . . . What wouldst thou do, old man?
> Think'st thou that duty shall have dread to speak
> When power to flattery bows? To plainness honor's bound
> When majesty falls to folly. Reserve thy state,
> And in thy best consideration check
> This hideous rashness. . . .   (I.i.146–51)

If the final lines of the Folio are Edgar's call for Albany to retain the royal responsibilities that are his and no one else's, then the Folio *King Lear* may end—as the Quarto *King Lear* must end—with an open silence.[21] In the Folio, however, the silence is Albany's rather than Edgar's, for the Folio gives Albany no words to speak in response to (what might be) Edgar's call for him to obey the time.

During that silence, Albany may or may not act in a way that shows that Edgar's words to him are more effective than Kent's to Lear. Without violating the words of the Folio *King Lear*, Albany may or may not reverse his declared intent and silently take it upon himself to "rule in this Realme, and the gor'd state sustaine." The words of the Folio do not specify what action Albany takes if such a silence occurs during a performance of *King Lear*, but what the audience sees Albany do will generate meanings and effects that will profoundly determine how the play ends.

Should Albany silently assent to Edgar's appeal, the audience will see him assume, without speaking a word, responsibility for ruling England, a responsibility that he has twice tried to evade by using words. The political order that then begins to be established under Albany will be similar to that which can emerge at the end of the Quarto *King Lear* if Albany's response to Edgar's silence there is to declare that he will himself obey the time. A son-in-law who has proved more faithful than two of Lear's daughters, Albany provides not only a degree of moral authority but also a continuity in succession, which together can lessen the impact of Cordelia's death, by showing that men are able to organize themselves to continue national life in a cosmos whose gods are not always just: "As flies to wanton boys are we to th'gods; / They kill us for their sport" (IV.i.36–37). Somewhat paradoxically, Albany's silent acceptance of royal responsibility would enable the Folio *King Lear* to offer a final affirmation of the power of language that cannot occur if, as the Quarto allows, Albany says he will accept that burden. It would be Edgar's act of speaking rather than (as in the Quarto) the fact of his silent refusal that would move Albany to check the deep, powerful impulse to be free of the burdens of rule that he has twice voiced and that Lear indulged, despite Kent's pleas, during the opening scene.

Albany's silence also allows the possibility that, at the end of the Folio *King Lear*, he persists in acting out that impulse just as Lear did at the start of the play. Albany could wordlessly but unmistakably indicate that he will not rule. He could, for example, simply exit alone and without saying anything after Edgar has finished emphasizing the need to "speake what we feele." Alternatively, Albany in his silence could avoid giving any response, verbal or gestural, to Edgar's appeal. If he does, the last words Albany speaks when he calls on others to "rule in this Realme, and the gor'd state sustaine" remain the last indication of his intentions. In either case, Edgar's words to Albany would have proved no more effective than Kent's to Lear during the opening scene, and the power of language would thus be undercut rather than affirmed. Albany's silence permits the Folio *King Lear* to end, as the Quarto is also capable of ending, with no one willing to take on the burden of rule, with no one willing to assume the task of reestablishing the social order shattered by forces unleashed by Lear's refusal to continue to endure that burden. *King Lear* is a play that opens with those who soon show themselves to be evil eagerly accepting the power that Lear, in his desire to "unburdened crawl towards death," makes available to them. In both its Quarto and its Folio version, *King Lear* is a play that can end with those whose goodness has been tested and defined by events refusing to take up that power after Lear dies.[22]

□   □   □

For some the reunion of Cordelia and Lear and their final pairing in death offers a profoundly moving affirmation of the extraordinary power of human love to withstand what the world inflicts on mankind and what mankind inflicts on itself. Robert Egan, for example, explains that

> the order of love has survived the transition . . . from the context of pure artifice surrounding the image of Lear and Cordelia reunited to the context of absolute reality surrounding the image of Lear and Cordelia dead. It is the latter, a dark and painful emblem, which *King Lear* finally holds up to us; but by its unrelenting reflection of the real world's chaos that image retains the integrity necessary to communicate into our world an uncompromised vision of moral order.[23]

The Folio gives any affirmation of human love additional force by providing Lear with lines—absent from the Quarto—that make it possible to argue, with A. C. Bradley, that the agony in which Lear dies is "not one of pain but of ecstasy," "an unbearable *joy*"[24] arising from his certainty that Cordelia lives. In the Folio Lear's last words are: "Do you see this? Looke on her? Looke her lips, / Looke there, looke there."

In both the Quarto and the Folio, Lear himself declares that the possibility that Cordelia lives is "a chance which do's redeeme all sorrowes / That ever I have felt" (Folio). The love that holds Lear and Cordelia together at the end of the play may itself be sufficient to "redeeme" all that the audience has seen Lear, Cordelia, and others suffer, thereby giving what they have endured a kind of meaning and placing it within an order that is moral. The pairing of father and daughter testifies to the human capacity to join with another. A *King Lear* that fashions from what must be Edgar's silence in the Quarto or from what can be Albany's silence in the Folio an ending in which one or the other agrees to sustain the state shows that capacity expressing itself in the act of beginning the construction of a political order. However, a *King Lear* that fashions from those same silences an ending in which neither Albany nor Edgar is willing to sustain the state places the pairing of Lear and Cordelia and the affirmation of love it makes possible within an extremely bleak universe. There is no certainty of cosmic justice and no sign of a political order that unites man's ability to organize a society with the capacity to love as that capacity survives, after the deaths of Lear and Cordelia, in the persons of Kent the faithful servant, Albany the faithful son-in-law, and Edgar the faithful son. The love that humans can give and receive may be affirmed, but its impact is sharply, fiercely limited.

For Lynda E. Boose, the final pairing of Lear and Cordelia is not a sign of transcendent, redeeming love but a piercing illustration of

> the tragic failure of the family unit to divide, recombine, and regenerate. The only respite from pain the tragedy offers is the beauty of Lear's reunion with Cordelia, but that reunion takes place at the cost of both the daughter's life and the future life of the family. . . . In *King Lear*, the father who imagined that he "gave his daughters all" extracts from his daughter at the end of the play the same price he demanded in the opening scene—that she love her father all.[25]

A *King Lear* that ends with Albany or Edgar agreeing to rule England lessens the impact of the family's failure to recombine and regenerate by showing the state recombining and regenerating even after all that has occurred. By contrast, a *King Lear* that ends with Albany and Edgar refusing to rule increases that impact by showing the state, as well as the family, failing to recombine and regenerate. Their refusals leave a kingless England facing a political chaos that is the analogue in society of the cosmic senselessness that can reveal itself most nakedly in the deaths of Cordelia and Lear. *King Lear* can show the basic groupings of family and state, within which humans seek to shelter themselves, shattering as mankind seeks to endure and survive the storms unleashed within a world devoid of political and cosmic order. Such a *King Lear* leaves its audiences, as well as the surviving characters, to find shelter in and take comfort from nothing more and nothing less than the elementary human capacity to feel for and with one another as we endure what time imposes. What solace there is lies in the thought that we shall not have to bear anything like that "most" which "the oldest hath borne."

King Lear is a play that announces the approach of its own conclusion. When the mortally wounded Edmund declares, "The wheel is come full circle" (V.iii.175), his words serve, Stephen Booth has noted, as "an almost explicit statement that the dramatic entity is complete."[26] A little later, Kent, upon seeing Lear bearing Cordelia's corpse, asks, "Is this the promised end?" (V.iii.264). The final moments of *King Lear* offer three open silences that stage traditions, editorial practices, and habits of interpretation have almost obliterated: the silence that both the Folio and the Quarto specify must come after Lear asks that "this button" be undone, the silence that the Quarto requires of Edgar, and the silence that the Folio allows for Albany. Once those silences are faced directly, they force those who study, teach, and perform the play to rephrase Kent's question and to ask, What is "the promised end" of *King Lear* itself? What is the conclusion specified for the play by its constituent parts?

The answer must be that *King Lear* gives us no single "promised end," no one conclusion that is the inevitable result of the relationships among its elements. Instead, by virtue of its final silences, *King Lear* gives us a variety of possible endings, each with its own coherence, each with its own validity. Kent or Albany or Edgar may undo Lear's button, or Kent or Albany or Edgar may undo Cordelia's button. An anonymous soldier or attendant may undo Lear's button or undo Cordelia's. A combination of characters might undo "this button," or the button might remain undone. The play—in both its Quarto and its Folio version—may end with the beginning of a new political order centered on Edgar or with the beginning of a new political order centered on Albany, but either version may also end with Albany and Edgar refusing to participate in the construction of even the beginning of a political order.

Each of the endings that the silences make possible alters the structure of *King Lear*. By establishing different links between the play's final moments and its opening scene, each ending specifies different but equally valid ways in which "the wheel is come full circle." Each ending of *King Lear* also generates different correspondences among the characters, correspondences that in turn alter the audience's sense of the value and limits of human love. Each ending, by means of the structure it defines and the correspondences among characters it brings into focus, articulates a different vision of mankind's ability to unite—in a political order based on ties of love, or on little more than the knowledge that all men suffer—to confront and endure an existence that can bring, after excruciating suffering, a death as senseless and wasteful as Cordelia's and as heartrending as Lear's. Just as *King Lear* denies its characters the comforting certainty that "the gods are just," so it denies us the comfort of knowing that the play moves to a single, certain, "promised" end. One response to that denial is to reduce the uncertainty to a comfortable level by developing and then submitting unquestioningly to stage traditions, editorial practices, and habits of interpretation that minimize the impact of the open silences that mark the final moments of *King Lear*. The other response is to face directly and to bear fully—in our common love for Shakespeare's play—the challenge presented to us by those silences and by the uncertainty they generate.

6. A Different Paradigm

The challenge posed by the open silences of *King Lear* is like that posed by the open silences of *Measure for Measure* and, somewhat less forcefully, by those of *The Tempest*, *Twelfth Night*, and *A Midsummer Night's Dream*. Individually and collectively, these silences challenge us to come to terms with the freedom, with the capacity for sometimes conflicting multiplicity, that they help to generate and to which they mutely testify. No mode of analysis that takes the words of a Shakespearean playtext (or, in such cases as *King Lear*, playtexts) as its exclusive point of reference will be adequate to meet that challenge. Literary in its assumptions, procedures, and conclusions, such textual analysis must either ignore or dismiss as insignificantly peripheral the numerous, at times contradictory, sets of meanings and effects made possible by silences that are established by the words of a playtext but then float free of those words and take on specific shape and coherence only during a performance of the play. The preceding chapters have demonstrated a method for meeting that challenge, a method that combines close analysis of the words of a Shakespearean playtext with equally rigorous analysis of the details of particular performances arising from that playtext.

Ultimately, however, the challenge is more than one of methodology. It is, fundamentally, a matter of ontology and epistemology—of determining what a play is and how we can best proceed to know it. Facing that challenge requires that we fashion, or find, a way of thinking and speaking—a conceptual model that can accommodate the insights provided by literary analysis of Shakespeare's playtexts yet overcome the biases and limitations of such analysis in order to embrace the specifically theatrical nature of Shakespeare's plays. The paradigm must enable us to come to terms with the capacity of a Shakespearean play to retain its identity as it changes significantly from production to production, even from performance to performance. It must enable us to understand how, to give one example,

Measure for Measure can sometimes end with Isabella silently accepting the Duke's proposals of marriage and can at other times end with Isabella rejecting those proposals. The paradigm must also allow for the fact that a single Shakespearean play—*King Lear*, for example—can have more than one playtext, each significantly different from the other(s), each with its own coherence. In addition, the paradigm must provide a way of understanding the relationship between playtext(s) and performance(s) that goes beyond simply equating the play itself with either and assigning secondary status to the other. Finally, the paradigm must clarify how those involved in performing a Shakespearean play and those who are their audience bring to fulfillment, during the moments of a given performance, a process that Shakespeare initiated but did not himself specify in all significant detail. In particular, the paradigm must accommodate the role of the audience in that process, acknowledging (as Prospero does) that the responses of the audience determine whether the communal "project" that each Shakespearean play becomes during performance succeeds or fails.

I believe we can develop the paradigm that we need by redeploying the principles of complementarity and superposition that quantum physicists formulated during the early decades of this century as they sought to understand atomic and subatomic entities and processes. The application of principles of quantum physics to the study of Shakespeare's plays must, on first glance (and even second), seem farfetched, but it is consistent with cultural patterns laid down as a result of the development of printing with movable type toward the end of the fifteenth century in Europe and the related emergence and eventual dominance of modern science, especially physics.

Shakespeare and his contemporaries were among the first playwrights in history to have the words of their plays published in print. Francis Bacon, in 1625, identified printing with movable type as one of three Renaissance "inventions" that had already "changed the appearance and the state of the whole world."[1] Among the things that printing "changed" was the relationship between the plays and those who make up their audiences. Before the advent of printing, the only way most people could know a play was to gather with others at a specified time and place for a performance. Gutenberg's invention made the words of a play widely available for reading by individuals at times and places of their own choosing. As more printed copies of the words of plays became available to an increasingly literate public, attending a performance became an option rather than a necessity—an alternative to the more convenient activity of reading. In the process of giving plays what might be called a second audience composed of readers, printing fostered, and eventually made possible the institutionalization of, a radical change in the prevailing conception of what a play was. Richard Schechner has characterized that change as an inversion of "the ancient relationship between doing and script":

> In the West the active sense of script was forgotten . . . and the doings of a particular production became the way to present a drama in a new way. Thus, scripts no longer functioned as a code for transmitting action through time; instead the doings of each production became the code for re-presenting the words-of-the-drama. Maintaining the words intact grew in importance; how they were said, and what gestures accompanied them, was a matter of individual choice, and of lesser importance.[2]

Printing encouraged and ultimately compelled us to accept a definition that equates a play with its words rather than its performances. In Shakespeare's plays, the density and richness of the words made that definition all the more irresistible.

Printing also helped to change "the appearance and the state of the whole world" by contributing, in ways described by scholars as diverse in their methods and assumptions as Marshall McLuhan and Elizabeth L. Eisenstein,[3] to the development of modern science, especially the physics that Sir Isaac Newton brilliantly brought to fruition. In *Mathematical Principles of Natural Philosophy* (1687), Newton synthesized the work of Copernicus, Galileo, Kepler, and Descartes and united celestial and terrestrial mechanics. Newton's physics enabled mankind to see the universe as a system capable of being understood fully by precisely describing the location of any or all of its parts in space and time and then determining, by means of equations based on Newton's famed simple principles, the past and future movements of those parts through space and time. Because it was used successfully to describe and predict phenomena in the natural world—particularly the movements of the planets—Newtonian physics became for Western civilization the most compelling example of how mankind can gain reliable knowledge. Newton's assumptions and procedures became the norm not just for various kinds of scientific inquiry but also for other fields of knowledge.

Printing facilitated the extension of Newtonian assumptions and procedures to the study of Shakespeare's plays. By making the words of those plays available—to readers at different times and in different places—in multiple copies characterized by a degree of uniformity never before known in history, printing ended the association of those words with a particular moment and a particular place. It became possible and then increasingly easy to regard Shakespeare's words as existing in that uniform space and uniform time in which Newtonian physics locates the subjects of its inquiries. The assumption of uniform time and space allows Newtonian physics to insist on methods of inquiry and proof that can be repeated. The results of physicist *A*'s experiment are accepted as valid only if identical or at least compatible results emerge when physicists at other times and in other places repeat that experiment. The existence of uniform[4] copies of the words of Shakespeare's plays makes it possible for people dispersed in time and space to repeat the act of reading those words and, like Newtonian physicists, to arrive at conclusions that may confirm, qualify, or contradict those of other readers.

Performances of a Shakespearean play—as distinct from the printed words of the play—defy Newtonian assumptions and procedures. An experiment valid in Paris will prove equally valid when repeated in Copenhagen tomorrow, and printed words remain the same whether one reads them in London in 1623 or in New York in 1983. What occurs during tonight's performance of *A Midsummer Night's Dream*, however, is not and cannot be identical to what happened during a performance of the play a decade ago in Los Angeles nor to what will happen during tomorrow night's performance in London. No performance can be identical to another—not even performances given by the same actors working with the same director in the same theater. Each performance must and will vary from every other—sometimes subtly, sometimes markedly, sometimes insignificantly, sometimes profoundly—in details like timing, movement, delivery, gesture, grouping, and pacing. Such variety results from unavoidable changes that occur almost daily, not just in what the individual performer does and how he does it but also in the interactions among the performers as well as those between them and audiences whose temper and composition shift from one performance to the next. Because performances exist only at specific times and in specific places, they cannot be positioned, individually or collectively, in that uniform space and time which Newtonian physics made such a dominant feature of Western analysis. For the same reason, performances also elude methods of inquiry and proof founded on the Newtonian criterion of repeatability. Each performance is unique—its place and time, its participants, and its audience are peculiar to it. Watching a performance is, therefore, an activity that, unlike conducting an experiment or reading printed words, cannot be repeated.

"Truth," Newton insisted, "is ever to be found in simplicity, and not in the multiplicity and confusion of things."[5] In Newtonian physics, simplicity functions as what Gerald Holton has called a thema: a fundamental but nonverifiable conception that guides the preselection of facts, hypotheses, and explanatory methods.[6] Working within the thema of simplicity, Newton took planetary movements that centuries of observers had seen as erratic and presented them as complex composites resulting from the interplay of many motions, each of which is orderly in the sense of conforming to simple principles that can be formulated mathematically. The thema of simplicity obliges those who embrace it to view particular phenomena as specific manifestations of underlying principles of order that are abstract and relatively simple. Those principles become more general and more valid as they become increasingly simple.

Performances, because of their essential particularity and their inherent variety, partake of that "multiplicity and confusion of things" in which "truth" of the kind valued by the thema of simplicity is not to be found. Thus, the thema of simplicity channels attention away from performances and to the words of the play. Fixed in print, those words stand detached from the particulars of where and when and how. Thus abstracted, they can yield that simplicity in which, Newton says, "truth is ever to be found." The thema of simplicity converts those words, thus abstracted, into the play's underlying principle of order, and the details of any performance become more or less faithful manifestations of that principle at a given time and place. The details of one performance of a play frequently conflict with those of another performance of it—for example, in one performance Hippolyta may associate herself with Theseus' treatment of Hermia but in another performance she may not. The thema of simplicity attributes such conflicts to the failure of those performing the play to adhere to the play's principle of order, to the printed words that should, according to the thema, determine what happens each time the play is performed.

The editing of Shakespeare's plays offers additional evidence of the shaping influence of the thema of simplicity. Eighteen of Shakespeare's plays, among them *A Midsummer Night's Dream* and *King Lear*, exist in Quarto and Folio versions. Since the eighteenth century, editors have sought to provide for each of Shakespeare's plays, including those eighteen, a standard "authorized" text that reflects (what are presumed to have been) Shakespeare's intentions. For a play that exists in multiple versions, the "authorized" text is presented as that Shakespearean original of which the Quarto and Folio versions are more or less corrupt derivatives that engender confusion because of their conflicting multiplicity.

Indeed, the history of Shakespeare studies, including the editing of his plays, testifies to a centuries-long effort—rarely challenged until the 1960s[7]—to understand Shakespeare's plays in terms compatible with the assumptions, procedures, and themata that, with the success of Newtonian physics, have become the norms of scholarly inquiry endorsed by Western culture. According to those norms, performances of Shakespeare's plays are not appropriate objects of study. Because they are radically variable and radically particular, performances have generally been relegated to the periphery of Shakespearean studies or excluded totally. In synergistic combination, printing and the norms of inquiry validated by Newtonian physics have disposed Western culture to accept a definition of drama that equates a play with its words as they are presented in print to form a text. That definition endorses words, rather than performances, as the appropriate focus for any effort to study Shakespeare's plays.

□ □ □

The synthesis that Newton achieved in 1687 endured as the basis for post-Renaissance physics until early in the twentieth century, when two developments prompted a reassessment. One development was Einstein's special theory of relativity (1905) and general theory of relativity (1915). According to these theories, the space and time coordinates by which we make the kinds of measurements essential to Newtonian physics vary from one frame of reference to another. Einstein showed that space and time are not—as Newton had assumed—separate and uniform continua but instead constitute a single space–time continuum that, far from being uniform, changes in the vicinity of large bodies of matter. The theories of relativity compelled physicists to recognize that the laws of Newtonian physics are not universally valid but hold only for frames of reference within which, for example, velocities do not approach the speed of light.

However, even as it revealed the limits of Newtonian physics, relativity operated within and confirmed themata common to both. Relativity is consistent with the thema of simplicity fundamental to Newtonian physics. Einstein demonstrated that what men had previously thought were the simplest, most elementary physical laws are in fact special cases, particular manifestations, of laws that are even simpler and are valid for an even wider range of phenomena. Einstein also shared with Newton a commitment to causality, a thema according to which every phenomenon results from the operation of a universal principle under a given set of conditions. Relativity and Newtonian physics also include the thema of completeness, which specifies that, in Einstein's words, "every element of the physical reality must have a counterpart in the physical theory."[8] Because of the themata they have in common (particularly the thema of completeness), Newtonian physics and relativity are varieties of what Gary Zukav calls "classical physics."[9]

The second development that prompted a reassessment of Newtonian physics began when physicists began to probe the atomic structure of matter. They soon encountered, at that elementary level of physical reality, phenomena that radically contradict Newtonian physics. The atom, they came to realize, is a physical system with features that are, as J. Robert Oppenheimer put it, "wholly at variance with the properties of Newtonian dynamics."[10] Physicists found the principles of Newtonian physics insufficient to explain such things as the stability, discontinuity, and discreteness characteristic of atomic systems, even though the validity of Newtonian physics for entities and processes involving aggregates of those same atomic systems remained indisputable. The paradox that nature presents—of a physical world that conforms to Newtonian laws even though the most elementary entities of which it is constituted defy those laws—forced physicists such as Planck, Bohr, Heisenberg, de Broglie, Pauli, Schrödinger, Dirac, Born, and Oppenheimer to develop between 1900 and 1927 a new theory of physics, the quantum theory.

Quantum theory breaks fundamentally not just with Newtonian physics but also with those themata which make it and relativity examples of classical physics. Quantum theory does not have that one-to-one correspondence between theoretical elements and physical realities, that completeness, essential to the physics of Newton and Einstein. In quantum theory there is not a theoretical element for each individual event that actually happens on the atomic level. Quantum theory is not only incomplete, but it also recognizes that completeness cannot be achieved at that level of nature because what happens to or within an individual atom cannot be described or predicted. Oppenheimer described the incompleteness of quantum physics in this way:

> We learned to accept, as we later learned to understand, that the behavior of an atomic system is not predictable in detail, that of a large number of atomic systems with the same history, in, let us say, the same state statistical prediction was possible as to how they would act . . . but that nowhere in our battery of experimental probings would we find one to say what one individual atom would in fact do.[11]

What Niels Bohr termed the "individuality of atomic processes"[12] also means that the thema of repeatability does not and cannot apply at the quantum level of reality. At the macrophysical level, valid experiments, when repeated, yield the same results. "In the study of atomic phenomena, however," Bohr pointed out,

> we are presented with a situation where the repetition of an experiment with the same arrangement may lead to different recordings.[13]

> The fact that in one and the same well-defined experimental arrangement we generally obtain recordings of different individual processes thus makes indispensable the recourse to a statistical account of quantum phenomena.[14]

For example, an experiment can be set up in which a diffracted electron strikes a fluorescent screen, but the electron diffracted will not always strike where its predecessor did each time the experiment is performed. After many repetitions of the experiment, physicists will know with certainty that electrons will strike the screen in different places and that all of the electrons will strike the screen within a region that can be specified. They will also know what a number of electrons will do, but they will not be able to predict exactly where within that specified region of the screen any one electron will strike.

Quantum theory permits one to predict the distribution of many individual atomic events; it can specify the region within which every electron will strike and outside of which no electron will strike. But quantum theory cannot predict the outcome of individual events; it does not tell in advance the precise spot that a single electron will actually strike. The knowledge that quantum theory yields is inherently statistical and probabilistic. Heinz Pagels offers this analogy: one can predict how many times a specific hand of cards gets dealt on the average, and one can estimate the probability of receiving a specific hand when the cards are dealt, but, even with such knowledge, one cannot predict the particular cards one will actually receive each time a hand is dealt.[15] Quantum theory enables us to predict exactly how a large number of electrons or other atomic entities will behave in a given set of circumstances, and we know the probability—without ever having the certainty—that an individual atomic entity will do this or do that, strike this spot on the fluorescent screen and not that one.

The individuality of quantum phenomena on which quantum theory insists also shatters the causality that long has been the unquestioned foundation of classical physics. The most striking illustration of that causality is Newton's physics. It incorporates the most rigorous form of causality, called determinism, the theory that everything in the physical world is involved in and determined by a sequence of cause-and-effect relationships. For Newton, Oppenheimer explained,

> the physical world was a world of differential law, a world connecting forces and motions at one point and one instant with those at an infinitely near point in space and point of time; so that the whole course of the physical world could be broken down into finer and finer instants, and in each the cause of change assigned by a knowledge of forces.[16]

Every event in the physical world results from the interplay of matter and forces, and every event is both the result and the cause of other events. Newton's principles made it possible to predict with extreme accuracy, from our knowledge of the state of a physical system as defined at a given moment by measurable quantities, the state of that system at any subsequent time. The ability to determine what the future will be on the basis of available knowledge of the present persuaded physicists after Newton that they could understand fully the causes of those things and events that make up the physical world. At the quantum level, however, the detailed and complete causality of classical physics proved to be, in Bohr's words, "too narrow a frame to embrace the peculiar regularities governing individual atomic processes."[17] Physicists cannot mount experiments that enable them to predict what an individual atom will do, and they cannot cause a diffracted electron to strike a predetermined spot on a fluorescent screen and no other.

The causality of classical physics presupposes, Bohr points out, "the unrestricted divisibility of the course of phenomena in space and time and the linking of all steps in an unbroken chain of cause and effect."[18] It also presumes the capacity to know, with whatever degree of exactness is required, such information as the position and momentum of an entity at any given moment. Heisenberg's uncertainty principle demonstrates, however, that exact knowledge of the kind that deterministic causality requires is unavailable at the atomic level, because time, space, energy, and momentum are not infinitely divisible into ever-smaller units, into "finer and finer instants." Heisenberg shows that the more precisely we are able to fix the point in space at which a quantum entity is located at a given moment, the less certain we become about its momentum (the velocity at which its mass is moving through space) at that same moment. Conversely, Heisenberg also shows that the more certain we are about the entity's momentum at any instant, the less certain we must be about its position at that moment.[19] Heisenberg's uncertainty principle destroyed the proud assumption of classical physics that the exact place and time of every event in the universe can be exactly calculated. The destruction of that assumption required, in turn, renunciation of deterministic causality. The uncertainty principle also made it compellingly clear that individual atomic events are not predictable in principle—that is, their unpredictability was not simply attributable to computational or experimental difficulties.

Quantum theory reverses "the direction of the arrow of explanation."[20] For Newton and Einstein, in their common commitment to the thema of simplicity, evidence of chaos and uncertainty in nature arose from and was explained by an underlying order. Beneath "the multiplicity and confusion of things" they sought, and found, order. At the atomic level of nature, however, physicists came upon a realm of entities and processes that defy both precise measurement and individual prediction. It is not a realm devoid of order and regularity, but the order and regularity manifest there must be understood as arising from and applying only to the aggregate of a large number of atomic events, each of which is subject to a degree of randomness that can be statistically calculated with exquisite precision but can never be eliminated to give certainty in any individual instance. Faced with such order and regularity in the atomic systems on which all properties of matter must ultimately depend, physicists put aside the thema of simplicity that had long served well as the primary explanatory thema of classical physics. In its place they accepted, sometimes reluctantly, a different explanatory thema, the thema of fundamental probabilism in nature. "The ontological ladder was," as Holton puts it, "once more turned around."[21] Instead of chaos arising out of elementary order, order in nature was now seen to arise from elementary chaos—from the formless turmoil of the ongoing creation, transformation, and annihilation of elementary particles.

□   □   □

The definition that equates a play with the words that constitute its playtext incorporates the themata that physicists relinquished in order to come to terms with physical reality at the quantum level. The thema of simplicity establishes the playtext as that abstract principle of order underlying the multiple (often confusingly varied) performances of the play. That playtext, rather than any performance of the play, becomes the appropriate focus of analysis, the place where, in Newton's words, "truth" about the play "is ever to be found." The thema of completeness converts the playtext into a statement of theory and creates the expectation that there is or must be a one-to-one correspondence between each physical detail of every performance and an element in the theory. If there is no such correspondence, either the details are considered trivial or the performance is considered invalid. The thema of causality encourages us to think of the playtext as the initial state of that artistic system which is the play and to regard performances as developments of that primary state—of the playtext. The assumption that follows is that study of the play in its primary state (as playtext) should yield all knowledge essential to the play and that such knowledge, in turn, will enable us to predict specific states that the play will assume when performed. According to the thema of causality, the playtext is the determining cause for each and for all of the individual events that together constitute a particular performance. Should a performance include events that are not seen as caused by the playtext, they are either dismissed as superfluous production values or taken as evidence of failure to respect the play itself.

The open silences of Shakespeare's plays demonstrate the limits of those themata and of the definition they give rise to. Barnardine's response after the Duke spares his life during the final scene of *Measure for Measure* is a crucial element in the play's definition of the relationship between justice and mercy, and according to the thema of simplicity we can best understand his response and the definition to which it contributes by referring to the words of the playtext. The playtext, however, establishes that Barnardine's response is a silence that may indicate anything from speechless gratitude to wordless indifference to unspoken incorrigibility. We can understand his silence and the relationship between mercy and justice that it helps to define only by putting aside the thema of simplicity and looking, not at abstract principles of order supposedly implicit in the playtext of *Measure for Measure*, but at specific performances of the play. We must, that is, look for "truth" in precisely those places where Newton, invoking the thema of simplicity, would say it cannot be found—in "the multiplicity and confusion of things."

Open silences also elude the themata of completeness and causality. Antonio, for example, may or may not be wordlessly included in the reordered society that forms at the end of *Twelfth Night*. If he is included there is no one-to-one correspondence between the gestures and movements that convey his inclusion and the words of the playtext, since those words give equal weight to the possibility that he is not included. If Antonio is not included, the gestures and movements that convey either his isolation or his withdrawal will likewise not correspond in any necessary or precise way to specific words in the playtext. There is, in other words, no one-to-one correspondence between every physical element that is part of a performance of *Twelfth Night* and the "theory" of the play supposedly articulated in the playtext. There is also no causal relationship between the words of *Twelfth Night* and the gestures or movements that establish whether Antonio is included. The playtext does not determine that one alternative (withdrawal) and not the others (inclusion, isolation) must happen during a specific performance. The words of *Twelfth Night* do not cause Antonio's inclusion, and they do not cause his isolation or his withdrawal. Analysis of the words of the playtext of *Twelfth Night* does not enable us to specify whether Antonio is included within Illyrian society as the play ends and does not enable us to describe or predict the gestures and movements during a performance that establish the fact of his inclusion, his isolation, or his withdrawal.

Open silences are particularly striking examples of elements in Shakespeare's plays that demonstrate the limited utility of information gained by applying modes of analysis founded on the themata of simplicity, completeness, and detailed causality. Open silences are not, however, the only such elements. There are fundamentally ambivalent passages, such as the words Hippolyta utters the only time she speaks during the opening scene of *A Midsummer Night's Dream*:

> Four days will quickly steep themselves in night,
> Four nights will quickly dream away the time;
> And then the moon, like to a silver bow
> New-bent in heaven, shall behold the night
> Of our solemnities.

As we saw in Chapter 1, analysis of her words does not enable us to say with certainty whether she shares Theseus' eagerness for their wedding day to arrive. Her words take on specific meaning only when she speaks them in a particular way during an actual performance. *King Lear* concludes with four lines that—regardless of differences between the Quarto and Folio versions—are similarly ambivalent:

> The weight of this sad time we must obey,
> Speak what we feel, not what we ought to say.
> The oldest hath [Quarto: have] borne most; we that are young
> Shall never see so much, nor live so long.

Whether the lines are assigned to Albany or to Edgar, they do not allow us to determine who, if anyone, rules England and what political order, if any, exists at the end of the play. Those lines, like Hippolyta's, take on specific meaning only when spoken within the context established during a particular performance by a host of aural, visual, and kinetic factors including intonation, pacing, enunciation, gestures, timing, facial expressions, movements, and groupings.

Even lines that are not fundamentally ambivalent present multiple possibilities. Consider the words with which Hamlet responds to appeals, first by Claudius and then by Gertrude, that he not return to Wittenberg: "I shall in all my best obey you, madam" (I.ii.120). The syntax is not complex and the vocabulary is not difficult; there is no doubt that Hamlet is saying he will remain at Elsinore. Yet his words embody additional possibilities that vary according to how the actor playing him actually says the words. If, as Nicol Williamson did in the movie based upon Tony Richardson's 1968 production, the actor places a heavy stress on "you" ("I shall in all my best obey *you*, madam"), the sentence emphasizes that Hamlet's obedience is to his mother rather than to the new king who has just declared Hamlet to be "our chiefest courtier, cousin, and our son" (I.ii.117). Spoken in that way, the sentence becomes something other than what Claudius declares it to be when he says, "Why, 'tis a loving and a fair reply" (I.ii.121). It is an act of defiance. However, the actor might elect instead to make "obey" prominent, thereby establishing that Hamlet regards his assent as an act of filial duty rather than the "gentle and unforced accord" (I.ii.123) that, Claudius says, so pleases him that he orders cannon fired to announce each "jocund health that Denmark drinks to-day" (I.ii.125). Hamlet's assent might also be spoken so that the words convey his own sense of the limits of his ability to obey: "I shall *in all my best* obey you, madam." If so, the line anticipates Hamlet's inner struggle—between what he judges to be the best and the worst in himself. Analysis that focuses exclusively on the playtext does not allow us to discriminate among the possibilities that Hamlet's words establish. It cannot, in other words, enable us to determine precisely what the sentence means.

□   □   □

If we are to understand the multiplicity generated by the freedom inherent in Shakespeare's plays, we must put aside assumptions and methods shaped by the themata of simplicity, completeness, and causality. In their place, we should adopt those themata incorporated in quantum physics as the principles of superposition and complementarity. They can contribute to a paradigm that will enable us to accept Shakespeare's plays as systems that display pattern and regularity and have an inherent capacity for multiplicity in such features as gesture, intonation, timing, movement, pacing, enunciation, and grouping that are powerfully significant in establishing what meanings are conveyed and what effects are produced. In Shakespeare's plays we see processes, structures, and behavior that are largely patterned but not entirely so. Particular novelty exists within general order.

A superposition is the imposition of one thing (or more) on another, such as when a photographer double-exposes film. Quantum systems exist as coherent superpositions. As Gary Zukav has explained,

> a coherent superposition . . . is not simply the superposition of one thing on another. A coherent superposition is a thing-in-itself which is as distinct from its components as its components are from each other.[22]

As an example of coherent superposition, Zukav describes an experiment in which light is polarized.[23] If we place a filter that polarizes light vertically either in front of or behind a filter that polarizes light horizontally, no light will pass through the sequence of filters. If we take a filter that polarizes light diagonally and place it either before or after the other two, the situation does not change. No light emerges from either sequence of three filters. If, however, we place the filter that polarizes light diagonally *between* the other two, the situation changes profoundly. Light does pass through such a sequence. This demonstrates that diagonally polarized light is not simply a combination of horizontally and vertically polarized light. It is a coherent superposition of horizontally and vertically polarized light; it exists apart from either yet includes both of them.

The principle of superposition requires that we think of a quantum entity as being an ensemble of various coexistent substates and properties rather than having, as classical physics requires, one mode of existence and a single set of fixed properties. Heisenberg's uncertainty principle demonstrates why that is the case. As we specify the position of an electron with greater precision, our uncertainty about its momentum increases. We find that we must think of it as having a range of speeds at a given moment and location. Conversely, the more precisely we establish a particular speed for an electron, the more we must realize that it can be simultaneously in a number of positions. In other words, the electron exists as a coherent superposition of different positions and momentums, all of which contribute to its behavior.

The experiment referred to earlier, in which electrons strike a fluorescent screen, illustrates the superposition principle. Each electron moves at different speeds simultaneously and simultaneously occupies different points in space. As it moves toward the screen in that manner, it has the potential for striking the screen at different points within a predictable region. In movement, the electron is a system of potential substates corresponding to each point on the screen that it is capable of striking. The electron is, in other words, an aggregate of possible events, of possible collisions with the screen. When it strikes the screen, one of those events happens, one of those states becomes actual. That actualized state is called an *eigenstate*.

The transition from the possible to the actual, from multifaceted potentiality to single eigenstate, is a quantum jump, a leap into actuality out of an aggregate of possibilities. Physicists also speak of that transition as the collapse of the wave function. Quantum physicists devised mathematical constructs called probability waves by which they could predict the likelihood that any one of the aggregate of possibilities that constitute a quantum system will make the jump into actuality. When an electron ceases to move through space (when, for example, it strikes a fluorescent screen), all but one of the possibilities of the coherent superposition described by the probability wave collapse. What remains is a single actuality, a particular event, an eigenstate. Striking the screen, the electron stops behaving like a wave and behaves instead like a particle, a discrete entity with a location that can be precisely defined. The particlelike electron is the actualization of one of the possibilities, of one of the constituent substates, of the wavelike electron moving through space.

It is crucial to keep in mind that the superposition principle does not define a quantum system as "a set of different states, one of which it actually occupies, with discernment of that one by an act of observation"[24] (such as occurs when we see an electron strike a fluorescent screen). The principle declares that each quantum system is distributed over all of its possible substates until, with an act of observation, the system assumes a single state. The superposition principle and the related mathematical construct of probability waves changed the ontology of physics. Through them, quantum theory reintroduced into physics the concept of potentiality that physicists had abandoned when, following the example of giants like Galileo, Descartes, and Newton, they focused their attention on entities, events, and processes whose properties could be observed and measured. Probability itself was certainly not new, but the quantum concept of probability was, as Heisenberg has explained, "something entirely new in theoretical physics since Newton":

> Probability in mathematics or in statistical mechanics means a statement about our degree of knowledge of the actual situation. In throwing dice we do not know the fine details of the motion of our hands which determine the fall of the dice and therefore we say that the probability of throwing a special number is just one in six. The probability wave of Bohr, Kramers, Slater, however, meant more than that; it meant a tendency for something. It was a quantitative version of the old concept of "potentia" in Aristotelian philosophy. It introduced something standing in the middle between the idea of an event and the actual event, a strange kind of physical reality just in the middle between possibility and reality.[25]

At the most elementary level of physical reality, physicists found themselves dealing not just with observable and measurable events and systems but also with systems that are aggregates of possible events—with what is somehow already happening although it has not yet and may not become actual. Such systems have what Heisenberg terms "a tendency toward reality."[26] The scientific concept of reality was no longer limited to what one could actually perceive through the senses or with the refined instruments provided by technology.

The superposition principle provides the foundation for a new ontology for plays in general and for Shakespeare's plays in particular. That ontology, in contrast to the ontology implicit in the definition that states that a play is in essence its playtext, allows us to conceive of the relationship among a Shakespearean play, its playtext(s), and its performances in ways that accommodate rather than deny freedom and multiplicity. The play is a coherent superposition of coexistent potentialities. Standing in the middle between the idea of an event and the actual event, a play does not exist in a single mode—as a playtext—but as an ensemble of various possibilities that may overlap and even conflict with one another. *The playtext of a Shakespearean play is not its enduring essence abstracted from the particularities that inhere in all performances. It is a verbal (rather than mathematical) construct that describes that ensemble of possibilities.* It establishes a range, a distribution of possible events during a performance, including acts of speaking, but it does not determine in minute and complete detail all of the events that happen during a specific performance. A Shakespearean playtext, like the probability wave associated with an electron, permits us to form expectations about what will happen during a performance—expectations, not certainties. Although it is highly probable that the audience at the next performance of *King Lear* will see Kent undo Lear's button, it is by no means certain, as Trevor Nunn's 1976 production and Robin Phillips' productions of 1979 and 1980 proved.

A Shakespearean playtext is not a series of statements that specify in all respects—or even in all important respects—what must happen during performance. Its statements do specify what *cannot* happen, and in doing so they permit whatever possibilities are not prohibited. Shakespeare's Hamlet is prohibited from refusing to stay at Elsinore, and he is also prohibited from using any words other than those assigned to him to express his agreement to stay: "I shall in all my best obey you, madam." Those words allow, however, for important differences in meaning and effect within a wide range of possibilities, and we cannot know for certain which meaning and effect will be enacted when the line is delivered during a performance. A Shakespearean playtext prohibits a character from speaking during an open silence, but the playtext does not specify what the character does or thinks or feels during that silence. The playtext of *Measure for Measure* prohibits Isabella from saying that she will marry the Duke. It also prohibits her from saying that she will not marry the Duke and from saying that she will not make such a choice. Within those constraints, however, the playtext leaves her free to decide and to express her decision wordlessly. We cannot be certain in advance what her decision will be. The superposition principle requires that in place of certainties we accept alternative possibilities.

During a performance a Shakespearean play makes the quantum transition from multifaceted potentiality to a single actuality. Each performance is a realization—at a particular time and place through the talents of living human beings—of one of the many substates of which the play is a coherent superposition. Each actualization acquires its distinctive features—its fine details, structures, and pro-

cesses—as the result of choices made that implement specific possibilities from among the many possible meanings and effects established by open silences, as well as by lines like those which conclude
King Lear and like Hamlet's "I shall in all my best obey you,
madam." Each choice involves enacting one of a range of alternatives, and a given performance is a composite of choices made from
an array of possibilities. There must be, to take one example, some
response during the open silence that falls between Lear's request
"Pray you undo this button" and his words of thanks. During a
particular performance, the response might be for Albany to undo
Cordelia's button, but *King Lear* remains a play in which Albany
might undo Lear's button rather than Cordelia's, and a play in
which another character (Edmund, Kent, an anonymous soldier)
might undo either Lear's button or Cordelia's. Hamlet's statement
that he will remain in Elsinore likewise establishes a spectrum of
possibilities. Delivery of those words during performance entails
bringing one of their multiple possible meanings into focus while
blurring or suspending the others. In the playtext, Hippolyta's
words at the start of *A Midsummer Night's Dream* are ambiguous.
The wedding night that she says will come "quickly" may be one
that she anticipates with joy or distaste, eagerness or indifference,
or even dread. Those possibilities will narrow into a single actuality
when her words are spoken during a performance in a way that
establishes what the quality of her anticipation is and whether it
corresponds with Theseus' enthusiasm.

Each performance is an ensemble of specific choices made in pursuit of an integrity that will make them seem appropriate both individually and collectively. They define and embody one substate of
the play, which is itself an artistic system comprised of many substates but not confined to any one of them. The structure of a play
may vary from substate to substate, as the structure of *A Midsummer Night's Dream* does depending on which meaning and effects
emerge from Hippolyta's open silence. *Twelfth Night* may end with
Antonio accepted into Illyrian society or with him isolated or even
with him withdrawing from it; each ending alters the play's thematic emphasis and shadings of emotions. Prospero may leave his
island at the end of *The Tempest* for a perfected society in which he
will not need the powers that he has relinquished, but the society to
which he is about to return may equally well be one in which the

human capacity for evil has been temporarily checked, but not extirpated, by his exercise of the very powers that he no longer possesses. Even when *Measure for Measure* ends with Barnardine moved to speechless gratitude by the Duke's mercy and with Isabella silently accepting the Duke's offer of marriage, it remains capable of being a play in which the relationships between mercy and justice and between love, marriage, and law will be defined differently. Barnardine's silence may testify to a murderous incorrigibility that mercy cannot affect, and Isabella, by her silence, may refuse to renounce the religious life she was commencing at the start of the play in order to become the wife of the Duke. In the different substates that it is capable of assuming, *King Lear* may end with a political order centered on either Edgar or Albany, depending on which of them agrees, silently or verbally, to rule England. If neither agrees, it may end with England kingless and devoid of any political order.

The existence of more than one playtext for many of Shakespeare's plays generates another kind of multiplicity that the superposition principle enables us to accommodate rather than deny. It frees us from the assumption that the different versions of, say, *King Lear* are more or less corrupt derivatives of a primary version, now lost, which is the play as Shakespeare penned it and intended it. Using the superposition principle, we can regard both the Quarto and the Folio as legitimate although differing verbal descriptions of *King Lear*, each of which presents possibilities that the other obscures. Because of the influence of classical physics, the playtext has long served as a kind of blueprint for subsequent performances (that is, an abstract statement of what should take place during a performance), but even in Western culture, not every play has had a playtext on which performances of it were based. The commedia dell'arte, for example, flourished for centuries without playtexts, and Athol Fugard's *Sizwe Bansi Is Dead* is more recent proof that a play need not have a script before it is rehearsed and performed. Only after that play had its first run in Port Elizabeth, South Africa, in 1972 was its script settled upon and then fixed in print. The superposition principle allows us, if we wish, to think of a playtext not just as a blueprint but also as a distillate of the performances that preceded it. Such a perspective enables us to regard *King Lear* as a play with possible substates different enough that they have been distilled into and described by two different playtexts. The

cf. music

variety of substates that constitute *King Lear* exceeds the spectrum of possibilities that can be described by a single playtext, be it the Quarto or the Folio.

□   □   □

Whereas the superposition principle provides the basis for an ontology compatible with the multiplicity of performances and, in some cases, playtexts of Shakespeare's plays, the principle of complementarity provides the cornerstone of an epistemology capable of accommodating that multiplicity. Bohr formulated the principle of complementarity in 1927 and later characterized it as "a new mode of description" in which "any given application of classical concepts precludes the use of other classical concepts which in a different connection are equally necessary for the elucidation of the phenomena."[27] For example, describing an electron by using the classical concept of momentum prevents us, as Heisenberg demonstrated, from describing it by using the concept of position at a fixed point in space. "Within the scope of classical physics," Bohr pointed out,

> all characteristic properties of a given object can in principle be ascertained by a single experimental arrangement, although in practice various arrangements are often convenient for the study of different aspects of the phenomena. In fact, data obtained in such a way simply supplement each other and can be combined into a consistent picture of the behaviour of the object under consideration.[28]

Quantum phenomena, however, defy combination into a single "picture." We can know simultaneously both the position and the momentum of a planet, but we cannot know both simultaneously for an individual electron. In addition, electrons exhibit a fundamental duality. Under certain experimental conditions, an electron behaves like a particle—something discrete that occupies a sharply defined location in space. Under different experimental conditions, however, an electron behaves like a wave, oscillating and spreading out as it moves through space. Light has the same duality; it sometimes displays particlelike properties and sometimes wavelike properties. Wave and particle are concepts—"pictures"—that contradict one another and cannot be combined, yet when used to study electrons and light, each offers valid information that the other does not; both are equally necessary to understand light and electrons.

They must be regarded as complementary "in the sense that they represent equally essential knowledge about atomic systems and together exhaust this knowledge."[29] Oppenheimer has provided an account of complementarity in which he also clarifies its relationship to superposition:

> We have seen that in the atomic world we have been led by experience to use descriptions and ideas that apply to the large-scale world of matter . . . ideas like the position of a body and its acceleration and its impulse and the forces acting upon it; ideas like wave and interference; ideas like cause and probability. But what is new, what was not anticipated a half-century ago is that, though to an atomic system there is a potential applicability of one or another of these ideas, in any real situation only some of these ways of description can be actual. . . . All such ways of observing are needed for the whole experience of the atomic world; all but one are excluded in any actual experience.[30]

The multiplicity inherent in Shakespearean drama poses contradictions as irreconcilable as that between the electron as a wave and the electron as a particle. Isabella may in silence agree to or refuse to marry the Duke or she may refuse to make such a decision, but she cannot do all three simultaneously. A similar group of contradictory possibilities exists for every open silence. Barnardine may be silent out of gratitude or defiance or indifference. Prospero's brother, Antonio, may be wordlessly remorseful or wordlessly malevolent. Sebastian's beloved friend Antonio may, without speaking a word, be accepted into Illyria or rejected or simply ignored. Albany or Kent or Edgar or an anonymous soldier or soldiers or even some combination of those characters may undo Lear's button, or one, two, or several of them may undo Cordelia's instead. Ambivalent passages and the existence of multiple playtexts of the same play also generate possibilities that defy combination into a single consistent "picture," or reduction to an underlying principle or idea. During a performance the final words of *King Lear* must be spoken by either Edgar or Albany, each an alternative possibility that excludes the other. The words that one or the other must speak cannot, when delivered to an audience, mean simultaneously that Edgar will rule and that Albany will rule and that England will be kingless.

In *Shakespeare and the Common Understanding*—a book whose title alludes to Oppenheimer's *Science and the Common Understanding*—Norman Rabkin shows that a number of Shakespeare's plays that offer contradictory conceptual meanings "are built on visions of complementarity."[31] The principle of complementarity is also useful in dealing with other problems, including those posed by open silences and the existence of multiple playtexts of certain plays. When, as with *King Lear*, more than one playtext exists, editors have traditionally sought to combine or reduce them to a single playtext, thus blurring, if not obliterating, differences that are fundamentally antithetical. An alternative to such reductionism is to see differences between versions as standing in complementary relationship to each other. Either Edgar (Folio) or Albany (Quarto) can speak the final lines of *King Lear*, and we needlessly narrow our knowledge of that play if we fail to see that it allows both alternatives. The principle of complementarity enables us to conceive of each playtext of *King Lear* as a description of different systems of possibilities—different substates that the play can assume from one performance to another. Each playtext offers knowledge about the play that the other does not, and to have the best chance of fully understanding *King Lear*, we must attend to what both tell us about the play.

The various possible meanings and effects generated by open silences, and by ambiguous passages, also have a complementary relationship to one another. Each actualization of a specific possibility during a performance excludes other possibilities that are not only equally valid but also equally capable of providing necessary information about the play. If, for example, an anonymous soldier undoes Lear's button during a given performance, the meanings and effects of that act include those arising from the fact that an audience sees him do for Lear what neither Lear's son-in-law (Albany) nor Lear's faithful servant (Kent) nor Gloucester's faithful son (Edgar) was able or willing to do. Thus, the possibilities not enacted also contribute to our understanding of the action performed. Hippolyta, by the manner in which she speaks the only words assigned to her during the opening scene of *A Midsummer Night's Dream*, may convey that, like Theseus, she joyously anticipates their wedding night, but our knowledge about what those words convey, about the moment to which they contribute, and, ultimately, about the play itself is less than complete if we disregard the other possible meanings and effects that her words allow.

Composed of many specific actualizations drawn from among diverse, even contradictory possibilities, the various performances of a play—the different substates it actually assumes—are complementary to one another. Each performance can provide knowledge of the play that is not otherwise available, but the knowledge we gain from any performance is, no matter how valid and how fresh, also of necessity incomplete. A given performance can use Hippolyta's words at the start of *A Midsummer Night's Dream* and her ensuing silence to establish that she and Theseus are paired in harmony. We need to know that such harmony is a possibility, but we also need to know that another performance can, with equal validity, use Hippolyta's words and her silence to establish discord between Theseus and Hippolyta. If, at the conclusion of a performance of *Twelfth Night*, Antonio withdraws from Illyria or is left isolated onstage, the result is to set the heterosexual love that moves men and women to marry in opposition to the love that Antonio has for Sebastian. That possibility coexists with another. The men and women soon to be married can include Antonio in the society that their pairings will renew. Thus, *Twelfth Night* is also a play that can end by presenting the two kinds of love as compatible. When performed, either version of *King Lear* can conclude with either Edgar or Albany ruling England and thus with the restoration, after extraordinary suffering and loss, of the political stability that Lear shattered when he divided the kingdom. A performance of either version may instead end with no one willing to assume kingly responsibility for "the gor'd state" and with the instability that Lear initiated worsening indefinitely. The process of performance will actualize one of those possibilities, but *King Lear* remains a play that accommodates at least three endings: an England ruled by Edgar, an England ruled by Albany, an England ruled by no one at all.

The principle of complementarity also applies to the relationship between the performances of a play and its playtext(s). In performance and in print, the play presents itself to us in two radically different modes. The play when performed is a specific actualization of one of many possible substates; a playtext is a verbal construction that describes the range of possible states without actualizing any one of them. Each mode provides information that is necessary, valid, and not made available by the other. For example, a performance of *King Lear* tells us what no amount of analysis of either playtext can reveal: who undoes the button and whose button is undone. On the other hand, by making the words of the play available for sustained and repeated scrutiny, the Folio of *King Lear* enables us to trace a pattern of imagery that includes Lear's request, "Pray you undo this button," his earlier command, "Come, unbutton here" (III.iv.103),[32] and the lines in which he tells Gloucester of society's corruption:

> Through tattered clothes great vices do appear;
> Robes and furred gowns hide all. Plate sin with gold,
> And the strong lance of justice hurtless breaks;
> Arm it in rags, a pygmy's straw doth pierce it.   (IV.vi.161–64)

The pattern also includes the lines in which Lear initiates the competition among his daughters:

>   . . . Tell me, my daughters
> (Since now we will divest us both of rule,
> Interest of territory, cares of state),
> Which of you shall we say doth love us most, . . .   (I.i.48–51)

Lear's word "divest" links the shedding of garments with the surrender of royal power and responsibility.

Complementarity releases us from the need to declare that either the playtext or the performance is valid to the exclusion of the other, that one but not the other provides information needed for complete knowledge of the play. By allowing us to accept both the validity and the limits of what we can know through each of the modes by which a play is presented, complementarity validates a methodology that combines intense scrutiny of the playtext(s) with equally intense scrutiny of actual performances. Complementarity offers a different conception of clarity. In place of clarity achieved by a process of abstraction and simplification that reduces "the multiplicity and confusion of things" to a single principle or idea or model, complementarity seeks clarity that results from "the exhaustive overlay of different descriptions that incorporate apparently contradictory notions."[33] Clarity of that kind is far more compatible with Shakespeare's plays. It does not seek to restrict or eliminate the multiplicity of their performances and, frequently, their playtexts.

□   □   □

The ontology and epistemology that quantum physics validates can also accommodate the role the theater audience plays each time a Shakespearean play makes the transition, during a performance, from a multifaceted potentiality to a single eigenstate. The greatest difference between quantum physics and classical physics is that quantum physics recasts the role of the observer. Bohr has emphasized that

> indeed, the whole conceptual structure of classical physics, brought to so wonderful a unification and completion by Einstein's work, rests on the assumption, well adapted to our daily experience of physical phenomena, that it is possible to discriminate between the behaviour of material objects and the question of their observation.[34]

Such an assumption is consistent, Richard Schlegel has pointed out, with the doctrine of physical realism, which posits that "each part of nature has an existence intrinsic to itself, with its describable properties independent of our observation of it."[35] The assumption that entities exist and events occur independently of who observes them and of the processes and experimental arrangements by which they are observed is valid for nature on the large scale. We do not, for example, alter the path of a planet by observing it through a telescope. However, when we attempt to observe the path of an electron by using an electron microscope that bounces a gamma ray off it, we deflect the electron from the path it would otherwise have taken. We cannot in such a case discriminate between how the electron behaves (the path it takes) and how we observe it. The only path we can know for an electron is the one that, by the act of observation, we have to some extent caused it to take. Bohr declared that

> the fundamental difference with respect to the analysis of phenomena in classical and in quantum physics is that in the former the interaction between the objects and the measuring instruments may be neglected or compensated for, while in the latter this interaction forms an integral part of the phenomenon.[36]

The two-hole experiment, by showing that how we elect to observe an electron determines whether it behaves like a wave or like a particle, illustrates the breakdown at the quantum level of the concept of objectivity that is essential to classical physics and to physical realism.[37] A sheet of metal with two holes, each of which can be closed, is placed between a source that emits electrons and a screen that detects electrons. When hole 1 in the metal sheet is closed, electrons pass only through hole 2, and vice versa. Whichever hole is open, the pattern formed by the impact of electrons on the detecting screen is that of particles. When both holes are left open, the screen continues to detect individual electrons impacting as particles, but the pattern formed by those points of impact is no longer that of separate particles but that of waves. Paradoxically, if one electron at a time is sent toward the barrier when both holes are open, we find that it does not go through either hole 1 or hole 2, as a particle would, but through both holes simultaneously. Such behavior is consistent with that of a wave, yet we know that electrons are particles because they have such properties as mass and spin. An electron is a particle if one hole is open, but an electron is a wave if two holes are open. What its features are and what it is depend on the act of observation.

What is true of electrons is true of all quantum systems. The act of observation always collapses the probability wave of a quantum system. What exists as a coherent superposition of many possible substates exists, when observed, in a single state. On the quantum level, the act of observing results in an interaction that is integral to the phenomenon being observed, since the flow of energy into and out of the quantum system as a result of the act of observing is sizable in relation to energy changes that occur within the system as a result of the interaction of its parts. The flow of energy in and out of a large-scale system composed of many quantum entities as the result of observation is negligible compared with the energy changes that occur within the system as a result of the interaction of its parts. In that sense, one can speak of large-scale systems as being closed and of quantum systems as being open. The observation-interaction that occurs at the quantum level cannot be avoided, and it cannot be discounted in advance, for there is no possibility of predicting in individual instances what single state of the quantum system will emerge from the interaction. We know that the interaction must occur, but we cannot tell exactly what it will be. The existence of the observation-interaction means, Oppenheimer has told us, "that every intervention to make a measurement, to study what is going on in the atomic world, creates, despite all of the universal order of this world, a new, a unique, not fully predictable, situation."[38] Quantum physics reveals that at its most elementary level, physical reality is created in part by the act of observation and by those who engage in it.

Like those who observe quantum systems and events, members

of a theater audience participate in shaping the performance that they observe. They contribute to the performance and are integral to it in ways that members of a cinema audience or a television audience or a reading audience do not and are not. Those who watch Shakespeare's plays are often summoned to do more than be an inert and neutral presence. The Chorus of *Henry V* repeatedly calls upon those watching it to "piece out our imperfections with your thoughts" (Prologue, 23), to "play with your fancies," and to "work, work your thoughts" (III.Chorus 7, 25). Prospero, at the conclusion of *The Tempest*, admits that without the "gentle breath" of the audience's approval "my project fails," and he assigns to the audience powers over him that approach those they saw him exercise during the play. They can confine him or they can set him "free."

Unless they are as rigid and self-centered as Malvolio in his yellow stockings, actors attune themselves to their different audiences, emphasizing a certain gesture in response to one audience, playing it down for another, omitting it entirely for a third. The exchange, the interaction, between performers and audience determines the most precise features of the exact state that a play assumes during a particular performance. That interaction is as inescapable as the observation-interaction that is central to quantum physics, and its outcome is equally unpredictable. Like those who observe quantum phenomena, the members of a theater audience are, in immeasurable yet definite ways, both participants in and creators of the event that they have come together to watch. Each performance of a play is, therefore, despite the order arising from the playtext and from the rehearsed, patterned action of the performers, "a new, a unique, not fully predictable, situation."

The performance of a play is an open rather than a closed system—it is open to the influence of the energy, emotions, intelligence, and creativity not just of the actors but also of the audience. Norman Holland has analyzed the relationship between reader and text as a complex transaction involving the processes of defense, expectation, fantasy, and transformation.[39] The interaction between performers and audience that occurs during a performance undoubtedly involves the same or similar processes, but it is also certain to prove far more complex than the literary transaction, for two reasons. First, what occurs between actors and audience is an interaction rather than a transaction. It takes place between and among persons, not between a person and the printed words of a text. Second, the theatrical interaction, unlike the solitary, individualistic activity of reading, is a communal experience. The responses of each individual in the audience influence, and are influenced by, the responses of others in the audience. The collective response of the audience includes those individual responses but is not identical to them. Individual performers react not only to the responses (both individual and collective) of the audience but also to their fellow actors' reactions to those responses. This is not the place and I am not the person to undertake an analysis of the theatrical interaction, but the principles of superposition and complementarity provide an epistemological and ontological framework for such an analysis.

My application of the principles of superposition and complementarity to Shakespeare's plays is, I have no doubt, less compelling and less exact than their application to quantum systems and processes. That is so not only because my capacities fall short of those of the great quantum physicists, but also because, as Bohr has pointed out, quantum physics presents us with a "simpler situation" than those presented by "conscious individuals and human cultures."[40] Shakespeare's plays are among the most complex of mankind's creations. We who love, study, and perform those plays should neither assume nor insist that our progress in understanding them will be more rapid and less painstaking than that made over several decades by those from whose cumulative labors the achievements of quantum physics gradually emerged. An atom is not a play by Shakespeare, but the randomness of the former and the freedom of the latter generate multiplicity that poses problems for analysis that are of the same order. Quantum physics demonstrates that we can formulate precise, supple, and lucid ways of thinking and talking about the freedom and the multiplicity inherent in Shakespeare's plays.

Notes

Full bibliographic information for a book or article is given the first time it is mentioned in a note and again in the Bibliography.

Introduction

1. Ed. Geoffrey Shepherd (London: Thomas Nelson, 1965), p. 21.

2. *Ben Jonson*, ed. C. H. Herford, Percy Simpson. and Evelyn Simpson (Oxford: Clarendon Press, 1947), 8: 620–21.

3. Ibid., p. 625.

4. "I Love You. Who Are You? The Strategy of Drama in Recognition Scenes," *PMLA* 92 (1977): 304.

5. Princeton, N.J.: Princeton University Press, 1971.

6. London: Heinemann, 1974.

7. For a different but very useful discussion of silences within Shakespeare's plays, see chap. 4 ("Speaking Silences on the Shakespearean Stage") of Jean E. Howard, *Shakespeare's Art of Orchestration: Stage Technique and Audience Response* (Urbana and Chicago: University of Illinois Press, 1984), pp. 79–100. She describes various ways in which silence functions "as an active element in the dramatist's communication with the audience. And it is precisely because silence runs counter to our predominant expectation that speech will follow speech that it can produce powerful effects if skillfully used" (p. 97). None of the silences that she looks at is an open silence. In *Shakespere's [sic] Silences* (Cambridge, Mass.: Harvard University Press, 1929), pp. 3–63, Alwin Thayler discusses silences in terms of their contribution to credible characterization and to narrative design.

8. "The Eminent Text and Its Truth," trans. Geoffrey Waite, *Bulletin of the Midwest Modern Language Association* 13 (1980): 6.

Chapter 1

1. For a perceptive discussion of the ambiguity of time and man's perception of it in this play, see James E. Robinson's article, "The Ritual and Rhetoric of *A Midsummer Night's Dream*," *PMLA* 83 (1968): 380–91.

Less helpful is Anne Paolucci's essay, "The Lost Days in *A Midsummer Night's Dream*," *Shakespeare Quarterly* 38 (1977): 317–26.

2. This production was revived in 1962 and provided the basis for a 1969 film of the play that was designed for both British cinema and U.S. television. Michael Mullin discusses the shift from stage to screen in "Peter Hall's *A Midsummer Night's Dream*," *Educational Theatre Journal* 28 (1975): 529–34. Jack J. Jorgens devotes a chapter of *Shakespeare on Film* (Bloomington: Indiana University Press, 1977) to Hall's film, and he describes Hippolyta as "domestic and dull, the director having obliterated all traces of her conflict with Theseus" (p. 54). I did not see either stage production, but I have studied the promptbooks of both and have seen the film several times.

3. I saw the play performed once, but I had no opportunity to study the promptbook.

4. Andrew Veitch, *Guardian* (London, Manchester), 8 July 1980, p. 9.

5. After opening in Stratford-upon-Avon in 1970, this production toured North America, was made part of the RSC's 1971–72 London repertoire, and began a one-year world tour in 1973. My comments are based on a performance I saw in London in August 1971, and on the promptbook for the world tour production, edited by Glen Loney and published as *Peter Brook's Production of William Shakespeare's* A Midsummer Night's Dream *for the Royal Shakespeare Company: The Complete and Authorized Acting Edition* (Chicago: Dramatic Publishing Company, 1974). Loney observes: "This version is perhaps the most definitive because it represents the refinements and simplifications which the production achieved in the Paris rehearsals for the tour and the later modifications introduced as the show traveled to such cities as Budapest, Helsinki, and Los Angeles. It is interesting to note that the production always moved in the direction of greater simplicity—rather than greater complexity—from its earliest moments at Stratford. . . . The unnecessary and the extraneous did not survive, and they are not represented in this edition" (p. 3a).

6. In an interview published in Loney's edition, Alan Howard, who played Theseus and Oberon, says of Hippolyta: "she apparently comes to this court and discovers that although he has said he is going to wed her in a *different* way, he appears to be making an extraordinarily barbaric judgment against another woman" (p. 42).

7. This production was part of the television series entitled "The Shakespeare Plays."

8. For a discussion of the phenomenon of doubling, see Stephen Booth, "Speculations on Doubling in Shakespeare's Plays," in Philip C. McGuire and David A. Samuelson, eds., *Shakespeare: The Theatrical Dimension* (New York: AMS Press, 1979), pp. 103–31. An expanded version of Booth's article was published as appendix 2 of his King Lear, Macbeth,

Indefinition, and Tragedy (New Haven, Conn.: Yale University Press, 1983), pp. 129–55.

9. This principle is akin to what C. L. Barber has called "the saturnalian pattern," consisting of "a basic movement which can be summarized in the formula, through release to clarification" (p. 4). His *Shakespeare's Festive Comedy: A Study of Dramatic Form and Its Relation to Social Custom* (Princeton, N.J.: Princeton University Press, 1959) is a masterpiece to which I am deeply indebted. *A Midsummer Night's Dream* was the subject of three books between the mid-1960s and the mid-1970s: David P. Young, *Something of Great Constancy: The Art of* A Midsummer Night's Dream (New Haven, Conn.: Yale University Press, 1966); Stephen Fender, *Shakespeare:* A Midsummer Night's Dream (London: Edward Arnold, 1968); and T. Walter Herbert, *Oberon's Mazed World* (Baton Rouge: Louisiana State University Press, 1977).

10. The shift from disorder to order can be sudden and total because there is a pattern to the confusion in which the characters are caught. In *The Court Masque* (Cambridge: Cambridge University Press, 1927), Enid Welsford describes that pattern as a dance:

> The plot is a pattern, a figure, rather than a series of human events occasioned by character and passion, and this pattern, especially in the moonlight parts of the play, is the pattern of a dance. . . . The appearance and disappearance and reappearance of the various lovers, the will-o'-the-wisp movement of the elusive Puck, form a kind of figured ballet. The lovers quarrel in a dance pattern: first, there are two men to one woman and the other woman alone, then a brief space of circular movement, each one pursuing and pursued, then a return to the first figure with the position of the women reversed, then a cross-movement, man quarreling with man and woman with woman, and then, as a finale, a general setting to partners, including not only the lovers but fairies and royal personages as well. (pp. 331–32)

The pairings of the young lovers are constant because the love juice remains in Demetrius' eyes. That fact illustrates that the order that emerges toward the end of act IV, like the disorder that preceded it, rests upon impulses and affections that are capable of changing swiftly, completely, and even randomly. In *A Midsummer Night's Dream*, order and disorder are not so much antitheses of one another as mirror images of one another. Discord is not extinguished by, but "translated" into, concord.

11. The motif of women engaged in conflicts deserves specific mention. *A Midsummer Night's Dream* opens soon after a battle in which the Athenian army under Theseus has vanquished Hippolyta and her army of women. When the audience first sees Titania, she is engaged in a struggle

that pits her and her attendants against Oberon and his. Oberon triumphs by using the love juice to bring Titania's sexual energies to such a pitch that she, doting on Bottom, no longer prizes the boy or the love that bound her to his mother. In victory Oberon reclaims Titania as his wife and takes the boy for himself. During act III, Hermia and Helena come to the point where they are ready to fight one another. Each woman, in order to gain the man she wants, disregards the love and loyalty that since childhood have made them virtually one. "So we grew together, / Like to a double cherry, seeming parted, / But yet a union in partition" (III.ii.208–10). Each subordinates those ties to the desire for a different kind of intimacy and union, to the imperatives of sexual love. From a Freudian perspective, the women in the play can be said to grow up as each emerges from a state in which relationships with other women are valued to one in which relationships with men become paramount. One could also argue, however, that the motif of women who either cease to do battle with men or come to do battle with each other implies a vision, a fantasy, of male domination.

12. The harmony that Theseus and Hippolyta either have from the start or eventually establish is not, it must be stressed, synonymous with uniformity—with the obliteration of all differences. The two characters differ during the rest of act V over a number of points—the truth of the lovers' "story of the night" (line 23), the appropriateness of having the rude mechanicals perform, the role of an audience's imagination—but those differences are now (if they were not earlier) part of a larger harmony that makes concord of potential discord.

13. Shakespeare calls attention to this process by reversing it when Bottom, playing Pyramus, arrives at Ninus' tomb. Bottom describes the moonlight, in which the audience was to imagine Pyramus standing, by using words that in fact describe the sunlight actually illuminating the daytime performance of the play of Pyramus and Thisby and of *A Midsummer Night's Dream*:

> Sweet moon, I thank thee for thy sunny beams;
>   I thank thee, moon, for shining now so bright;
> For, by thy gracious, golden, glittering gleams,
>   I trust to take of truest Thisby sight.   (V.i.265–68)

14. It is easy, tempting, and correct to say that "Pyramus and Thisby," particularly Quince's delivery of the Prologue, is a classic example of performers abusing what a playwright has written. It is also true, however, that even though it is thoroughly botched, the rude mechanicals' performance of that play helps to make *A Midsummer Night's Dream* itself a success in performance.

Chapter 2

1.   Olivia's previous uses of the phrase "my lord" during the final scene reflect the initial conflict between feudal allegiances and marital bonds. It is unclear whether she is referring to Duke Orsino or to the person she thinks is her husband:

> *Olivia:* What would my lord, but that he may not have,
> Wherein Olivia may seem serviceable?
> Cesario, you do not keep promise with me.
> *Viola:* Madam?
> *Duke:* Gracious Olivia—
> *Olivia:* What do you say, Cesario?— Good, my lord—
> *Viola:* My lord would speak; my duty hushes me.   (V.i.98–101)

2.   Cf. II.v.21–76.

3.   These themes have been discussed by C. L. Barber, "Testing Courtesy and Humanity in *Twelfth Night,*" in C. L. Barber, *Shakespeare's Festive Comedy* (Princeton, N.J.: Princeton University Press, 1959), pp. 240–61; Joseph H. Summers, "The Masks of *Twelfth Night,*" *University Review* 22 (1955): 25–32, repr. in Walter N. King, ed., *Twentieth Century Interpretations of* Twelfth Night (Englewood Cliffs, N.J.: Prentice-Hall, 1968), pp. 15–23, and in Leonard F. Dean, ed., *Shakespeare: Modern Essays in Criticism* (New York: Oxford University Press, 1967), pp. 134–43; L. G. Salingar, "The Design of *Twelfth Night,*" *Shakespeare Quarterly* 9 (1958): 117–36, abridged and repr. in King, *Twentieth Century Interpretations of* Twelfth Night, pp. 24–30; John Hollander, "*Twelfth Night* and the Morality of Indulgence," *Sewanee Review* 68 (1959): 220–38, repr. in King, *Twentieth Century Interpretations of* Twelfth Night, pp. 77–89, and in Alvin B. Kernan, ed., *Modern Shakespearean Criticism: Essays on Style, Dramaturgy, and the Major Plays* (New York: Harcourt Brace Jovanovich, 1970), pp. 228–41; John Russell Brown, "Directions for *Twelfth Night,*" *Shakespeare's Plays in Performance* (London: Edward Arnold, 1966), pp. 107–29, abridged and repr. in *Shakespeare: The Theatrical Dimension*, pp. 225–38.

4.   John Cairns, directing the Contact Theatre Company's 1974 production of *Twelfth Night* at the University Theatre in Manchester, England.

5.   I saw one performance of this production, and I have studied slides of it.

6.   I have seen the film several times but have had no opportunity to study the shooting script.

7.   I did not see a performance of this production, but I have studied the promptbook.

8. I did not see this production, but I have studied slides of it as well as the promptbook.

9. Reviewing this production in the *Guardian* (London, Manchester) of 24 August 1974, Michael Billington wrote: "William Dudley's plain box set confronts us throughout with a sketch of an ambisextrous Narcissus figure gazing into a pool" (p. 8). His account tallies with that of J. W. Lambert, who gave this description of the set in the *Sunday Times* (London) of 25 August 1974: "The stage, in William Dudley's setting, is a great golden-tawny box; the Illyrians, in Deirdre Clancy's costumes, play out their dreams and follies in a graceful Hilliard world dominated by the image of Narcissus gazing into the pool" (p. 27). Ralph Berry links the Narcissus figure with the production's emphasis on the theme of illusion and eroticism in *Changing Styles in Shakespeare* (London: George Allen and Unwin, 1981), pp. 115–16.

10. I saw a performance of the 1969 production, but the only prompt-books in the Shakespeare Centre Library are for the 1970 revival at the Aldwych and the performances given during the 1972 tour of Japan. I did not see either. Stanley Wells fully and intelligently discusses this production in *Royal Shakespeare: Four Major Productions at Stratford-upon-Avon*, Furman Studies (Manchester: Manchester University Press, 1976), pp. 43–63. Also see Berry, *Changing Styles in Shakespeare*, pp. 113–14.

11. I saw a performance of this production, but I could not study the stage manager's book because of the festival's policy of restricting access to such documents until the production has been out of performance for ten years.

12. I saw the first U.S. telecast of this production in February 1980, and I have studied the edition of *Twelfth Night* (London: British Broadcasting Corporation, 1980; New York: Mayflower Books, 1980) that is keyed to that production.

13. The Folio has "*Exeunt*" before Feste sings—a stage direction that does not require that the stage be cleared before Feste begins singing and does not specify when each character exits. "*Exeunt*" allows the possibility that Antonio exits while Feste is singing. The freedom implicit in "*Exeunt*" becomes apparent if we contrast it with the stage direction that the Folio could have given at this same point but did not: "*Exeunt omnes; manet Feste.*"

14. In *Free Shakespeare* (London: Heinemann, 1974), p. 68, John Russell Brown succinctly describes several of the possibilities inherent in Andrew's silent exit and comments astutely on the dramatic potential of the Priest's presence.

15. I saw one performance of this production.

16. This account is based on my memory of the performance of the 1969 production that I saw. Stanley Wells, in *Royal Shakespeare*, describes the moment differently: "Sir Toby's rejection of Andrew's well-meant offer

of help was fierce and bitter: 'Will you help? an ass-head, and a coxcomb, and a knave? a thin-faced knave, a gull!' It was followed by a long pause, giving Andrew an opportunity to register his disillusionment before Sir Toby was helped off by his new wife, with a disconsolate Sir Andrew, pathetically offering a final bow to Olivia, bringing up the rear" (p. 55). The promptbook for the 1969 production is missing, and the one for the 1970 revival at the Aldwych does not conclusively specify the details of Andrew's exit. In a certain sense, however, it is immaterial which of us is accurate, since what I describe is certainly one of the possibilities allowed by Andrew's silent exit, whether or not it was the possibility enacted during Barton's 1969 production.

17. Hands's decision to have Toby and Andrew remain onstage is not incompatible with the Folio text, which does not specify that they must exit. It allows for the possibility that Sebastian's entrance checks their departure(s), freezing them as well as the others in amazement.

18. Although the Folio text does not specify that Maria is present at any time during the final scene, it is not unusual for her to be onstage, and if she is, she usually helps Toby exit or goes after him when Olivia orders, "Get him to bed, and let his hurt be looked to." The justification for having her present seems to be Fabian's revelation that Toby and she are married, but that revelation is part of an account of what has happened that does not square with what the audience has seen and heard:

> Good madam, hear me speak,
> And let no quarrel, nor no brawl to come
> Taint the condition of this present hour,
> Which I have wond'red at. In hope it shall not,
> Most freely I confess myself and Toby
> Set this device against Malvolio here,
> Upon some stubborn and uncourteous parts
> We had conceived against him. Maria writ
> The letter, at Sir Toby's great importance,
> In recompense whereof he hath married her.   (V.i.345–54)

However, Fabian was not present when the "device against Malvolio" began to take shape during act II, scene iii, and Maria proposed using a counterfeit letter on her own (II.iii.134–48), without any "great" importuning from Sir Toby. More effectively than any other production I have seen, Hands's production alerted the audience to the possibility that Fabian is not above reworking some details and fabricating others in hopes of ensuring that no one is punished for the trick played on Malvolio. However, in order to have all major characters remain visible during all of Feste's song, Hands ignored the "*Exeunt*" that comes before Feste begins singing.

19. The conflict between Malvolio and Feste comes to a head immedi-

ately after Olivia seeks to console Malvolio by saying, "Alas, poor fool, how have they baffled thee!" (V.i.359). "Poor fool" is the last thing Malvolio wants anyone, let alone Olivia, to call him. While he is absorbing what Olivia says, the last of the scene's encounters takes place when Feste the fool steps forward to confront Malvolio the "poor fool." Feste reveals that "I was one, sir, in this interlude, one Sir Topas, sir; but that's all one. . . . And thus the whirligig of time brings in his revenges" (V.i.361–66). Malvolio's response is to promise vengeance of his own.

20. The concept of authorial intentions has been challenged from various directions. Stephen Orgel, in "What Is a Text?" (*Research Opportunities in Renaissance Drama* 24 [1981]: 3–6), questions the assumption that the text of a Shakespearean play reflects Shakespeare's intentions and no one else's. That assumption, he points out, is incompatible with what we know about theatrical and publishing practices in Shakespeare's time, thanks to G. E. Bentley, *Profession of Dramatist in Shakespeare's Time, 1590–1642*; and E. A. J. Honigmann, *The Stability of Shakespeare's Text* (Lincoln: University of Nebraska Press, 1965). In *A Critique of Modern Textual Criticism* (Chicago: University of Chicago Press, 1983), Jerome J. McGann mounts a more general challenge by demonstrating the inadequacy of using the concept of authorial intentions as the basis for resolving the difficulties encountered when editing virtually any text in English or in any other modern vernacular language. For Roland Barthes and Michel Foucault, the concept of authorial intentions must be abandoned because it restricts our capacity to understand how a text generates meanings. See Roland Barthes, "The Death of the Author," in *Image, Music, Text*, trans. Stephen Heath (New York: Hill and Wang, 1977), pp. 142–48; Michel Foucault, "What Is an Author?" in Josué V. Harari, ed., *Textual Strategies: Perspectives in Post-Structuralist Criticism* (Ithaca, N.Y.: Cornell University Press, 1979), pp. 141–50.

Chapter 3

1. Although throughout this chapter I refer to Ariel as "him," Ariel could also be played as "an airy spirit" who is female or even androgynous.

2. The important point is that Caliban voices these sentiments. His words may not be sincere, or if they are sincere, his resolve may not last, but these possibilities should not blur the contrast between what he says and what Antonio does not say.

3. I saw a performance of this production and viewed a videotape of it. The festival's regulations prohibit examining the stage manager's book of a production until ten years after the last performance.

4. For a thorough discussion of the importance of memory and remembering in *The Tempest*, see Douglas L. Peterson, *Time, Tide, and Tempest: A Study of Shakespeare's Romances* (San Marino, Calif.: Huntington

Library, 1973). I found the following works especially helpful: Robert
Egan, *Drama within Drama: Shakespeare's Sense of His Art in* King Lear,
The Winter's Tale, *and* The Tempest (New York: Columbia University
Press, 1975); Howard Felperin, *Shakespearean Romance* (Princeton, N.J.:
Princeton University Press, 1972); Michael Goldman, *Shakespeare and the
Energies of Drama* (Princeton, N.J.: Princeton University Press, 1972);
Joan Hartwig, *Shakespeare's Tragicomic Vision* (Baton Rouge: Louisiana
State University Press, 1972); Alvin B. Kernan, *The Playwright as Magi-
cian: Shakespeare's Image of the Poet in the English Public Theater* (New
Haven, Conn.: Yale University Press, 1979); Barbara A. Mowat, *The Dra-
maturgy of Shakespeare's Romances* (Athens: University of Georgia Press,
1976); and Thomas F. Van Laan, *Role-playing in Shakespeare* (Toronto:
University of Toronto Press, 1978). I am also indebted to Northrop Frye, *A
Natural Perspective: The Development of Shakespearean Comedy and Romance* (New York: Columbia University Press, 1965); and to Frank Kermode, "Introduction," *The Tempest*, Arden edition, 6th ed. (Cambridge,
Mass.: Harvard University Press, 1958), pp. xi–xciii.

5. The modern practices of punctuation that most editors of *The Tempest* follow tend to dilute that richness. Note how the use of periods and
dashes in the following examples establishes definite syntactical ties and
points toward shifts in address—which are often reinforced by editorially
added stage directions—in places where the colons of the Folio leave such
matters fruitfully unclear.

In the Pelican Shakespeare:

> I'll deliver all;
> And promise you calm seas, auspicious gales,
> And sail so expeditious that shall catch
> Your royal fleet far off.—My Ariel, chick,
> That is thy charge. Then to the elements
> Be free, and fare thou well!—Please you draw near.   (V.i.313–18)

In *The Riverside Shakespeare*, G. Blakemore Evans, textual ed. (Boston:
Houghton Mifflin, 1974):

> I'll deliver all,
> And promise you calm seas, auspicious gales,
> And sail so expeditious, that shall catch
> Your royal fleet far off. [*Aside to Ariel.*] My Ariel, chick,
> That is thy charge. Then to the elements
> Be free, and fare thou well!—Please you draw near.   (V.i.314–19)

In *Shakespeare in Performance: An Introduction through Six Major
Plays*, ed. John Russell Brown (New York: Harcourt Brace Jovanovich,
1976):

I'll deliver all;
And promise you calm seas, auspicious gales,
And sail so expeditious that shall catch
Your royal fleet far off. [*Aside to* ARIEL] My Ariel, chick,
That is thy charge. Then to the elements
Be free, and fare thou well. [*To the others*] Please you, draw near.

                                              (V.i.313–18)

6.   I did not see a performance of this production, but I have studied the promptbook.

7.   *Times* (London) *Educational Supplement*, 23 October 1970, p. 25.

8.   *Sunday Times* (London), 18 October 1970, p. 37.

9.   Barton focused the issue by cutting Prospero's next sentence: "Do not approach / Till thou dost hear me call." Ariel's reply ("Well: I conceive") became, then, a response not to Prospero's instructions but to his statement of love.

10.   The Shakespeare Centre Library in Stratford-upon-Avon has a copy of the program. Its pages are not numbered.

11.   *Illustrated London News*, 31 October 1970, p. 29.

12.   Prospero begins his explanation of who Miranda and he are by saying, "Obey, and be attentive" (I.ii.38). While describing Antonio's treachery, he breaks off several times to call for Miranda's attention:

"I pray thee mark me."   (line 67)
"Dost thou attend me?"   (line 78)
"Thou attend'st not? . . . I pray thee mark me!"   (lines 87–88)
"Dost thou hear?"   (line 106)

13.   I saw this production when it was first broadcast in the United States, and I have studied the edition of *The Tempest* keyed to that production that was published in the United States (New York: Mayflower Books, 1980).

14.   Quoted in Henry Fenwick, "The Production," published as part of the Mayflower edition of *The Tempest*, p. 25.

15.   The difference in what Prospero can feel as a man and what Ariel can feel as a spirit is made explicit early during the final scene:

Ariel: Your charm so strongly works 'em,
           That if you now beheld them, your affections
           Would become tender.
Prospero: Dost thou think so, spirit?
     Ariel: Mine would, sir, were I human.

> Prospero: And mine shall.
>   Hast thou, which art but air, a touch, a feeling
>   Of their afflictions, and shall not myself,
>   One of their kind, that relish all as sharply
>   Passion as they, be kindlier moved than thou art?
>   (lines 17–24)

In a theatrical context that emphasizes that difference, Ariel's inquiry "Do you love me, master? No?" becomes an expression not of his need or desire to be loved but of his curiosity about whether what Prospero feels for him is that emotion humans call love.

16. Anne Barton discusses the limits of Prospero's powers in her note in the program for her husband's 1970 production of *The Tempest* for the RSC.

17. Cf. I.ii.16–186.

18. A similar use of "rough" occurs in *Hamlet* when Hamlet tells Horatio, "There's a divinity that shapes our ends, / Rough-hew them how we will—" (V.ii.10–11).

19. John Russell Brown, *Shakespeare in Performance*, p. 605.

20. In her note in the RSC program for her husband's production, Anne Barton says of *The Tempest*: "A play standing somewhat apart from the other final romances, it seems to reject their essential optimism." The open silences of the final scene certainly permit such a rejection, but they do not compel it. She is absolutely correct when she observes: "To perform it [*The Tempest*] in the theatre, even to try and talk about it, is inevitably to add to its substance by filling in gaps and silences left deliberately by the dramatist."

21. In "*The Tempest* and the Concept of the Machiavellian Playwright," *English Literary Renaissance* 8 (1978): 43–66, Richard Abrams discusses the difference between Prospero's treatment of humans and his treatment of the spirits who are summoned to perform the masque: "Prospero's dramaturgy scarcely resembles his handling of the human characters in the story whom he immobilizes or moves strategically about the island, but never obliges to enact his commands. . . . In ruling his actors, Prospero is absolute, dictatorial; as a 'potent' tyrant, he bids his henchman Ariel 'bring the rabble' and 'Incite them to quick motion' (IV.i.37, 39)" (p. 60).

Chapter 4

1. This production was revived for the 1976 season, but since I did not see the revival, I shall discuss only the original production.

2. She had entered earlier, with the newly married Angelo and Mariana.

3. Michael Billington, *Guardian* (London, Manchester), 5 September 1974, p. 10.

4. The actor playing Barnardine (Dan Meaden) also played both Mistress Overdone and Francisca, the nun with whom Isabella is speaking when Lucio brings news of Claudio's imprisonment. The tripling of roles juxtaposed the chastity of a nun to the extremes of carnality embodied in the madame and the murderer who refuses to die.

5. The note was on the rear cover of the program.

6. The Duke's assignment of Barnardine to Friar Peter's hand was especially significant in this production because the Duke had earlier taken Barnardine's hand in his when forgiving his act of murder.

7. In this production Friar Peter was renamed Friar Thomas.

8. See particularly IV.ii.104–9, when the Duke confidently declares in an aside that the message from Angelo, which the Provost has just received, is Claudio's pardon. The Duke then discovers that it reiterates the order that Claudio be executed and adds the stipulation that Claudio's head be sent to Angelo.

9. Here and in the next passage quoted, Hack combines into a single exchange lines that are separated in Shakespeare's playtext: V.i.371–73 and V.i.403–7; V.i.412–14 and 421–22. In addition to rearranging Shakespeare's words, he also changes them. For example, Shakespeare's V.i.403–7 read:

> The very mercy of the law cries out
> Most audible, even from his proper tongue,
> "An Angelo for Claudio, death for death!"
> Haste still pays haste, and leisure answers leisure,
> Like doth quit like, and Measure still for Measure.

10. I follow here the Pelican edition; the Folio gives the lines as follows:

> If he be like your brother, for his sake
> Is he pardon'd, and for your lovelie sake
> Give me your hand, and say you will be mine,
> He is my brother too: . . .

11. If, however, a production effectively establishes that the Duke is under pressure or that he feels pain because of the suffering he is inflicting on Isabella, the audience's judgment of him softens. Davis, for example, tempered any inclination the audience might have to dislike the Duke by having the camera register in telling close-up the supremely confident Duke's pained surprise when what he expected to be Angelo's letter pardoning Claudio turned out to be an order for his swift execution. Giles's pro-

duction justified the Duke's tactics by opening with a kind of dumb show that established the breakdown of order in Vienna. A blind man entered and was mugged beneath corpses dangling from scaffolds. That blind man, the audience subsequently learned, was the Duke.

12. For example, in Giles's production, Isabella deliberated and looked first at the Duke, then at Mariana, and finally at Angelo before turning back and speaking to the Duke.

13. What the Duke and Isabella are wearing when he proposes to her is an important factor in giving her silences meaning and effect. In most productions, Isabella wears a nun's habit throughout the play, but Shakespeare's playtext allows some leeway. Isabella is not, when the audience first sees her, a full-fledged member of "the votarists of Saint Clare," and Francisca, the nun with whom Isabella is speaking when Lucio calls, asks her to deal with him precisely because "you are yet unsworn" (I.iv.5, 9). Kyle's production emphasized Isabella's free decision to don religious garb before undertaking the effort to save her brother's life. Isabella wore secular dress during the scene, but at the end she exited with Francisca in order to put on the nun's habit she was carrying in her arms.

In the productions directed by Phillips and Davis, the Duke doffed his friar's garments completely once he was unhooded and wore secular garb (in Phillips' production, a military uniform) when proposing to an Isabella who was dressed in a nun's habit. In those specific contexts, the proposed marriage seemed to entail a union of the secular and the religious. The Duke in both Giles's and Hack's productions wore his friar's robes, with the hood thrown back, when he proposed to an Isabella dressed in a nun's habit. The method of costuming muted any sense of the proposed marriage as a merger of church and state. Hack, by having the Duke put on the golden robes of state before proposing to an Isabella whom the audience never saw in religious garb, made the proposal of marriage a purely secular assertion of Vincentio's ducal power.

14. See Henry Fenwick's essay, "The Production," in the edition of *Measure for Measure* prepared as a companion to the television production: *The BBC-TV Shakespeare:* Measure for Measure (London: British Broadcasting Corporation, 1979; New York: Mayflower Books, 1979), p. 25.

15. Adding to the sense of festivity was the silent presence of Elbow, the malapropian constable. It was he who took Isabella into custody and, with the Provost, brought in the Duke disguised as a friar.

16. See chap. 8 of Josephine Waters Bennett, *Measure for Measure as Royal Entertainment* (New York: Columbia University Press, 1968); also pertinent are pp. 44–47. In *The Problem of* Measure for Measure*: A Historical Investigation* (London: Vision Press, 1976; New York: Barnes and Noble, 1976), Roselind Miles surveys critical and theatrical treatments of the play. Other books devoted exclusively to the play include Darryl F.

Gless, Measure for Measure, *the Law and the Covenant* (Princeton, N.J.: Princeton University Press, 1979); Nigel Alexander, *Shakespeare:* Measure for Measure (London: Edward Arnold, 1975); William B. Bache, Measure for Measure *as Dialectical Art* (Lafayette, Ind.: Purdue University Press, 1969); David L. Stevenson, *The Achievement of Shakespeare's* Measure for Measure (Ithaca, N.Y.: Cornell University Press, 1966), and Mary Lascelles, *Shakespeare's* Measure for Measure (London: Athlone Press, 1953).

My early thinking about this play was influenced greatly by Francis Fergusson's chapter, "Philosophy and Theatre in *Measure for Measure*," in *The Human Image in Dramatic Literature* (Garden City, N.Y.: Doubleday, 1957). Of the many articles on *Measure for Measure*, I found three especially valuable: Marvin Rosenberg, "Shakespeare's Fantastic Trick: *Measure for Measure*," *Sewanee Review* 80 (1972): 51–72; James Trombetta, "Versions of Dying in *Measure for Measure*," *English Literary Renaissance* 6 (1976): 60–76; and Jane Williamson, "The Duke and Isabella on the Modern Stage," in Joseph G. Price, ed., *The Triple Bond* (University Park: Pennsylvania State University Press, 1975), pp. 149–60. In his chapter on *Measure for Measure* in *Changing Styles in Shakespeare*, Ralph Berry discusses the productions directed by Hack and Phillips and offers a particularly valuable assessment of John Barton's 1970 production for the RSC. That production concluded with "Isabella alone on stage, unresponsive to the Duke's overtures, silently resistant," and in so doing "launched a complete theatrical re-examination of the text" (pp. 40–41). Jonathan Miller's 1975 version of his famed production of *Measure for Measure*, Berry observes, continued and, in a sense, completed that re-examination. In Miller's production, Isabella backed away in horror from the Duke when he proposed the second time, and thus the production "appeared to terminate a line of inquiry, leaving the possibilities only of imitation. Ever since 1975, Isabellas have continued to express doubts about the Duke, with varying degrees of emphasis" (p. 45). In chap. 5 of *Renaissance Drama and a Modern Audience* (London: Macmillan, 1982), pp. 61–75, Michael Scott discusses British productions of *Measure for Measure* during the 1970s, including those directed by Barton, Miller, Kyle, Hack, and Davis.

17.   The Duke's entrance on horseback provides an excellent example of how the technical resources of television can visually complement and enhance a pattern of imagery established by the words of Shakespeare's playtext. Consider the following passages, which relate riding a horse to governing a city and controlling sensual appetites:

> Whether it be the fault and glimpse of newness,
> Or whether that the body public be
> A horse whereon the governor doth ride,
> Who, newly in the seat, that it may know
> He can command, lets it straight feel the spur;

> Whether the tyranny be in his place,
> Or in his eminence that fills it up,
> I stagger in— . . .   (I.ii.153–60)
>   I have begun,
> And now I give my sensual race the rein.   (II.iv.159–60)

18. Alexander Leggatt's description of the final scene of this production in "The Extra Dimension: Shakespeare in Performance," *Mosaic* 10 (1977): 37–49, establishes the context for Isabella's final isolation:

> The scene began (again, this was a nineteenth-century setting) with jolly band music and much twirling of parasols to greet the Duke's return; with its colour and bustle, it looked like the conventional comic finale. As the scene advanced, the revelations became more painful and complicated, business was contrived so that more and more characters left the stage and did not return. (At the scandalous accusations of the women against Angelo, a party of children was whisked off by their nursemaid.) Towards the end some half-dozen figures were left—and finally Isabella stood alone, tearing off her nun's headdress with an expression of bewilderment and dismay. The gradual filling of the stage, so basic to the traditional comic ending, was reversed; the effect was of deliberate parody, underlying the sense of unease, even failure, that lies beneath the apparent satisfaction of the scene as written. (pp. 46–47).

19. Suzanne Langer, *Feeling and Form* (New York: Charles Scribner's Sons, 1953); Northrop Frye, *The Anatomy of Criticism* (Princeton, N.J.: Princeton University Press, 1957); and Frye, "The Argument of Comedy," *English Institute Essays, 1948,* ed. D. A. Robertson, Jr. (New York: Columbia University Press, 1949), pp. 58–73.

20. Berners W. Jackson, in a review of Giles's production, published in the *Hamilton Spectator* (Ontario), 28 June 1969, p. 25.

Chapter 5

1. A third playtext from Shakespeare's time, the Second Quarto, was printed in 1608 (according to its title page), but experts now agree that it was actually printed in 1619 from a copy of the 1608 Quarto. Differences between the two Quartos are attributed to changes made by the compositor in 1619 and therefore the 1619 changes have no authority.

2. The 1608 Quarto gives the corresponding line as "O thou wilt come no more, never, never, never." Differences between the Quarto and the Folio

with regard to the final moments of *King Lear* include differences in Shakespeare's use of open silence. Accordingly, when quoting lines that come after the announcement of Edmund's death, I use either the Quarto or the Folio rather than any modern edition of *King Lear* that blurs such differences by conflating the two playtexts. When citing quotations from the Folio, I follow *The Norton Facsimile: The First Folio of Shakespeare*, ed. Charlton Hinman (New York: Norton, 1968; London: Paul Hamlyn, 1968). When citing quotations from the Quarto of 1608, I use *Shakespeare's Plays in Quarto: A Facsimile Edition of Copies Primarily from the Henry E. Huntington Library*, ed. Michael J. B. Allen and Kenneth Muir (Berkeley and Los Angeles: University of California Press, 1981). When quoting lines that come before the announcement of Edmund's death, I use Harbage, *William Shakespeare: The Complete Works*.

3.   Berkeley and Los Angeles: University of California Press, 1972, p. 319. For further discussion of "Pray you undo this button," see Maurice Charney, "Shakespeare's Unpoetic Poetry," *Studies in English Literature* 13 (1973): 199–207. Also see two essays in Gary Taylor and Michael Warren, eds., *The Division of the Kingdoms: Shakespeare's Two Versions of* King Lear (Oxford: Clarendon Press, 1983): Michael Warren, "The Diminution of Kent," pp. 59–73; and Thomas Clayton, " 'Is this the promis'd end?' Revision in the Role of the King," pp. 121–41.

I am deeply indebted to Rosenberg, *The Masks of* King Lear. I also found very helpful Maynard Mack, King Lear *in Our Time*, first paperback edition (Berkeley and Los Angeles: University of California Press, 1965); Steven Urkowitz, *Shakespeare's Revision of* King Lear (Princeton, N.J.: Princeton University Press, 1980); and Stephen Booth, "On the Greatness of *King Lear*," in Janet Adelman, ed., *Twentieth Century Interpretations of* King Lear (Englewood Cliffs, N.J.: Prentice-Hall, 1978), pp. 98–111. An expanded version of Booth's essay appears in his King Lear, Macbeth, *Indefinition, and Tragedy*, pp. 3–57.

Other works devoted exclusively to *King Lear* include Rosalie L. Colie and F. T. Flahiff, eds., *Some Facets of* King Lear: *Essays in Prismatic Criticism* (Toronto: University of Toronto Press, 1974); S. L. Goldberg, *An Essay on* King Lear (New York: Cambridge University Press, 1974); and John Reibetanz, *The Lear World: A Study of* King Lear *in Its Dramatic Context* (Toronto: University of Toronto Press, 1977).

4.   The Folio assigns these words to Kent. In the Arden edition of *King Lear* [based on the edition of W. J. Craig, 8th ed., rev. (Cambridge, Mass.: Harvard University Press, 1952), repr. with minor corrections, 1955; repr. with further corrections, 1957, 1959], Kenneth Muir, like most modern editors, follows the Folio and defends his choice by observing: "Q[uarto], impossibly, gives the words to Lear who is already beyond speech" (p. 218 n). What Muir dismisses as an impossibility is, however, something

that, within the context of the Quarto playtext, has its own coherence and logic, since the Quarto, unlike the Folio, does not specify that Lear dies after asking that the button be undone. See Michael Warren's discussion of Lear's death in the Quarto and Folio in "The Diminution of Kent," pp. 70–71; and Thomas Clayton's discussion of the same subject in " 'Is this the promis'd end?' " pp. 128–38. Both essays are in Taylor and Warren, *The Division of the Kingdoms*.

5. *Shakespeare in the Theatre* (Cambridge: Cambridge University Press, 1978), pp. 103–4. I did not see a performance of this production, but I have examined the promptbook. In "Shakespeare's Unpoetic Poetry," Charney summarized an exchange of letters in the *Times Literary Supplement* (November and December 1952) about whether the button is Lear's or Cordelia's.

6. "The Catharsis of *King Lear*," in Leonard Dean, ed., *Shakespeare: Modern Essays in Criticism*, rev. ed. (New York: Oxford University Press, 1967), p. 366; repr. from *Shakespeare Survey 13*, ed. Allardyce Nicoll (Cambridge: Cambridge University Press, 1960), pp. 1–10.

7. The stage manager's scripts for the six productions of *King Lear* performed since 1950 by the Royal Shakespeare Company offer evidence that confirms the strength of this tradition. One contains the direction "Kent to Lear," three note that "Kent undoes button," and the other two say nothing—an absence of comment that indicates that who undoes the button is a settled matter requiring no statement specifying a particular directorial choice made from among a variety of alternatives. In Nunn's 1976 production, it was Kent who undid Cordelia's button.

8. For a full discussion of the resonances and ramifications of these lines, see Booth, "On the Greatness of *King Lear*," in Adelman, *Twentieth Century Interpretations of* King Lear, pp. 102–3; and his King Lear, Macbeth, *Indefinition, and Tragedy*, p. 16.

9. For a discussion of the tradition that has Kent undo Lear's button, see the new Cambridge edition of *King Lear*, ed. John Dover Wilson and George Ian Douthie (Cambridge: Cambridge University Press, 1960), pp. 274–75; and Kenneth Muir, letter, *Times Literary Supplement*, 21 November 1952, p. 761.

10. Harbage here follows the Folio. The corrected Quarto reads, "off, off, you lendings, come on." The uncorrected Quarto reads, "off, off, you leadings, come on bee true." See Clayton's discussion of these lines in " 'Is this the promis'd end?' " in Taylor and Warren, *The Division of the Kingdoms*, pp. 121–41.

11. I saw a performance of this production each year, but the stage manager's script was not available for study.

12. "The Diminution of Kent," in Taylor and Warren, *The Division of the Kingdoms*, p. 71, reads: "it is not clear from 'you' who undoes the

button, or even, given the range of possible states of Lear's mind, whether the button is actually undone." Warren expanded that observation in a suggestion he offered after reading the typescript of this book.

13. The Quarto reads: "Rule in this kingdome, and the goard state sustaine."

14. In the Quarto, Lear speaks these words (cf. note 4), but that does not alter the fact that Albany says nothing.

15. In *Shakespeare's Revision of* King Lear, Steven Urkowitz analyzes the Quarto and the Folio as "distinct dramatic documents" (p. 13), rather than as more or less corrupt versions of a lost primal text. The differences between them, he argues, "are the result of Shakespeare's own revision" (p. 15) and reflect Shakespeare's processes of composition. Michael Warren also rejects the assumption of a primal text of *King Lear* and reaches a more radical conclusion in "Quarto and Folio *King Lear* and the Interpretation of Edgar and Albany," in David Bevington and Jay L. Halio, eds., *Shakespeare: Pattern of Excelling Nature* (Newark: University of Delaware Press, 1978; London: Associated University Presses, 1978), pp. 95–107. Warren declares: "Conflated texts such as are commonly printed are invalid and should not be used for either production or interpretation. . . . What we as scholars, editors, interpreters, and servants of the theatrical craft have to accept and learn to live by is the knowledge that we have two plays of *King Lear* sufficiently different to require that all further work on the play be based on either Q[uarto] or F[olio], but not the conflation of both" (p. 105). Also see Gary Taylor, "The War in *King Lear*," *Shakespeare Survey* 33, ed. Kenneth Muir (Cambridge: Cambridge University Press, 1980), pp. 27–34. All of the essays in *The Division of the Kingdoms*, which Warren and Taylor edited, are concerned with the issue of differences between Quarto and Folio *King Lear*.

16. Urkowitz observes that having Albany deliver the final speech "is perfectly consistent with Albany's characterization in the Quarto," whereas having Edgar deliver the last speech "is consistent with other variants in the Folio increasing Edgar's role in the scene while reducing Albany's" (p. 125). The RSC productions of *King Lear* in 1950 and 1953 solved the dilemma in a manner perfectly consistent with the editorial principle of conflating the Quarto and the Folio: Albany spoke the first two lines, Edgar the last two. The result of such conflation, however, was a theatrical moment utterly different from what either the Quarto or the Folio offers.

17. Warren, in "Quarto and Folio *King Lear*," assumes that Edgar's silence means that he is unwilling or unable to accept the crown and that Albany's words mean that he will rule: "In Q[uarto], then, Edgar concludes the play stunned to silence by the reality of Lear's death . . . so that Albany reluctantly but resolutely accepts the obligation to rule: 'The weight of this sad time we must obey' " (p. 323). My point is that Edgar's silence allows

those meanings to emerge during a performance but does not prohibit other alternatives. Urkowitz says nothing about Edgar's silence, but he is alert to the ambiguities posed by the fact that it is Albany who speaks the play's final lines: "In the Quarto, Albany says that he gives the rule of the realm to Edgar and Kent, but he takes upon himself the responsibility of closing the scene. He says he abdicates, but we see him still in authority. According to the Quarto, Albany's second abdication seems suddenly inconclusive. This is not an unthinkable ending for *King Lear*" (p. 125).

18. Stampfer, "The Catharsis of *King Lear*," p. 10. Nicholas Brooke also explores the nihilistic implications of *King Lear* in "On Moral Structure vs. Experience," in Adelman, *Twentieth Century Interpretations of King Lear*, pp. 125–27. Brooke notes: "The final sense is that all moral structures, whether of natural order or Christian redemption, are invalidated by the naked fact of experience. . . . We are left with unaccommodated man indeed; naked, unsheltered by any consolation whatsoever" (p. 127). "On Moral Structure vs. Experience" is reprinted from Brooke, *Shakespeare:* King Lear (London: Edward Arnold, 1963), pp. 58–60.

19. For widely used editions of *King Lear* that follow the Folio in assigning the final lines to Edgar, see *William Shakespeare: The Complete Works*, gen. ed. Alfred Harbage, Pelican text revised; *The Complete Works of Shakespeare*, rev. ed., ed. Hardin Craig and David Bevington (Glenview, Ill.: Scott, Foresman, 1973); *The Riverside Shakespeare*, textual ed. G. Blakemore Evans; *King Lear*, ed. G. K. Hunter (Harmondsworth, Middlesex: Penguin Books, 1972); and *King Lear*, ed. Kenneth Muir, Arden edition. Muir provides a note that summarizes the major arguments in support of assigning the final lines to either Albany or Edgar: "These lines are given to Albany by Q[uarto]; and critics have argued that the last speech should be given to the person of highest rank who survives. But Edgar has to reply to Albany's speech, and the words 'We that are young' come somewhat more naturally from his mouth than from that of Albany" (p. 219). Such reasoning does not solve the problem, however. Albany is the highest ranking survivor only if Edgar does not accept the throne. Nothing dictates that "Edgar has to reply" to Albany, and Edgar's reply does not have to be verbal.

20. For example, Warren, in "Quarto and Folio *King Lear*," concludes that Edgar's words in the Folio indicate his acceptance of the crown. In the Folio, Warren says, Edgar "comes forward as a future ruler when he enables Albany to achieve his objective of not ruling; F's Edgar is a young man of limited perceptions concerning the truth of the world's harsh realities, but one who has borne some of the burdens and appears capable of handling (better than anybody else) the responsibilities that face the survivors" (pp. 104–5).

Rosenberg, in *The Masks of* King Lear, is more responsive than Warren to the ambiguity of what Edgar says at the conclusion of the play in the Folio edition:

> The weight of the kingdom is thrust on the ambiguous Edgar; and he responds with an ambiguity that is characteristic. He is as the time is— he speaks of time as Edmund did: 'The weight of this sad time we must obey; / Speak what we feel, not what we ought to say.' How much in other times has he spoken as he felt? How much as he ought? What kinds of *ought* have shaped his ambivalences—toward Lear in madness, toward his father, toward Edmund? This new king, in abetting the old king's unreason, and in painfully testing Gloster, has played many roles. Does he play one now? He does not resolve uncertainty, rather intensifies it.   (p. 322)

However, as his reference to Edgar as "This new king" shows, Rosenberg does not allow the ambiguity of what Edgar says to include the possibility that Edgar may be voicing his refusal to rule the kingdom.

21.   The Quarto specifies that Edgar must be silent, but in the Folio Albany's open silence can be established only if, with the last words an audience hears, Edgar calls for Albany to retain royal power. Edgar's silence in the Quarto is required, Albany's in the Folio permitted.

22.   I should like at this point to note another possibility arising from the fact that in both the Quarto and the Folio, the speaker of the play's final lines uses "we." Both Albany and Edgar may be using "we" in the royal sense or even with reference to all who have witnessed the final events of the play; however, "we" may also refer specifically to Albany and Edgar, and this interpretation allows the possibility that the two of them agree to rule together. That possibility, if enacted, establishes a correspondence between the bipartite political order with which the play closes and the order that Lear seeks to establish during the opening scene when he calls upon Albany and Cornwall to "part" the coronet between them. The correspondence may, if the production emphasizes the moral goodness of Edgar and Albany in contrast to the perversity of Edmund, Cornwall, Goneril, and Regan, provide the basis for a certain degree of optimism. This final sharing of authority is (can be) better than the first one. The same correspondence may, however, prompt a more pessimistic response if the audience's attention is focused not on the personalities involved in the division of the kingdom but on the fact of division itself. The play closes with a second division of the kingdom and thus has come full circle, ending with what could well be the start of the same process whose consequences the audience has just seen played out.

23.   *Drama within Drama: Shakespeare's Sense of His Art in* King Lear, The Winter's Tale, *and* The Tempest, p. 55.

24.   *Shakespearean Tragedy* (1904; repr., New York: Fawcett World

Library, 1965), p. 241. In "The Salvation of Lear," *ELH* 15 (1948): 93–109, O. J. Campbell argues that *King Lear* is

> a sublime morality play [since] its action prepares Lear not for a life of stoic tranquillity on this earth, but for the heavenly joy of a redeemed soul. The meaning of Cordelia's execution comes to Lear slowly and painfully. At first he is filled with despair at losing her . . . but suddenly he makes the blessed discovery that Cordelia is not dead after all, that the breath of life still trembles on her lips. . . . In the joy of this discovery the old man's heart breaks in a spasm of ecstasy. For only to earthbound intelligence is Lear pathetically deceived in thinking poor Cordelia alive. Those familiar with the pattern of the morality play realize that Lear has discovered in her unselfish God-like love the one companion who is willing to go with him through Death up to the throne of the Everlasting Judge. This knowledge enables Lear to meet death in a state of rapture.   (p. 107)

25. "The Father and the Bride in Shakespeare," *PMLA* 97 (1982): 335.

26. "On the Greatness of *King Lear*," in Adelman, *Twentieth Century Interpretations of* King Lear, p. 100; Booth, King Lear, Macbeth, *Indefinition, and Tragedy*, p. 7.

Chapter 6

1. Aphorism 129, *Novum Organum*, Book 1, *Selected Writings of Francis Bacon*, ed. Hugh G. Dick (New York: Random House, 1955), p. 538. The other two "inventions" are gunpowder and the magnetic compass.

2. "Drama, Script, Theatre and Performance," *Essays on Performance Theory, 1970–1976* (New York: Drama Book Specialists, 1977), p. 38.

3. Marshall McLuhan, *The Gutenberg Galaxy: The Making of Typographic Man* (London: Routledge and Kegan Paul, 1962); Elizabeth L. Eisenstein, *The Printing Press as an Agent of Change: Communications and Cultural Transformations in Early-Modern Europe*, 2 vols. (Cambridge: Cambridge University Press, 1979).

4. In using the word "uniform," I do not mean to suggest that every printed copy of a given play was or is identical to every other. Copies of the Quarto *King Lear* differ among themselves, as do copies of the Folio *King Lear*. What I mean by "uniform" is that a certain number of copies of a given play exist that are uniform among themselves even if they differ from other copies of the same play. To use a current example: copies of the Pelican edition of *King Lear* display uniformity among themselves, even as they differ from copies of the Riverside *King Lear*.

5. This sentence is from a "Treatise on Revelation," which Newton did not publish. The treatise can be found in appendix A of Frank E. Manuel, *The Religion of Isaac Newton* (Oxford: Clarendon Press, 1974), pp. 107–25. The sentence is on page 120 and is also quoted in Gerald Holton, *The Scientific Imagination: Case Studies* (Cambridge: Cambridge University Press, 1978), pp. 272–73.

6. *Thematic Origins of Scientific Thought: Kepler to Einstein* (Cambridge, Mass.: Harvard University Press, 1973). Also see Holton, *The Scientific Imagination*, pp. 2–14. On pp. 296–97 of that work, Holton discusses, with the aid of a diagram, how Newton drew on earlier and contemporary developments in mathematics, physics, and philosophy and how he in turn contributed to later developments in those and other fields, including chemistry and political science. My discussion of the impact of the Newtonian synthesis on the study of Shakespeare's plays is, in essence, an extension of Holton's analysis.

7. See particularly Bernard Beckerman, *Shakespeare at the Globe, 1599–1609* (London: Collier Books, 1962); J. L. Styan, *Shakespeare's Stagecraft* (Cambridge: Cambridge University Press, 1967); John Russell Brown, *Shakespeare's Plays in Performance*.

8. Albert Einstein, Boris Podolsky, and Nathan Rosen, "Can Quantum-Mechanical Description of Physical Reality Be Considered Complete?" *Physical Review* 47 (1935): 777–80. Quoted in Gary Zukav, *The Dancing Wu Li Masters: An Overview of the New Physics* (New York: William Morrow, 1979), p. 276. Einstein never accepted the implications of quantum theory, but his 1905 paper demonstrating that light behaves like a particle (photon), as well as a wave, contributed greatly to the development of quantum theory.

9. *The Dancing Wu Li Masters*, p. 25. In *The Revolution in Physics: A Non-Mathematical Survey of Quanta*, trans. Ralph W. Niemeyer (New York: Noonday Press, 1953; repr. Westport, Conn.: Greenwood Press, 1969), pp. 99–100, Louis de Broglie applies the term "classical physics" to both Newtonian and relativistic physics since, as he emphasizes, a principle of both is that "each observer can represent the totality of physical phenomena in a framework of space and of time which is well defined and completely independent of the nature of the entities which enter into it" (p. 100).

10. *Science and the Common Understanding* (New York: Simon and Schuster, 1954), p. 42.

11. Ibid., p. 47.

12. "Biology and Atomic Physics, 1937," in Bohr, *Atomic Physics and Human Knowledge* (New York: John Wiley, 1958; London: Chapman and Hall, 1958), p. 18.

13. "The Connection between the Sciences, 1960," in Bohr, *Essays*

1958–1962 on Atomic Physics and Human Knowledge (New York: John Wiley, 1963), p. 18.

14. "Light and Life Revisited, 1962," in Bohr, *Essays 1958–1962*, p. 25.

15. *The Cosmic Code: Quantum Physics as the Language of Nature* (New York: Simon and Schuster, 1982), p. 86.

16. *Science and the Common Understanding*, p. 11.

17. "Natural Philosophy and Human Cultures, 1938," in Bohr, *Atomic Physics and Human Knowledge*, p. 25.

18. "The Rutherford Memorial Lecture, 1958," 1961 elaboration, in Bohr, *Essays 1958–1962*, p. 59.

19. For a different exposition of Heisenberg's uncertainty principle, see Pagels, *The Cosmic Code*, pp. 85–91. My exposition closely follows that which Heisenberg himself gave in his book *The Physicist's Conception of Nature*, trans. A. J. Pomerans (London: Hutchinson, 1958; New York: Harcourt, Brace, 1958):

> It was discovered that it was impossible to describe simultaneously both the position and the velocity of an atomic particle with any pre-scribed degree of accuracy. We can either measure the position very accurately—when the action of the instrument used for the observa-tion obscures our knowledge of the velocity, or we can make accurate measurements of the velocity and forego knowledge of the position. The product of the two uncertainties can never be less than Planck's constant. This formulation makes it quite clear that we cannot make much headway with the concepts of Newtonian mechanics, since in the calculation of a mechanical process it is essential to know simultane-ously the position and velocity at a particular moment, and this is precisely what quantum theory considers to be impossible.
>
> (pp. 39–40)

20. Holton, *The Scientific Imagination*, p. 21.

21. Ibid.

22. *The Dancing Wu Li Masters*, p. 285. In *Superposition and Interac-tion: Coherence in Physics* (Chicago: University of Chicago Press, 1980), Richard Schlegel gives this explanation of the principle of superposition:

> In direct words, without reference to solutions of equations, we can say that in the mechanics of classical physics a particle can have only one set of dynamic variables at a given time. Its position, velocity, momentum, or energy is single-valued. This statement is in accord with our commonsense notions about material particles: for a given ob-server, at a given time, a body is at one and only one position and has a particular velocity and energy. An assertion to the effect, for example,

that a particle may simultaneously have a wide range of momentum values p, even for a single observer, would be regarded as outright nonsense in classical physics.

Yet, in quantum theory we find that we do have such an ambiguity for the momentum, and also for other dynamical variables of a particle. We speak of the state of the particle, or other physical system, as being defined by the value of one or more appropriate descriptive magnitudes. And empirical considerations have required in quantum theory the principle that a particle or system may exist in more than one dynamical state. This multiplicity of states, *any one of which would be the only possible one in classical physics*, is the central content of the superposition principle in quantum theory. . . . The formation of an electron wave packet by superposition of many different momentum states, the existence of a particle at different positions (as when it passes through separated layers of a crystal in a diffraction apparatus), and the superposition of possible trajectories for a photon in passing through a system of slits are ready instances of the kind of physical superposition that we find in nature.   (pp. 25–26)

23.   *The Dancing Wu Li Masters*, pp. 278–85.

24.   Richard Schlegel, "Quantum Physics and Human Purpose," *Zygon* 8 (1973): 206. In this article Schlegel gives the best explanation of the superposition principle for the nonphysicist that I have seen. For my understanding of quantum theory in general, I am indebted to Schlegel's *Completeness in Science* (New York: Appleton-Century-Crofts, 1967); his *Inquiry into Science: Its Domains and Limits* (Garden City, N.Y.: Doubleday, 1972); and his "Progress and Completeness in Science," *Centennial Review* 22 (1978): 375–88.

25.   *Physics and Philosophy: The Revolution in Modern Science* (New York: Harper and Brothers, 1958), p. 41.

26.   Ibid., p. 181.

27.   *Atomic Theory and the Description of Nature* (New York: Cambridge University Press, 1934), p. 10. Quoted in Schlegel, *Completeness in Science*, p. 172.

28.   "Quantum Physics and Philosophy: Causality and Complementarity, 1958," in Bohr, *Essays 1958–1962*, p. 5.

29.   Bohr, "Unity of Knowledge, 1954," in Bohr, *Atomic Physics and Human Knowledge*, p. 74.

30.   *Science and the Common Understanding*, pp. 86–87.

31.   New York: The Free Press, 1967; London: Collier Macmillan, 1967; repr. Chicago: University of Chicago Press, 1983, p. 27. Rabkin's focus is upon Shakespearean playtexts; his more recent book, *Shakespeare and the Problem of Meaning* (Chicago: University of Chicago Press, 1981),

also concentrates on thematic meanings as they emerge from the study of Shakespearean playtexts.

32. For an analysis of how Quarto and Folio differ at this point and of how the Folio develops the pattern of clothing and nakedness in ways that the Quarto does not, see Thomas Clayton's " 'Is this the promis'd end?' Revision in the Role of the King," in Taylor and Warren, *The Division of the Kingdoms*, pp. 121–41.

33. Holton, *Thematic Origins of Scientific Thought*, p. 108.

34. "Biology and Atomic Physics, 1937," in Bohr, *Atomic Physics and Human Knowledge*, p. 19.

35. "Quantum Physics and Human Purpose," p. 203.

36. "Unity of Knowledge, 1954," in Bohr, *Atomic Physics and Human Knowledge*, p. 72.

37. For a fuller discussion of this experiment, see Pagels, *The Cosmic Code*, pp. 135–45. In *The Dancing Wu Li Masters*, pp. 85–102, Zukav discusses a similar experiment involving light rather than electrons.

38. *Science and the Common Understanding*, p. 62.

39. Holland's books include *Psychoanalysis and Shakespeare* (New York: McGraw-Hill, 1966); *The Dynamics of Literary Response* (New York: Oxford University Press, 1968); *Poems in Persons: An Introduction to the Psychoanalysis of Literature* (New York: Norton, 1973); and *Five Readers Reading* (New Haven, Conn.: Yale University Press, 1975).

40. "Quantum Physics and Philosophy," in Bohr, *Essays 1958–1962*, p. 7.

Bibliography

Abrams, Richard. "*The Tempest* and the Concept of the Machiavellian Playwright." *English Literary Renaissance* 8 (1978): 43–66.

Adelman, Janet, ed. *Twentieth Century Interpretations of* King Lear. Englewood Cliffs, N.J.: Prentice-Hall, 1978.

Alexander, Nigel. *Shakespeare:* Measure for Measure. London: Edward Arnold, 1975.

Bache, William B. Measure for Measure *as Dialectical Art*. Lafayette, Ind.: Purdue University Press, 1969.

Bacon, Francis. *Selected Writings of Francis Bacon*. Ed. Hugh G. Dick. Book 1, *Novum Organum*. New York: Random House, 1955.

Barber, C. L. *Shakespeare's Festive Comedy: A Study of Dramatic Form and Its Relation to Social Custom*. Princeton, N.J.: Princeton University Press, 1959.

Barthes, Roland. "The Death of the Author." In *Image, Music, Text*, trans. Stephen Heath. New York: Hill and Wang, 1977, pp. 142–48.

Barton, Anne. Note in the program for John Barton's 1970 production of *The Tempest* for the Royal Shakespeare Company.

Beckerman, Bernard. *Shakespeare at the Globe, 1599–1609*. London: Collier Books, 1962.

Bennett, Josephine Waters. Measure for Measure *as Royal Entertainment*. New York: Columbia University Press, 1968.

Bentley, G. E. *The Profession of Dramatist in Shakespeare's Time, 1590–1642*. Princeton, N.J.: Princeton University Press, 1971.

Berry, Ralph. *Changing Styles in Shakespeare*. London: George Allen and Unwin, 1981.

Bevington, David, and Jay L. Halio, eds. *Shakespeare: Pattern of Excelling Nature*. Newark: University of Delaware Press, 1978; London: Associated University Presses, 1978.

Billington, Michael. Review of Keith Hack's 1974 production of *Measure for Measure* for the Royal Shakespeare Company. *Guardian* (London, Manchester), 5 September 1974, p. 10.

———. Review of Peter Gill's 1974 production of *Twelfth Night* for the Royal Shakespeare Company. *Guardian* (London, Manchester), 24 August 1974, p. 8.

Bohr, Niels. *Atomic Physics and Human Knowledge*. New York: John Wiley, 1958; London: Chapman and Hall, 1958.

———. *Atomic Theory and the Description of Nature*. New York: Cambridge University Press, 1934.

———. *Essays 1958–1962 on Atomic Physics and Human Knowledge*. New York: John Wiley, 1963.

Boose, Lynda E. "The Father and the Bride in Shakespeare." *PMLA* 97 (1982): 325–47.

Booth, Stephen. King Lear, Macbeth, *Indefinition, and Tragedy*. New Haven, Conn.: Yale University Press, 1983.

———. "On the Greatness of *King Lear*." In *Twentieth Century Interpretations of* King Lear, ed. Janet Adelman. Englewood Cliffs, N.J.: Prentice-Hall, 1978, pp. 98–111. Expanded version in Stephen Booth, King Lear, Macbeth, *Indefinition, and Tragedy*. New Haven, Conn.: Yale University Press, 1983, pp. 3–57.

———. "Speculations on Doubling in Shakespeare's Plays." In *Shakespeare: The Theatrical Dimension*, ed. Philip C. McGuire and David A. Samuelson. New York: AMS Press, 1979, pp. 103–31. Expanded version in Stephen Booth, King Lear, Macbeth, *Indefinition, and Tragedy*. New Haven, Conn.: Yale University Press, 1983, pp. 129–55.

Bradley, A. C. *Shakespearean Tragedy*. 1904. Repr. New York: Fawcett World Library, 1965.

Broglie, Louis de. *The Revolution in Physics: A Non-Mathematical Survey of Quanta*. Trans. Ralph W. Niemeyer. New York: Noonday Press, 1953. Repr. Westport, Conn.: Greenwood Press, 1969.

Brooke, Nicholas. "On Moral Structure vs. Experience." In *Twentieth Century Interpretations of* King Lear, ed. Janet Adelman. Englewood Cliffs, N.J.: Prentice-Hall, 1978, pp. 125–27. Repr. from Nicholas Brooke, *Shakespeare:* King Lear. London: Edward Arnold, 1963, pp. 58–60.

———. *Shakespeare:* King Lear. London: Edward Arnold, 1963.

Brown, John Russell. "Directions for *Twelfth Night*." In *Shakespeare's Plays in Performance*. London: Edward Arnold, 1966, pp. 107–29. Abr. repr. in *Shakespeare: The Theatrical Dimension*, ed. Philip C. McGuire and David A. Samuelson. New York: AMS Press, 1979, pp. 225–38.

———. *Free Shakespeare*. London: Heinemann, 1974.

Brown, John Russell, ed. *Shakespeare in Performance: An Introduction through Six Major Plays*. New York: Harcourt Brace Jovanovich, 1976.

Brown, John Russell. *Shakespeare's Plays in Performance*. London: Edward Arnold, 1966.

Campbell, O. J. "The Salvation of Lear." *ELH* 15 (1948): 93–109.

Charney, Maurice. "Shakespeare's Unpoetic Poetry." *Studies in English Literature* 13 (1973): 199–207.

Clayton, Thomas. " 'Is this the promis'd end?' Revision in the Role of the King." In *The Division of the Kingdoms: Shakespeare's Two Versions of King Lear,* ed. Gary Taylor and Michael Warren. Oxford: Clarendon Press, 1983, pp. 121–41.

Colie, Rosalie L., and F. T. Flahiff, eds. *Some Facets of* King Lear*: Essays in Prismatic Criticism.* Toronto: University of Toronto Press, 1974.

David, Richard. *Shakespeare in the Theatre.* Cambridge: Cambridge University Press, 1978.

Dean, Leonard F., ed. *Shakespeare: Modern Essays in Criticism.* Rev. ed. London: Oxford University Press, 1967.

Egan, Robert. *Drama within Drama: Shakespeare's Sense of His Art in* King Lear, The Winter's Tale, *and* The Tempest. New York: Columbia University Press, 1975.

Einstein, Albert, Boris Podolsky, and Nathan Rosen. "Can Quantum-Mechanical Description of Physical Reality Be Considered Complete?" *Physical Review* 47 (1935): 777–80.

Eisenstein, Elizabeth L. *The Printing Press as an Agent of Change: Communications and Cultural Transformations in Early-Modern Europe.* 2 vols. Cambridge: Cambridge University Press, 1979.

Felperin, Howard. *Shakespearean Romance.* Princeton, N.J.: Princeton University Press, 1972.

Fender, Stephen. *Shakespeare:* A Midsummer Night's Dream. London: Edward Arnold, 1968.

Fenwick, Henry. "The Production." *Measure for Measure.* By William Shakespeare. London: British Broadcasting Corporation, 1979; New York: Mayflower Books, 1979, pp. 18–25.

———. "The Production." *The Tempest.* By William Shakespeare. London: British Broadcasting Corporation, 1980; New York: Mayflower Books, 1980, pp. 18–26.

Fergusson, Francis. *The Human Image in Dramatic Literature.* Garden City, N.Y.: Doubleday, 1957.

Foucault, Michel. "What Is an Author?" In *Textual Strategies: Perspectives in Post-Structuralist Criticism,* ed. Josué V. Harari. Ithaca, N.Y.: Cornell University Press, 1979, pp. 141–60.

Frye, Northrop. *The Anatomy of Criticism.* Princeton, N.J.: Princeton University Press, 1957.

———. "The Argument of Comedy." In *English Institute Essays, 1948,* ed. D. A. Robertson, Jr. New York: Columbia University Press, 1949, pp. 58–73.

———. *A Natural Perspective: The Development of Shakespearean Comedy and Romance.* New York: Columbia University Press, 1965.

Gadamer, Hans-Georg. "The Eminent Text and Its Truth." Trans. Geoffrey White. *Bulletin of the Midwest Modern Language Association* 13 (1980): 3–10.

Gless, Darryl F. Measure for Measure, *the Law and the Covenant*. Princeton, N.J.: Princeton University Press, 1979.

Goldberg, S. L. *An Essay on* King Lear. New York: Cambridge University Press, 1974.

Goldman, Michael. *Shakespeare and the Energies of Drama*. Princeton, N.J.: Princeton University Press, 1972.

Hartwig, Joan. *Shakespeare's Tragicomic Vision*. Baton Rouge: Louisiana State University Press, 1972.

Heisenberg, Werner. *The Physicist's Conception of Nature*. Trans. A. J. Pomerans. London: Hutchinson,1958; New York: Harcourt, Brace, 1958.

———. *Physics and Philosophy: The Revolution in Modern Science*. New York: Harper and Brothers, 1958.

Herbert, T. Walter. *Oberon's Mazed World: A Judicious Young Elizabethan Contemplates* A Midsummer Night's Dream, *with a Mind Shaped by the Learning of Christendom Modified by the New Naturalist Philosophy and Excited by the Vision of a Rich, Powerful England*. Baton Rouge: Louisiana State University Press, 1977.

Hobson, Harold. Review of John Baron's 1970 production of *The Tempest* for the Royal Shakespeare Company. *Sunday Times* (London), 18 October 1970, p. 37.

Holland, Norman. *The Dynamics of Literary Response*. New York: Oxford University Press, 1968.

———. *Five Readers Reading*. New Haven, Conn.: Yale University Press, 1975.

———. *Poems in Persons: An Introduction to the Psychoanalysis of Literature*. New York: Norton, 1973.

———. *Psychoanalysis and Shakespeare*. New York: McGraw-Hill, 1966.

Hollander, John. "*Twelfth Night* and the Morality of Indulgence." *Sewanee Review* 68 (1959): 220–38; repr. in *Twentieth Century Interpretations of* Twelfth Night, ed. Walter N. King. Englewood Cliffs, N.J.: Prentice-Hall, 1968, pp. 77–89. Also repr. in *Modern Shakespearean Criticism: Essays on Style, Dramaturgy, and the Major Plays*, ed. Alvin B. Kernan. New York: Harcourt Brace Jovanovich, 1970, pp. 228–41.

Holton, Gerald. *The Scientific Imagination: Case Studies*. Cambridge: Cambridge University Press, 1978.

———. *Thematic Origins of Scientific Thought: Kepler to Einstein*. Cambridge, Mass.: Harvard University Press, 1973.

Honigmann, E. A. J. *The Stability of Shakespeare's Text*. Lincoln: University of Nebraska Press, 1965.

Howard, Jean E. *Shakespeare's Art of Orchestration: Stage Technique and Audience Response*. Urbana and Chicago: University of Illinois Press, 1984.

Jackson, Berners W. Review of David Giles's 1969 production of *Measure for Measure* for the Stratford Festival. *Hamilton Spectator* (Ontario), 28 June 1969, p. 25.

Jonson, Ben. *Ben Jonson.* Ed. C. H. Herford, Percy Simpson, and Evelyn Simpson. 11 vols. Oxford: Clarendon Press, 1947.

Jorgens, Jack J. *Shakespeare on Film.* Bloomington: Indiana University Press, 1977.

Kernan, Alvin B., ed. *Modern Shakespearean Criticism: Essays on Style, Dramaturgy, and the Major Plays.* New York: Harcourt Brace Jovanovich, 1970.

———. *The Playwright as Magician: Shakespeare's Image of the Poet in the English Public Theater.* New Haven, Conn.: Yale University Press, 1979.

Keyssar, Helene. "I Love You. Who Are You? The Strategy of Drama in Recognition Scenes." *PMLA* 92 (1977): 297–306.

King, Walter N., ed. *Twentieth Century Interpretations of* Twelfth Night. Englewood Cliffs, N.J.: Prentice-Hall, 1968.

Knapp, Elizabeth. Review of John Barton's 1970 production of *The Tempest* for the Royal Shakespeare Company. *Times* (London) *Educational Supplement,* 23 October 1970, p. 25.

Lambert, J. W. Review of Peter Gill's 1974 production of *Twelfth Night* for the Royal Shakespeare Company. *Sunday Times* (London), 25 August 1974, p. 27.

Langer, Suzanne. *Feeling and Form.* New York: Charles Scribner's Sons, 1953.

Lascelles, Mary. *Shakespeare's* Measure for Measure. London: Athlone Press, 1953.

Leggatt, Alexander. "The Extra Dimension: Shakespeare in Performance." *Mosaic* 10 (1977): 37–49.

Loney, Glen, ed. *Peter Brook's Production of William Shakespeare's* A Midsummer Night's Dream *for the Royal Shakespeare Company: The Complete and Authorized Acting Edition.* Chicago: Dramatic Publishing Co., 1974.

McGann, Jerome J. *A Critique of Modern Textual Criticism.* Chicago: University of Chicago Press, 1983.

McGuire, Philip C., and David A. Samuelson, eds. *Shakespeare: The Theatrical Dimension.* New York: AMS Press, 1979.

Mack, Maynard. King Lear *in Our Time.* 1st paperback ed. Berkeley and Los Angeles: University of California Press, 1965.

McLuhan, Marshall. *The Gutenberg Galaxy: The Making of Typographic Man.* London: Routledge and Kegan Paul, 1962.

Manuel, Frank E. *The Religion of Isaac Newton.* Oxford: Clarendon Press, 1974.

Miles, Roselind. *The Problem of* Measure for Measure: *A Historical Investigation.* London: Vision Press, 1976; New York: Barnes and Noble, 1976.

Mowat, Barbara A. *The Dramaturgy of Shakespeare's Romances.* Athens: University of Georgia Press, 1976.

Muir, Kenneth. Letter. *Times Literary Supplement,* 21 November 1952, p. 761.

Mullin, Michael. "Peter Hall's *A Midsummer Night's Dream.*" *Educational Theatre Journal* 28 (1975): 529–34.

Newton, Isaac. "Treatise on Revelation." Unpublished by Newton. Published as appendix A in Frank E. Manuel, *The Religion of Isaac Newton.* Oxford: Clarendon Press, 1974, pp. 107–25.

Oppenheimer, J. Robert. *Science and the Common Understanding.* New York: Simon and Schuster, 1954.

Orgel, Stephen. "What Is a Text?" *Research Opportunities in Renaissance Drama* 24 (1981): 3–6.

Pagels, Heinz. *The Cosmic Code: Quantum Physics as the Language of Nature.* New York: Simon and Schuster, 1982.

Paolucci, Anne. "The Lost Days in *A Midsummer Night's Dream.*" *Shakespeare Quarterly* 38 (1977): 317–26.

Peterson, Douglas L. *Time, Tide, and Tempest: A Study of Shakespeare's Romances.* San Marino, Calif.: Huntington Library, 1973.

Price, Joseph G., ed. *The Triple Bond: Plays, Mainly Shakespearean, in Performance.* University Park: Pennsylvania State University Press, 1975.

Rabkin, Norman. *Shakespeare and the Common Understanding.* New York: The Free Press, 1967; London: Collier Macmillan, 1967. Repr. Chicago: University of Chicago Press, 1983.

———. *Shakespeare and the Problem of Meaning.* Chicago: University of Chicago Press, 1981.

Reibetanz, John. *The Lear World: A Study of* King Lear *in Its Dramatic Context.* Toronto: University of Toronto Press, 1977.

Robinson, James E. "The Ritual and Rhetoric of *A Midsummer Night's Dream.*" *PMLA* 83 (1968): 380–91.

Rosenberg, Marvin. *The Masks of* King Lear. Berkeley and Los Angeles: University of California Press, 1972.

———. "Shakespeare's Fantastic Trick: *Measure for Measure.*" *Sewanee Review* 80 (1972): 51–72.

Salingar, L. G. "The Design of *Twelfth Night.*" *Shakespeare Quarterly* 9 (1958): 117–36. Abr. repr. in *Twentieth Century Interpretations of* Twelfth Night, ed. Walter N. King. Englewood Cliffs, N.J.: Prentice-Hall, 1968, pp. 24–30.

Schechner, Richard. "Drama, Script, Theatre and Performance." In *Essays on Performance Theory, 1970–1976*. New York: Drama Book Specialists, 1977, pp. 36–62.

Schlegel, Richard. *Completeness in Science*. New York: Appleton-Century-Crofts, 1967.

———. *Inquiry into Science: Its Domains and Limits*. Garden City, N.Y.: Doubleday, 1972.

———. "Progress and Completeness in Science." *Centennial Review* 22 (1978): 375–88.

———. "Quantum Physics and Human Purpose." *Zygon* 8 (1973): 200–220.

———. *Superposition and Interaction: Coherence in Physics*. Chicago: University of Chicago Press, 1980.

Scott, Michael. *Renaissance Drama and a Modern Audience*. London: Macmillan, 1982.

Shakespeare, William. *The Complete Works of Shakespeare*. Rev. ed. Ed. Hardin Craig and David Bevington. Glenview, Ill.: Scott, Foresman, 1973.

———. *King Lear*. Ed. G. K. Hunter. Harmondsworth, Middlesex: Penguin Books, 1972; repr. 1973, 1974, 1976, 1977 (twice), 1979 (twice), 1980, 1981.

———. *King Lear*. Ed. Kenneth Muir. Arden edition. Based on the edition of W. J. Craig. 8th ed., rev. Cambridge, Mass.: Harvard University Press, 1952; repr. with minor corrections, 1955; repr. with further corrections, 1957, 1959.

———. *King Lear*. Ed. John Dover Wilson and George Ian Douthie. New Cambridge ed. Cambridge: Cambridge University Press, 1960.

———. *The Norton Facsimile: The First Folio of Shakespeare*. Ed. Charlton Hinman. New York: Norton, 1968; London: Paul Hamlyn, 1968.

———. *The Riverside Shakespeare*. Textual ed. G. Blakemore Evans. Boston: Houghton Mifflin, 1974.

———. *Shakespeare's Plays in Quarto: A Facsimile Edition of Copies Primarily from the Henry E. Huntington Library*. Ed. Michael J. B. Allen and Kenneth Muir. Berkeley and Los Angeles: University of California Press, 1981.

———. *The Tempest*. Ed. Frank Kermode. Arden edition, 6th ed. Cambridge, Mass.: Harvard University Press, 1958.

———. *William Shakespeare: The Complete Works*. Gen. ed. Alfred Harbage. The Pelican text revised. New York: Penguin Books, 1969; repr. 1975. Repr. New York: Viking Press, 1977.

Sidney, Sir Philip. *A Defense of Poesy*. Ed. Geoffrey Shepherd. London: Thomas Nelson, 1965.

Stampfer, Judah. "The Catharsis of *King Lear*." In *Shakespeare Survey* 13, ed. Allardyce Nicoll. Cambridge: Cambridge University Press, 1960, pp. 1–10.

Stevenson, David L. *The Achievement of Shakespeare's* Measure for Measure. Ithaca, N.Y.: Cornell University Press, 1966.

Styan, J. L. *Shakespeare's Stagecraft*. Cambridge: Cambridge University Press, 1967.

Summers, Joseph H. "The Masks of Twelfth Night." *University Review* 22 (1955): 25–32; repr. in *Twentieth Century Interpretations of* Twelfth Night, ed. Walter N. King. Englewood Cliffs, N.J.: Prentice-Hall, 1968, pp. 15–23; also repr. in *Shakespeare: Modern Essays in Criticism*, ed. Leonard F. Dean. New York: Oxford University Press, 1967, pp. 134–43.

Taylor, Gary. "The War in *King Lear*." In *Shakespeare Survey* 33, ed. Kenneth Muir. Cambridge: Cambridge University Press, 1980, pp. 27–34.

———, and Michael Warren, eds. *The Division of the Kingdoms: Shakespeare's Two Versions of* King Lear. Oxford: Clarendon Press, 1983.

Thayler, Alwain. *Shakespere's [sic] Silences*. Cambridge, Mass.: Harvard University Press, 1929.

Trewin, J. C. Review of John Barton's 1970 production of *The Tempest* for the Royal Shakespeare Company. *Illustrated London News*, 31 October 1970, p. 29.

Trombetta, James. "Versions of Dying in *Measure for Measure*." *English Literary Renaissance* 6 (1976): 60–76.

Urkowitz, Steven. *Shakespeare's Revision of* King Lear. Princeton, N.J.: Princeton University Press, 1980.

Van Laan, Thomas F. *Role-playing in Shakespeare*. Toronto: University of Toronto Press, 1978.

Veitch, Andrew. Review of Celia Brannerman's 1980 production of *A Midsummer Night's Dream* for the New Shakespeare Company at the Open Air Theatre in Regent's Park, London. *Guardian* (London, Manchester), 8 July 1980, p. 9.

Warren, Michael. "The Diminution of Kent." In *The Division of the Kingdoms: Shakespeare's Two Versions of* King Lear, ed. Gary Taylor and Michael Warren. Oxford: Clarendon Press, 1983, pp. 59–73.

———. "Quarto and Folio *King Lear* and the Interpretation of Edgar and Albany." In *Shakespeare: Pattern of Excelling Nature*, ed. David Bevington and Jay L. Halio. Newark: University of Delaware Press, 1978, pp. 95–107.

Wells, Stanley. *Royal Shakespeare: Four Major Productions at Stratford-upon-Avon*. Furman Studies. Manchester: Manchester University Press, 1976.

Welsford, Enid. *The Court Masque*. Cambridge: Cambridge University Press, 1927.

Williamson, Jane. "The Duke and Isabella on the Modern Stage." In *The Triple Bond: Plays, Mainly Shakespearean, in Performance*, ed. Joseph

G. Price. University Park: Pennsylvania State University Press, 1975, pp. 149–69.

Young, David P. *Something of Great Constancy: The Art of* A Midsummer Night's Dream. New Haven, Conn.: Yale University Press, 1966.

Zukav, Gary. *The Dancing Wu Li Masters: An Overview of the New Physics*. New York: William Morrow, 1979.

Index

Compositor: Wilsted & Taylor
Text: Sabon 10/12
Display: Sabon
Printer: Edwards Brothers, Inc.
Binder: Edwards Brothers, Inc.